The Baroque Technotext

First published in the UK in 2020 by
Intellect, The Mill, Parnall Road, Fishponds, Bristol, BS16 3JG, UK

First published in the USA in 2020 by
Intellect, The University of Chicago Press, 1427 E. 60th Street,
Chicago, IL 60637, USA

A catalogue record for this book is available from the British Library.

Cover designer: Alex Szumlas
Copy editor: MPS
Frontispiece image: Olivier Richon (1989),
A Devouring Eye, C type print, 24 in. × 30 in.
Production manager: Laura Christopher
Typesetting: Newgen

Print ISBN 978-1-78938-165-8
ePDF ISBN 978-1-78938-166-5
ePub ISBN 978-1-78938-167-2

Printed and bound by 4edge, UK.

This is a peer-reviewed publication.

Contents

About the Book

To focus on *what* is represented is to relish the *zuhanden* where the reader depends on the author to provide a product they can enjoy without much thought to its construction. When readers begin asking *how* of their representational texts, they become invested in the process of its making and the assumptions they adopted while interacting with those texts, placing them in a *vorhanden* state.[1] Readers start to see how they read as a layer that affects what they understand. In that spirit, I write this book not just to argue for the relevance of the baroque as a point of comparison to technotextual literature, but to act out baroque reason and assume baroque tropes as structurally foundational.[2]

In charting relevant baroque aesthetic practices, I catalogue five concepts[3] explored in twentieth-century post-structuralist thought but which are ultimately based on baroque aesthetic practices. I apply each concept to technotexts that demonstrate how literature exercises baroque aesthetic techniques to adjust to digital culture and emerging models of subjectivity and textuality. While this theoretical backing and application to a technotext constitute the bulk of the book that follows, I prime each chapter with a discussion of a nonliterary text spurred on first by personal experience, thus grounding the theme of the following chapter. Concepts presented as theoretical or abstract are also quotidian. By including some workaday observations and nonliterary texts, I hope to make clear that baroque aesthetic techniques are not only at work in literature, or even just artistic expressions across media, but affect human perception and perceptions of humanness. While each chapter is separate and complete on its own, there are many overlaps and resonances across their limits. The book's structure can result in a dizzying, labyrinthine experience, but an unavoidable one when acting out the baroque, not just discussing it. The chapters are essentially fugal: five chapters, five melodic themes, with the personal experience and nonliterary text introducing each theme. The theoretical portion of the chapter develops the theme, and the application of theoretical concepts to technotexts resolves the theme.

From its beginnings, I imagined the book as a Jacob's ladder – a line of blocks looped to move cyclically even if they appear to exist linearly. Because the baroque makes clear its critique on representation when it shifts between exposing and obscuring the frame, perspective or medium, so too does this book attempt to show the moment when the Jacob's ladder reveals itself as a circle of blocks tumbling upon one another. The end of one chapter flips the block over to its reverse so that 'Monad' closes with the idea of representation folding in on itself, while '*Mise en Abyme*' opens with representation unfolding outwards. '*Mise en Abyme*' closes with the idea of looking *at* the materiality of representation, while '*Trompe l'Oeil*' opens with the reverse approach of looking *through* material structures to reach the supposed content. Even closing with accumulation in the final chapter 'Collections and Navels' flips back into the opening chapter 'Monads', which begins with the idea of choice and arrangement. Turning the chapters over into one another helps replicate the inclusivity and variety of the baroque ellipse[4] over the unity and stability of the classical circle.

The book is condensed in the prologue and expanded in its chapters. Its introduction, like a perturbance on a baroque pearl, is an outgrowth of the chapters and an expansion of the title. Once you arrive at the chapters, the book is a cycle, you can start with any chapter as your entry point. If you start with 'Choice', you start with constructing identity. 'Mirrors' would begin the journey with exposing functions of representation. Commencing with 'Illusion' sets the starting line at immersion and its pleasures. Originating at 'Surface' is to begin with criticizing hegemony. Setting forth from 'Code' is to start with the blunt claim of meaninglessness. Begin where you like. You will always end in a conceptually oppositional place from where you began.

If you do not care for the Jacob's ladder or ellipse metaphor, you could also imagine the book as a looped tour of Gilles Deleuze's Allegory of the Baroque House. The first floor of the house contains all possibilities available in the universe and the second floor includes only those possibilities that a subject has chosen or that chance and circumstance foisted upon them. Going up the stairs narrows one's reality and supports a *zuhanden* state of ignoring form to exercise a function. Going down the stairs reveals one's second-floor reality as only one possible iteration, given the infinite recombinations available on the first floor and ushers in *vorhanden* moments of interrogating form to infer multiple functions. By doing and then undoing – of walking upstairs and downstairs in Deleuze's baroque house – we can experience the representational crisis the baroque embodies. Technotexts also encourage readers to run up and down those stairs by imbricating literary content with its material substrate. This book uses this vertical movement to replicate the repeatedly changing states between *zuhanden* and *vorhanden* that make the baroque technotext both perplexing and pleasurable. 'Choice' and 'Illusion' run upstairs. 'Mirrors' and 'Surface' travel downstairs. 'Code' sits midway through the staircase considering which way to go.

As you move through the book, there are a handful of concepts that appear across chapters. I do not repeatedly explain these concepts, so, instead, you may find it helpful to know the location of its most detailed explanation:

- Allegory of the Baroque House pp. 25–26
- ellipse pp. vii n4, 121–22
- major and minor strategies pp. 119–21
- monad pp. 24–27
- technotext pp. 6–8
- *vorhanden* and *zuhanden* pp. vii n1, 7.

Otherwise, traditional chapter summaries immediately follow and the prologue that condenses the entire book to one page appears after the introduction.

Chapter Summaries

'Choice' opens with the conundrum of choosing from 94 vodka bottles and a brief reading of Jaco Van Dormael's 2009 film, *Mr. Nobody*, to address the crucial role of choice and arrangement in building subjective perspectives.

'Monads' considers how Gottfried Leibniz's monadology inspired Deleuze's *The Fold* and a reimagined subjectivity that perceives all entities as entangled with one another but differentiated only via their perspective. Entities establish their perspective by the choices and circumstances they make or experience. To bridge these differences, entities find resonant harmonies with one another and communicate through allegory.[5] The chapter culminates with a close reading of David Clark's net.art work, *88 Constellations for Wittgenstein (to be played with the Left Hand)*, an insistently digressive, recursive, born-digital meta-biography of Ludwig Wittgenstein as a showcase of monadic subjects who are inherently allegorical and rife with harmonic potential.

'Mirrors' starts with a misguided use of a disposable camera and continues into a reading of match cuts and applications of mirrors in Joe Wright's 2012 film, *Anna Karenina*.

'*Mise en Abyme*' borrows the concept of the mirrorish from Jean-François Lyotard as a broader explanation for what one experiences more specifically in the literary and visual trope of *mise en abyme*. While the mirrorish unfolds higher dimensions, the *mise en abyme* reveals co-centric layers of representation. The chapter closes with an analysis of Kevin Gold's interactive sci-fi novel in app form, *Choice of Robots*, specifically regarding how paratextual features such as running metadata function textually.

'Illusion' moves on to the robo-telemarketer before providing a brief exploration of the augmented reality app NOAD as a return to baroque challenges of the divide between representation and reality.

'*Trompe l'Oeil*' takes up illusory practices of the *quadratura*, *bel composto* and *trompe l'oeil* that mean to smooth over media boundaries[6] and erase the presence of the frame so that illusion is easily mistaken for or bleeds into reality. Here I exercise Jacques Derrida's idea of the *parergon* as a frame that oscillates between being part of and separate from the work it frames. The chapter closes with an extended reading of a cross-media collaboration between artist Izhar Patkin and poet Agha Shahid Ali as they treat the veil as a conceit between media and cultures in *The Wandering Veil*. Patkin and Ali worked with metaphors in reverse and circular patterns, addressing the subject of the veil as a *parergon* that obscures and reveals.

'Surface' begins with the shame and pride of global capitalism and mass media consumption followed by a concise review of Björk's app album *Biophilia* and its accompanying musico-scientific educational program as a reimagined view of musical instruction.

'Minoring' begins by focusing on William Egginton's minor strategy of baroque reason, a strategy predicated on admitting the presence of artifice even in what seems real. Egginton's minor strategy is akin to Deleuze and Guattari's broader concept of 'minor literature' where minority refuses hierarchy and decenters the human subject to see the potential paradigm the object might adopt if freed from anthropocentrism. Closing out the chapter is an interpretation of Jonathan Safran Foer's *Tree of Codes* and its parent text, Bruno Schulz's *The Street of Crocodiles*, as exemplars of minor literature, whose versioning leads to polyphony and hybridity, concepts commonly discussed in the postcolonial critique of the new world baroque and neobaroque in twentieth-century Latin American literature.[7]

'Code' opens with egg donation before providing a short study of Christian Bök's *The Xenotext* and its relationship to bio arts, which use and influence natural growth to serve human signifying practices.

After minoring undermines dominant narratives as artifice, cultures must rebuild through collecting or accumulating a mass that can then be arranged to a new narrative (essentially the 'Monad' chapter) or face the *horror vacui* of knowing that there is no meaning beyond the surface artifice. To exercise these ideas, 'Collections and Navels' takes up Mieke Bal's concept of the navel as the detail that overwhelms the larger image, meaning or story of a text and the *wunderkammer* as non-categorical ordering paradigm aimed at enticing curiosity rather than solidifying verifiable knowledge. In closing, I examine Chris Ware's *Building Stories*, a series of cartoon pieces to be read after being distributed across the reader's living space and Georges Perec's *An Attempt at Exhausting a Place in Paris*, a three-day log of the mundane happenings in Place Saint-Sulpice. Both pieces return the reader to a database aesthetic of compiling information that makes nonlinear connections and considers seemingly nonhuman ways of seeing.

NOTES

1. Martin Heidegger described the *zuhanden* and *vorhanden* in *Being and Time* as states of being and modes of seeing. The *zuhanden* or ready-to-hand obscures the particularity of the object and confines it to its function. In this pragmatic or utilitarian mode, humans instrumentalize objects for their purposes rather than contemplate those objects. The *vorhanden* or present-at-hand considers the nature and specificity of an object on its standing, thus noticing its construction and its potential unbridled by the expectations of a prescribed function.
2. See note 2 on page 138.
3. These concepts include: (1) Gilles Deleuze's *monad* derived from Gottfried Leibniz and exercised in Walter Benjamin's *The Origin of German Tragic Drama*, (2) Jean-François Lyotard's *mirrorish* related to baroque *mise en abyme*, (3) Jacques Derrida's *parergon* from baroque ornamentation and *trompe l'oeil*, (4) Deleuze and Félix Guattari's *becoming minor* from baroque repetition and reflection, and finally, (5) navel-gazing from Mieke Bal's thoughts on baroque embodied immersion in the broader context of collecting and the *wunderkammer*.
4. The ellipse in baroque architecture makes space appear illusory and flexible, so individuals cannot grasp a church's overall scale, as in Gian Lorenzo Bernini's Sant-Andrea al Quirinale (1658-72) whose elliptical floor plan is shockingly small compared to the imposing impression of its altar. The oval became so common to baroque church architecture that its overlapping and intercut use in Contanzo Michela's Chiesa di Santa Marta in Agliè creates so perplexing a space that its scale and design are hard to divine without an aerial view (Bailey 2012: 194). The dual foci of the ellipse make room for hybridity and multiple viewpoints that could reject established norms – a phenomenon well documented in neobaroque criticism of Latin American culture – and push aside balanced, circular models that implicitly act out monotheism and kingship.
5. For Walter Benjamin, the allegory is the main aesthetic element of modernity, and its roots were in the baroque. Similarly, for Christine Buci-Glucksmann, allegory predates modern art in recognizing the destructive principles enacted in fragments and the commanding presence of absence that undercuts reason (Buci-Glucksmann 1994: 71). Allegory helps one see the world as a theater of representation. For instance, Charles Baudelaire and Benjamin's manifestation of allegory in the *flâneur* shows the emptiness of modernity, hollowed out of the idea of progress thanks to the ambiguity of urban life and the expansion of commodity culture.
6. The baroque historical era includes ample works that transcend media. Italian baroque churches provide some of the most striking examples from Scipione Pulzone and Gaspare

Celio's 1590–97 frescos in the Passion Chapel of the Il Gésu church in Rome. There the painted Jesus gazes at the crucifix altarpiece from his location on a left panel of the chapel. He seems aware of the space beyond the limits of his panel (Bailey 2012: 154). The ceiling fresco in the Il Gésu church also utilizes painted stucco to build clouds that fall out of the frame that surrounds the heavenly imagery and painted shadows to trick viewers to think the clouds are real. Not only does the content of a representation seem to leap out from its frame, but one medium mimics another in Gian Lorenzo Bernini's *Ecstasy of Saint Teresa* in the Cornaro Chapel of the Santa Maria della Vittoria church. Though the altarpiece in this *bel composto* centers on a three-dimensional sculpture of Spanish Carmelite Saint Teresa and an angel, it can only be viewed from the front as if it were a painting. On the sides of the Cornaro Chapel appear oratories that include members of the Cornaro family in low-relief vaults and colonnades that borrow linear perspective from painting to feign depth (Bailey 2012: 163–64).

7. Much of the new world baroque and neobaroque criticism is predicated on the west's disillusionment with modernism that yielded the troubled term 'postmodernism'. Monika Kaup documents this disillusionment well in how Latin America used the break in western thinking toward postmodernism to consider an alternative modernism that challenges Eurocentric historicism (Kaup 2007: 228). Returning to the baroque is not a denial of modernity posited by the 'third world' that has not yet achieved modernity, but a reversal to the primal modernism of the baroque instead of the perceived progress of the 'civilizing myth of Enlightenment modernity' (Kaup 2007: 131).

Introduction: An Anamorphic Projection of the Title

When I was 8 years old, my neighbor's daughter, then completing her master's degree in psychology, asked if I would talk with her and draw her a few pictures. I only recall one drawing. She asked me to imagine a door and on the other side of that door would be pure potential. I drew letters that could fly with thin wings left uncolored. Each letter had a face. In the end, she did not seem too interested in what I drew, and I felt like I must have done whatever we were doing all wrong. I shrugged it all off at the time, but looking back now, I had taken the form of the letters and divested them of their semantic value and servitude to linguistic exchange. When I looked just to their form, I freed them from the expectations of their prescribed content and what could be more liberating and more terrifying than language unmoored?

Some twenty years later I found myself crammed into an 800-square-foot apartment in Queens, New York with two toddlers determined to overturn my bookshelves. I could no longer stand the daily ritual of re-alphabetizing my books and so altered the organizational paradigm to arrange them by color so that the children could pick up after themselves. This only introduced a new problem. While I knew the color of the binding of all my books and that of my partner's, he did not. He thought the color of the spine inconsequential to the book's meaning and so every time he went looking for a book, he had to ask the color of its spine. Eventually, he divorced his books from mine and placed them back in alphabetical order on the top shelves beyond the reach of our maniacal children. As simple as the book object seems, as a material form it braves a complex nexus of exchange well beyond the author's word.

In short, I have long dreamt, imagined, studied and thought about how language seems like both a magical abstraction and a precise object amidst complex functions. Looking at the linguistic content and the material qualities of literature at once is akin to looking at a visual illusion and simultaneously recognizing both interpretations. While both are always present, that is not how they are perceived. Because of the increasingly digital nature of literature's material substrate, we are in a position to reconsider the role of materiality in literary studies. Putting the material form on equal footing with the semantic meaning of language broadens literature's context and propels us to networked models of subjectivity and a more empathetic foundation for our understanding of humanness.

Reconciling Literary Study with Materiality

Consuming literature is more than a cognitive decoding of words and producing literature does not concern only the semantic value of the words strung together. The real material qualities of a literary text have and will remain deeply intertwined with the representational function of literature. While the technology of the codex form – of folded paper bound together – has historically become an invisible assumption of the literary form for most readers, writers and critics, digital technologies have reminded us all of the importance of reconsidering the material state of any text as central to its meaning-making. Though subfields like book history, bibliography, book arts and fine press printing have explored the material state of literature for some time, for most writers and critics, the form of the book and the material choices made in its production are not broadly considered part of the meaning-making process that authors embark upon or that critics retrace. For other critics like N. Katherine Hayles, the material state of literature must now play a central role in various literary practices. For Hayles:

> A critical practice that ignores materiality, or that reduces it to a narrow range of engagements, cuts itself off from the exuberant possibilities of all the unpredictable things that happen when we as embodied creatures interact with the rich physicality of the world.
>
> (Hayles 2002: 107)

This broader awareness of the meaningful nature of materiality in literature came to the forefront with the advent of the personal computer and the rise of media theory. For the likes of Loss Pequeño Glazier, digital media opens literature – and poetry in particular – to innovation through engagement with the medium. In such a way, meaning-making is obfuscated rather than transparent (Glazier 2008: 171). Both New Criticism's disregard for everything but the linguistic text and post-structuralism's deconstruction have oriented literary critics toward a theoretical rather than practical focus on textual materiality.

Attention to materiality is a niche in literary studies mainly because the appearance and function of the textual inscription are often considered outside of the author's purview. Publishers, printers and software designers make choices separate from the textual choices authors make, and more often than not, critics and scholars examine the author's role rather than the reader's, printer's, illustrator's, publisher's or editor's. Digital technologies from word processing to desktop publishing rejoined form and content decisions in such a way that mainstream authors outside of avant-garde or fine press book traditions may easily alter the appearance of their texts. As a consequence, authors now realize the semantic, aesthetic and emotive power of the form their content takes. Even seemingly minor design choices, like changing the font, size and orientation of text, remind writers of the compositional qualities of words on a page. The visual appearance of writing becomes neither arbitrary nor decorative, but what Johanna Drucker calls 'functional cognitive guides' (cited in Funkhouser 2012: 25). Once those decisions are recognized as more readily available to an author, material choices more readily become the object of literary and cultural study. While digital technologies ushered in a broader awareness of literature's material form, the interplay between form, content and medium is not new or exceptional. These moves are established in literature and rhetoric and have gained and lost prominence depending on current factors such as aesthetic movements, technological affordance or disciplinary methodologies.

Paying attention to digital materiality can change literature drastically. For Adelaide Morris and Thomas Swiss, new media poetry is different from print poetry because it needs to be programmed. Overlooking the code misses part of the poem's meaning. On the other hand, code proves unsettling because 'it catches us in a cleft between what we "see" and what we "know"' (Morris and Swiss 2009: 30). Moving from a conception of writing as the linguistic expression of a human's imagination to one in which language processing no longer involves humans can be a disorienting shift if we start from an anthropocentric understanding of language and expression. If one can author a program that generates poetry, what happens to the value of the human as a poet? Is the programmer the poet? Is the program the poet? Even in less forceful terms, just the sheer amount of paratext and metatext that writing on digital platforms produces challenges our understanding of the edge of the literary text. Without a binding to determine the boundaries of a textual object, where is the end of the text? Is the code part of the digital text? What about the URL? The browser settings? The operating system? The hardware? While materiality reminds readers and authors to think of the relationships between content and form as a part of textual production, programming tells us that we are in a space of executable processes among things and not dealing with things that magically appear.

Literary and cultural study's long disinvestment in the material qualities of the text was largely normalized because of eighteenth-century debates surrounding copyright and the meaning of the book. Lawyer William Blackstone draws the line of textual meaning in his *Commentaries on the Laws of England* in the late 1760s when he writes, '[t]he identity of a literary composition consists intirely [*sic*] in the *sentiment* and the *language* [...] the paper and print are merely accidents, which serve as vehicles' (cited in Calé 2011: 105). Historiographer and book historian, Roger Chartier, affirms that the western tradition divided 'the interpretation of texts' from 'the analysis of the technical and social conditions of their publication and circulation' (Chartier and Elton 2005: 40). Furthermore, the two critical approaches meant to bridge the divide – bibliography and deconstruction – have only enforced abstraction by either focusing on uncovering the ideal text in the former or, with the latter, investing more in conceptual categories than in the materiality of writing it insists upon (Chartier and Elton 2005: 40). Such divides between content and materiality are mirrored in the side-by-side development of humanities, computing and literary and cultural studies in the twentieth century, as Jerome McGann describes in his book, *Radiant Textualities*.

While digitizing and marking up archival documents for *The Rosetti Project*, McGann found that digitizing a document was more than maintaining its linguistic content; otherwise, a plain transcript would be sufficient. To document its meaning also meant to document its material realities – the paper, printer, distribution, reception, publication, revision, illustration and so forth. Beyond its role as a repository for analogue texts and tool for textual analysis, the computer recovers 'more "subjective" forms of analysis and interpretation, forms and procedures that have fallen into disuse under the pressure of neoclassical and scientistic models of thinking and imagining' (McGann 1998: 617).

The study of computing in the humanities, because of its close association with computational linguistics in the mid-twentieth century, did not interest literary or cultural studies until the mid-1990s. Even then, the connection lay in the investigation of expressive veins like hypertexts rather than in the attention to textual markup and editing that conversely found its home in library and archival sciences (McGann 2001: 4–5). Despite its foundational nature, scholarly editing, archival work or the materiality of their texts and tools remain the focus of few scholars. Instead, most focus on interpreting the meaning of literary and cultural works chiefly via their content (McGann 2001: 213). This tendency, however, seems to be changing as we recognize the convergence between the expressive possibilities of computers and the procedural capabilities of the human, made all the more prominent by the rise of digital humanities. As analogue and digital materiality become more entwined and interdependent, literary and cultural studies are bound to increase their attention to the complexity of textuality, both digital and analogue.

The growing convergence of content and materiality in contemporary digital studies is, to some extent, a return to older models of textual studies. For McGann, digital media takes textual scholarship back to philology, the foundation of literary and cultural studies before the shift to hermeneutics in the twentieth century. Recalling Donald McKenzie, McGann reminds us that 'documents carry the evidence of "the history of their own making". To the philologist, all possible meanings are a function of their historical emergence as material artefacts' (McGann 2009: 13). Turning to the past dredges up two significant assumptions that must be broadly accepted for the study of materiality to thrive: first, that materiality *is* meaningful content and not a neutral container and second, that textual study requires an attention to networks of forces that go well beyond the borders of an individual textual object.

Digital aesthetics and its analogue predecessors highlight the constructed nature of textuality such that 'texts and documents are not primarily understood as containers or even vehicles of meaning. Rather, they are sets of instantiated rules and algorithms for generating and controlling themselves and for constructing further sets of transmissional possibilities' (McGann 2001: 2). Of course, we did not need the computer to do this. Stéphane Mallarmé accomplished this by displacing assumptions of the book through typographic alterations (McGann 2001: 210). However, we did need to recognize that authorial content does not happen in a vacuum, and the networked capabilities of the computer provided a convenient daily reminder of such a context, making it easier to see texts as both semantic content and physical construction born from a network of constituents and factors often invisible in the textual object.

Recognizing the interplay between content and materiality opens textual study and book history outward to the communicative network that exists around any one text. In this case, a text is part of a more extensive process that includes not just authors, but printers, artists, engravers, vendors, distributors, designers, publishers, editors, agents, readers, paper mills, binders, translators, reviewers, libraries, shippers, smugglers, even government policy and taxation. To see the whole network in the production of a book is the foundation of what Robert Darnton calls the 'sociology of books',[1] which studies books not just for their form, but also for their process of transmission, production and reception (Chartier and Elton 2005: 37). In this case, book history goes beyond any one discipline to uncover a network of forces behind the communicative technology of the book as it cycles through the author, publisher, printer, shipper, bookseller and reader and in that process touching 'other systems, economic, social, political, and cultural, in the surrounding environment' (Darnton 1982: 67). The book is material and conceptual; its context extends well beyond the author, and its meaning is not exclusive to the language on the page.

Technotexts as a Focus

Certainly, this is all so overwhelming that it is no wonder that literary and cultural study struggle to incorporate the impact of digital technologies and its implications despite the genuine connection digital materiality has to existing interests in textuality, however old, niche or generally forgotten those may be. Nevertheless, there are conceptual tools to use to bridge the gap between material and meaning, form and function, media substrate and literary expression. Ultimately, this book uses two such tools as two foci that ground an elliptical path: the technotext, which I derive from N. Katherine Hayles's *Writing Machines*, and the baroque, which is ideologically characterized in Christine Buci-Glucksmann's *Baroque Reason: The Aesthetics of Modernity* and Gregg Lambert's *On the (New) Baroque*. The first brings us to the importance of more broadly focusing on the inscription media of literature and the second promotes baroque thinking as a more comprehensive framework for understanding representational crises of modernity. However, the first examines such media-conscious literature often through the lens of a modernist aesthetic and the second makes little to no mention of contemporary literature or digitality. While I come nowhere close to adopting a sociology of the book, I aim to provide a rereading of how literary and cultural study might more readily welcome material study if it considered the deep aesthetic and rhetorical work of the baroque, which is too often dismissed as spectacle without substance. If we believe it is worth paying increased attention to materiality as content, then the baroque offers a uniquely rich field of practices. Baroque thought and works actively flicker back and forth from *zuhanden* to *vorhanden* moments so that readers alternate between noticing materiality and being immersed in language. In the specific case of a technotext, which actively relates form and function, this baroque flickering mimics the technotext's functions.

The 'technotext' of *Baroque Technotext* originates from Hayles's efforts to provide a common framework for thinking about media-conscious literature across disciplines while also proposing a methodology for literary studies. Moreover, the term 'technotext' remedies the shortcomings of previously used terminology for such media-conscious literature. Unlike web 1.0 texts like Michael Joyce's 1987 *afternoon: a story* or Shelley Jackson's 1995 *Patchwork Girl* that lean on hypertext theory and its obsession with linking lexia, or units of reading, the technotext is not so narrowly defined. Neither is the technotext so disciplinarily defensive, unlike hypertext theory whose underlying objective was more or less to convince the literary community of the value of hypertexts as literary objects. Web 2.0 texts such as Christine Wilks's 2008 *Fitting the Pattern* or John Cayley's 2004 *Translation*, which use computational capacities of software more sophisticated than the link, such as animations, multimedia, flash or generators, have quickly outgrown hypertext theory. Espen Aarseth filled the void with his idea of the cybertext, which highlighted the computational and combinatorial function of ergodic literature, which requires nontrivial effort to navigate. However, such a focus on the computational and a bent toward video games rather than digital literary texts were ways to dethrone the literary critic in the space of digital textuality. Unlike technotexts, cybertexts were more interested in the capabilities of inscription technologies and their underlying processes than in what becomes inscribed on them.

Hayles's 'technotext' functions therefore as a broader term meaning 'a literary work [that] interrogates the inscription technology that produces it [so that] it mobilizes reflexive loops between its imaginative world and the material apparatus embodying that creation as a physical presence' (Hayles 2002: 25). In brief, a technotext is a piece of literature that recognizes its state as a material object and communicative technology. The purposeful relationship between the content of a literary text and its material state defines the technotext. The term and its related approach squash the paradoxical debate of which is primary: the content or the form, the writing or the inscription medium. While hypertext emphasized the former and cybertext privileged the latter, the technotext sees content and form as entwined, inseparable and simultaneous. Furthermore, while cybertexts did account for analogue literature like Raymond Queneau's *Cent Mille Milliards des Poemes* and hypertext theory did draw points of comparison with footnotes in printed books, the technotext makes clear that its manifestation could just as well be digital or analogue. Looking beyond the purely digital text recognizes bookish books and hybrid and transmedia narratives that resulted from interactions between print and digital composition. Even more, literary texts that do not question or interact with their material substrate are still subject to their materiality, which broadens the applicability of the technotext to virtually any literary object.[2]

In a way, digital technology's significance for writing is partly due to its effectiveness in turning writing from a ready-to-hand tool to a present-at-hand phenomenon, a phenomenon that Martin Heidegger called the *zuhanden* and *vorhanden* in *Being and Time* and Richard Lanham reframed as 'looking through' and 'looking at' in *The Electronic Word*. As states of being and modes of seeing, the *zuhanden*, ready-to-hand or 'looking through', obscures the particularity of the object and confines it to its function. In this pragmatic or utilitarian mode, humans instrumentalize objects for their own purposes rather than contemplate those objects. The *vorhanden*, present-at-hand or 'looking at', provides the theoretical mode that considers the nature and specificity of an object on its own standing, thus noticing its construction and its potential, unbridled by the expectations of a prescribed function. The technotext pushes literary study to recognize the *zuhanden* and *vorhanden* states of a literary text that is both a material form and a literary expression. The technotext reanimates representational practices for literature in ways that broaden our thoughts on authorship or intent, such that literary expression exists on a larger mediascape.

Technotexts beyond Modernism

Despite technotext's flexibility as a term, its close association with the modernist and avant-garde tradition limits its applications. Modernist aesthetics offered new media authors enough cultural capital to legitimate their literariness and to defend the substance of their content. Moreover, the computer does materialize and activate avant-garde tropes like the collage. It is no wonder that between the credentials they lend and the aesthetic similarities they hold with many digital literary texts, the avant-garde and modernism have served as relays and points of comparison for digital media for many literary scholars including Jay David Bolter, Richard Grusin, Lev Manovich, Glazier, Lanham, Hayles and Pressman. Pressman's *Digital Modernism* defends the value of electronic literature as legitimate because it draws from a modernist tradition.

Perhaps avant-garde's privilege stems from its association with critical and political action in terms of the analytical and thoughtful use of media. It is cast as a movement about content and ideas rather than the form or appearance that entertainment media is chastised for privileging. Coupling this with the advent of the computer as a celebration for the thoughtfully written text over immersive visual media can explain some biases against the baroque in imagining literature in a digital era. Scholars like Roberto Simanowski observe how hypertext scholars were first excited by the advent of the computer as a textual display to counter cinema and television's visual paradigm. However, as computers could handle increasingly larger image and video files, hypermedia became more prevalent. By 1999, Robert Coover, a hyperfiction enthusiast, predicts that hypermedia will 'suck the substance out of a work of lettered art, reduce it to surface spectacle' (cited in Simanowski 2011: 72). Many scholars link baroque aesthetics to this flattened sense of spectacle and surface that comes to define postmodern practices. For instance, Angela Ndalianis reboots discussions of hypertexts and their networked structure as akin to the baroque and its fascination with mazes and labyrinths (Ndalianis 2004: 122–26). In any case, such associations with the baroque are quite often treated pejoratively.

Several scholars cast the baroque as the thoughtless, commercialized enemy. Manovich calls such baroque media artists 'Generation Flash' in a self-same titled essay, casting such an artist as 'a parasite who lives at the expense of the commercial media – the result of collective craftsmanship of highly skilled people' uninterested in media critique (Manovich 2006: 212). While postmodernism is popularly conceived as the blending of high and low culture, in this regard, a strong hierarchy seems still in place. Manovich argues that 'the language of modernist abstraction and design [must be employed] to get away from figuration in general, and cinematographic language of commercial media in particular' to escape the 'baroque assault of commercial media' (Manovich 2006: 211, 209). There is no denying that the baroque is well encapsulated in the media spectacles of its time such as operas, theatrical machinery and fireworks displays, and those equivalents still permeate our own culture evident in political conventions, concerts and special effects movies (Wollen 2006: 15). Though these cultural practices counter analytical ideologies expressed in high modernism and supported by the academy, willingly overlooking the baroque as spectacle can be a dangerous oversight that threatens to separate further the academy from the everyperson.

This simplified characterization of the baroque as a spectacle without thought, significance, or symbolism and the avant-garde as a pure thought and a raw awareness of mediation overlooks the nuanced relationship between baroque and avant-garde aesthetics. Simanowski calls on Andrew Darley to differentiate avant-garde and commercial (baroque) aesthetics in film since they seem to carry similar interests in formal aspects of the medium. Darley claims their differences lie in what filmmakers foreground. At times, attention is drawn to the materiality of film in such elements as grain or focus but at other times it is the spectacle of the film achieved by smoothing out the material qualities that the former highlights (Darley 2000: 114). When one insists on making distinctions between baroque and avant-garde attention to the medium and materiality, the avant-garde attention to materiality is more frequently considered a thought-provoking exercise that tests the audience's patience while the baroque spectacle does not seem to require interpretation because it is distracting and pleasurable to the audience (Simanowski 2011: 82).

Regardless of their visual and stylistic differences, baroque and avant-garde experimental motives often get confused for one another because they are conceptually similar. Both experiment with language and focus on form. However, the avant-garde does so by questioning its genre. René Magritte's 1929 *La trahison des images (ceci n'est pas une pipe)* plays with the still life as a flashcard. The baroque conversely accomplishes this fixation through the use of rhetorical tropes. For example, Michelangelo Caravaggio's 1600 *Martyrdom of Saint Matthew* for the Contarelli Chapel in the church of Saint Luigi dei Francesi in Rome uses contemporary clothing in a historical painting, building on the rhetoric of immersive contemplation forwarded by Saint Ignatius's *Spiritual Exercises*. Both movements aim to surprise their viewers with the unexpected – the avant-garde for novelty's sake and the baroque to amaze the viewer (Sefami 2011: 5). Ultimately, their differing methods complement rather than contradict one another in pursuit of a shared goal. Moreover, both the baroque and avant-garde are chiefly concerned with what Andrès Sánchez Robayna calls 'la materialidad y de la concreción del lenguaje' (the materiality and the concision of language) (cited in Sefami 2011: 7).

While the connection between digital literary texts and modernism or the avant-garde is undoubtedly well founded, its scope is limiting. Many technotexts that fall outside of or can be read as beyond modernist or avant-garde traditions get left behind. Pressman's study on modernism though does hold conceptual parallels to many scholars of the baroque. She uses the term 'modernism' not as a historical period but as a movement arranged around the concept of the medium. She interprets Ezra Pound's mantra 'make it new' not as a press for novelty, pure media or experimentation, but as a process of recovering and renovating the past via media. In the same spirit, several scholars of the baroque from Friedrich Nietzsche and Eugenio d'Ors to Walter Benjamin and Gonzalo Celorio also release the term 'baroque' from its use for historical periodization to emphasize recursive processes of representation.

Baroque as the Other Focus

To adopt the baroque as the second focus of this elliptical study is not to overwrite a modernist style for a baroque one. Instead, the baroque is its own ideology that can relieve the technotexts of some of modernism's limitations. In her examination of baroque thought, Buci-Glucksmann looks at three critical ruptures in modernity: the seventeenth-century baroque, Charles Baudelaire's Paris and avant-garde art movements. Ultimately, their similarities lead her to subsume the avant-garde and modernism as one of several resurgences of baroque reason spurred on by a moment of crisis. Because the baroque understands reality as artificial and admits 'the precarious, catastrophic, uncertain and hazardous nature of all human existence' (Turner 1994: 8), it can process representational crises. What Buci-Glucksmann recognizes in the baroque is not the reason that modernism typically refers to – an enlightened reason. The baroque is rather 'a different reason, or even a different modernity, which appeals to the interstices of reason and feeling' (Buci-Glucksmann 1994: 160).

Despite the general criticism that the baroque is void of critical thought, substance or structure, Timothy Murray in *Digital Baroque* argues that the baroque gives deeper, broader, more elastic psychosocial properties to new media immersion and interactivity. New media and the baroque resonate because they both depend 'on a model of knowledge that is grounded less in the centrality of the thinking subject than in the flow and energetics of mania and possession in all of its mystical intensity' (Murray 2008: 46). For Murray, our inscription into data flows and the increasing intensity of those flows displace the thinking subject with data accumulation (Murray 2008: 46). The speed of data blurs distinctions in time while faltering distinctions between subject and ground in space, both of which confound the participant.

This indistinction harkens to baroque aesthetic practices that confuse reality and representation. In his opening characterizations of the baroque, Robert Harbison broadly claims

> Baroque architecture becomes painterly, seeking fluidity and indistinctness much more feasible in flickering brushwork than solid stone. Painters like Preti conceive spatial ambitions which would be more at home in architecture, and one finds poets treating language as a plastic medium.
>
> (Harbison 2000: 4)

Such transgressions of media are not only the result of the competition of the *paragone* debates of the Renaissance – centered on the superiority of painting, sculpture or architecture's tools and techniques over the others – but a reflection of the subversive power of paradigm shifting views. For instance, Johannes Kepler's discovery of the elliptical planetary orbits exploded single-center images of God or King (Kaup 2007: 238–39). Chief among those challenged norms is the divide between reality and representation, which *trompe l'oeil* artists such as Cornelius Gijsbrechts and Evert Collier exemplify in their work or that *quadraturista* painter Andrea Pozzo made famous with his false dome (1684–85) in the Saint Ignatius church in Rome (Bailey 2012: 194). Such representational crises open up the *horror vacui* that spurs on the decorative motive to distract from representational meaninglessness.

Immersive spectacle represents a misunderstood and underappreciated aesthetic, one whose 'extravagance and excessive decoration requires a sophistication – [Susan] Sontag calls it "a good taste of bad taste"' (Simanowski 2011: 82). It follows that in baroque moments – and for Peter Burke in the historical baroque in particular – theatricality abounds. Burke charts the use of the term 'baroque' among art historians as originating in the late nineteenth century used chiefly as a label for art that broke from Renaissance rules of representation. According to Burke, rather than espouse clarity, balance, unity and harmony, baroque works adopt the theatrical and spectacular as a response to a 'crisis of representation'. Such a representational crisis occurs among several other crises of the seventeenth century, including the Thirty Years War, bubonic plague outbreaks, urbanization, the astronomical discoveries of Kepler and Galileo Galilei as well as the Protestant Reformation and the subsequent Catholic Counter-Reformation. At that time, opera flourished in music, church and palace frescoes resembled theatrical scenery, architecture acted out movement and even in a literal sense, sculptors created spectators to look on to other sculptures. Spectacle is a survival strategy that leans into crisis.

While legitimizing spectacle is playing with fire, critics like Ndalianis look to how spectacular or commercial applications of the baroque possess potential to criticize culture beyond their capacity to elicit pleasurable illusion. Instead, Ndalianis traces what she calls the 'inherent Baroque dualism: the desire to be drawn into and duped by the illusion being produced while simultaneously being cognitively aware of the means of the illusion's construction' (Ndalianis 2008: 269). Ndalianis confronts new media commercialism as a critical approach to mediation. Where others have dismissed the neobaroque culture industry as void of meaningful thought and an easily adopted tool to prop up hegemony with spectacle and popular kitsch, Ndalianis explores how baroque aesthetic tropes – seriality, intertextuality, illusion, multimedia, spectacle, database or mass and allegory – and their tendency to admit mediation and construction are 'driven by an enigma that opens up a space of ambiguity rather than mastered clarity' (Ndalianis 2004: 157). Exposing the representational process and its theatricality helps spectators reconnect with bodily, physical and sensual abilities as an alternative reason. Baroque cultural criticism is keen on exploiting the dangers of making reality and representation indistinct. Enter the hyperbolic parody of newstainment or the steady move toward layering more dimensions in our media from three- and four-dimensional movie theaters to augmented and virtual reality games, all far from thoughtless and often downright perplexing. Encapsulated in baroque practice and aesthetics is a revolutionary self-awareness of life as a representational performance that cannot be tamed by an enlightened reason but instead felt and experienced by a baroque reason.

Baroque Reason as Modernity's Madness

Perhaps a more radical foundation in the baroque is to view it not as an alternative modernity, an alternate reason, but rather as encapsulating the central thought problem of modernity. For William Egginton the baroque is the aesthetic counterpart to the problem of modern thought that unsettles our culture: that knowledge is only accessible through appearances, and truth is only our best estimation of a world veiled by those appearances (Egginton 2010: 2). This necessary reliance on assumption constitutes modernity's core thought problem and thwarts reason's ability to achieve modernity by usurping myth, religion and universality. Rather than discipline the senses or undermine appearances, 'the Baroque makes a theater out of truth, by incessantly demonstrating that truth can only ever be an effect of the appearances from which we seek to free it' (Egginton 2010: 2). Thus, the return of the baroque is not a return of a style or a recycling of culture, but a mark of this thought problem rearing its ugly head. This crisis of truth and appearance manifests almost hyperbolically in the digital where computer-generated representations feign the real objects they replace and where artificial digital enhancements prove both ubiquitous and accepted as real.

When the distinction between reality and representation is lost, literature becomes what Michel Foucault calls a 'representation of representation' (cited in Lambert 2008: 87) leading to the postmodern state of duplicitous representation in intertext, metatext, pastiche, allusion, etc. Lambert cites Foucault's claim that the word 'literature', like the word 'baroque', has become generic and abstract. Compositional laws and definitional limits have dissolved to the point that Foucault claims literature 'breaks with the whole definition of *genres* as forms adapted to the order of representations, and becomes merely a manifestation of a language that has no other law than to affirm [...] its own precipitous existence' (cited in Lambert 2008: 41, original emphasis). At a digitally induced crisis, literature needs the baroque as both 'literature' and 'baroque' are words exhausted of their meaning, but not defeated by meaninglessness. Even when words lose their meaning, language is not freed from representation but folds language back on itself (Lambert 2008: 165). With representation's truth value undermined and language's power limited, representation is doomed to repeatedly render a retreating reality so well achieved in the *mise en abyme*.

> [R]epresentation suddenly discovers that external to itself are not things themselves, but rather another order of representation that is consequently much older and more dense. The window of language opens to a mirror that reflects back into the enigmatic space [of] language itself, at least into the depth of its historical sedimentation, all the way to its ever receding and inaccessible *origin*.
>
> (Lambert 2008: 166, original emphasis)

Here literature, and even language more broadly, is trapped in a self-referential loop akin to how the computer is accused of only replicating or remediating all other media. Ultimately, this state reaffirms Lambert's core understanding of the baroque as 'a kernel of madness in the form of Western critical reason' that undermines reason's power to maintain and describe a reality (Lambert 2008: xxxii). Instead, the baroque exaggerates markers of reason and unmoors itself from the idea of history or progress. The baroque revolts against the dominant culture through foiling representation by emphasizing its presence, calling the very rules of representation into question – not just their content but also their arbitrary nature. This questioning process bars one from establishing new rules since the concept of rule-making becomes farcical. What is left then but to play with, distort and recycle rules?

While this may all sound like depressing end times, the baroque also pivots back to beginnings like an apple on the counter, both dying for being plucked from the tree and living in the potential of its seeds. Looking at representational processes and rules – as the technotext does with its increased attention to materiality – offers a new-old potential for creating and understanding literature in the digital mediascape. Such a fresh understanding would unveil 'a sense of humor and an intellectual energy that no longer requires nostalgia, nor any of the old sentiments associated with the cult of European Literature' (Lambert 2008: xx). Representation remains a game whose rules are being rewritten in a mediascape where literature holds no place of privilege. Through the affordances of contemporary media and technology, Lambert claims we might realize the 'programmatic re-invention of a mode of writing identified by the different modern notions of "literary representation"' that twentieth-century movements from surrealism and futurism to the OuLiPo and LANGUAGE poets began but could not quite circle around to another beginning, to another baroque (Lambert 2008: 146).

NOTES

1. Robert Darnton traces the beginnings of this 'sociology of books' to the *Annales* school of socioeconomic history that turned bibliography's attention from rare and fine books to 'the most ordinary sort of books'. New Historicism does similar work for literary studies by examining 'the negotiations or transactions between literary works and the discourses or practices of the social world' and so stepping away from structuralist and semiotic readings (Chartier and Elton 2005: 38).
2. Ultimately, N. Katherine Hayles uses the concept of the technotext to legitimize her proposed literary methodology of media-specific analysis, later called comparative textual analysis in the co-edited 2013 anthology, *Comparative Textual Media*, where Hayles and Jessica Pressman's methodological project means to broaden the performance of materiality for literary studies while defending close reading strategies.

Prologue

And so the cycle begins pivoting around opposites. We collect and accumulate to excess until overwhelmed. We reconstitute our *monadic* vantage point by choosing and thus narrowing our perspectives. Once we feel self-assured of our distinction, we notice that our dissimilarity from our environment is the result of representational framing and so we perceive representational practices everywhere as though trapped in an endless *mise en abyme*. Just as that self-awareness of our state as a representational or theatrical product might eradicate our vantage point, we turn to restore our perspective by immersing ourselves in the illusionist practices of *trompe l'oeil* so that our viewpoint seems central and grounded in what appears embodied and real. As we fall into accepting illusion as reality, we swivel back around toward exaggerating or emptying out realist practices. Instead, we critique the normalizing power of unquestioned conventions and representations by employing a *minor* strategy. And when we tire of denigrating reality as representation and accept that truth value and universal meaning does not hide behind the veil, we face the *horror vacui*: that despite the overwhelming mass of information, there is no meaning. We seek solace again in collecting and accumulating to excess to differentiate our vantage point as separate from that of others and from the environment that surrounds us.

And so the cycle begins again pivoting around opposites, drawing wobbly ellipses in baroque fashion. It was the digital that disrupted literatures settled into the print medium, and it is through baroque practices and their aptitude for embracing such wobblings that we might understand the technotext, which, teetering around the dual foci of context and form, reimagines literature's place in a digital mediascape.

CHOICE

A visit to the grocery store is anxiety producing. There are just too many choices. In a quick grocery run, I have the pleasure of sifting through 378 types and sizes of breakfast cereals, 437 yogurts and 94 vodkas. I have lost count of how many times I have asked my partner to pick up such and such at the store, and he comes back with the wrong brand, variety, flavor, size, etc. because my text just said 'almond milk'. I am half convinced that the onslaught of Facebook birthday messages one receives is only partly due to convenience but otherwise a dodge of that greeting card aisle that can easily turn into a fifteen-minute trap. A teenage me had the time to sort through and select a card for my father that featured a flowchart with options like 'Is today your birthday? YES – Did you get what you wanted? NO – This card is not for you. Put it down'. It was appealing to see so many potential outcomes coexist and eventually lead to yet another arbitrary outcome. The process of choosing became farcical. Of course, he thought the card was hysterical, and everyone in the family went through the flowchart, laughing at the ridiculousness of choosing yes/no options. Given that my father liked the card so much and has always been a sap for romantic comedies, some fifteen years later, I thought he would be just as pleased with the movie Mr. Nobody.

***

Jaco Van Dormael's 2009 film, *Mr. Nobody*, lays out a narrative structure akin to a flowchart for the life of the main character, Nemo Nobody, which is dependent upon the woman he chooses to marry: Jeanne, Elise or Anna. As Nemo knows the universe will begin contracting at 5:50 a.m. on 12 February 2092, and time will move backwards, he is pressured to decide what life is worth reliving, based on memories of his pasts, which are actually projected futures. So the viewer filters through the insights of one 9-year-old Nemo, multiple teen versions of Nemo, several 34-year-old versions of Nemo and one 118-year-old Nemo. One choice branches to several others, rendering choice less meaningful. In Van Dormael's assessment, the pleasure of the film lies in connecting disparate storylines that lead one to imagine more story branches (toutlecineTLC 2010). Van Dormael thought cinema simplified reality with basic answers whereas it should be honest about the complexity and ambiguity of human life (La Biennale di Venezia Channel 2009). Given that impetus, the film is dense. Rather than summarize and interpret the content of these timelines, it is more useful here to consider how the film presents choice.

Choice is the main character of *Mr. Nobody*. One can read Nemo as the imagined projection of a definitive moment of decision making: with his parents' divorce, does the 9-year-old Nemo go with his mother or stay with his father? Nemo is a set piece or frame that starts as a boy on a train platform and ends as an old man in a hospital admitting he exists only in the mind of that boy at that moment. All the bifurcations that occur in between are moves through a flowchart that continues to expand with each response.

Suspending the effects of a choice by considering the implications of unlimited potential choices traps reality in a thought project. Nemo does not exist in the archives or records of 2092 because his child self never made a choice on that train platform. A definitive life does not happen. Instead, multiple potential lives with Nemo's three possible wives play out hypothetically, much to the frustration of the news reporter soliciting old Nemo's life story. When the reporter presses old Nemo to clarify whether he chose to go with his mother or stay with his father, old Nemo has no response. Near the end of the film, the reporter asks old Nemo which is the right life. Old Nemo responds: 'Each of these lives is the right one. Every path is the right path. Everything could have been anything else, and it would have just as much meaning' (Van Dormael 2009).

Multiplying these hypotheticals leads to many overlaps in the storyline and overwhelms viewers with choices. Just shy of the halfway point of the theatrical cut of the film, Nemo, then married to Elise, takes his three children to school and encounters Anna driving beside him. He stops for a train crossing and in that train is another Nemo, this time a pool cleaner searching for Anna. This Nemo finds Anna in a train station, after being delayed when he calls an ambulance to retrieve a deceased homeless woman, who was alive in another timeline. When the homeless woman lives, Nemo misses his opportunity to reconnect with his soulmate, Anna. Beyond the storylines overlapping, the grammar of the film replicates itself where a shot of adult Anna and Nemo kissing against a wall and then tumbling into bed repeats the match cut used to capture a sexual encounter they shared as teenagers.

The exponential bifurcation of choices leads to the central paradox of the film: an insignificant event or decision can have drastic implications just as dramatic coincidences or cosmic alignments frequently lead to the commonplace. We see the first side of the paradox rather explicitly when Nemo's financially driven consumer choice to purchase cheaper jeans costs a Brazilian man his factory job. That Brazilian man can then boil an egg at home during business hours, which results in a rainstorm in Canada that destroys the note containing Anna's phone number. The other side of the paradox is more obscured. In each version of Nemo's life, he is a heterosexual, British male with a romantic disposition and above average intelligence born to the same parents, who in each version divorce. This character and his baseline context remain unaltered.

While one could attribute such similarity to continuity, Van Dormael's treatment of the one of Nemo's lives brings home the second side of the film's paradox. Nemo's many timelines collapse in a series of quick cuts near the end of the film, Nemo the science-fiction author drowns at his desk. This scene blends into Nemo drowning in his car, which exists in a timeline with Elise and with Anna, before he narrowly escapes to resurface in a bathtub in Jeanne's timeline where he is assassinated. The gunshot cuts into a respirator code of comatose Nemo, which fades into the meteorite shower that pulverizes the Mars shuttle where a fictional Nemo character, encased in the comatose Nemo's imagined science-fiction novel in one of Elise's timelines, meets a fictional scientist Anna. He circles back to find himself dead inside the sunken car before waking up in 2092. Ultimately, despite his choices, he has the same beginning and the same end. The middle of the story does not affect the beginning and is of little consequence to the end. Choice is both significant, in that it can drastically alter one's life toward different paths, and inconsequential, because those paths eventually narrow to similar ends. Nemo dies, usually in water.

This two-sided paradox bookends the film. Early in the film 9-year-old Nemo stands before a bakery window and decides that he will not choose which pastry to buy because all possible purchases exist until he chooses. Before we see 9-year-old Nemo in front of the bakeshop, we hear infant Nemo narrating immediately after adult science-show-host Nemo narrates an episode on The Big Crunch – the contraction of the universe and the possibility of a temporal quantum dimension. Infant Nemo follows up:

> If you mix the mashed potatoes and the sauce, you can't separate them later. It's forever. The smoke comes out of Daddy's cigarette, but it never goes back in. We cannot go back. That's why it's hard to choose. You have to make the right choice. As long as you don't choose, everything remains possible.
>
> (Van Dormael 2009)

This premise opens up the full exploration of the married lives he has with each woman. Having seen all the choices that result from selecting a guardian from his divorced parents, by the close of the film, old Nemo and the reporter watch the world around them float away, to which old Nemo says, '[t]he child is taking it apart. He doesn't need it anymore. Before he was unable to make a choice because he didn't know what would happen. Now that he knows what will happen, he is unable to make a choice' (Van Dormael 2009). Instead of choosing which parent to live with, Nemo decides that he will shuffle the deck further back in time so that another life that he has not yet played out will unfold. Rather than staying at the station with his father or taking the train with his mother, Nemo runs down the road to blow a leaf that might trigger another initial anomaly of life-altering effect, like the one his father attributes to meeting his wife – slipping on a leaf. Despite the many lives Nemo experiences, there are still infinitely more possibilities, given a slightly different presentation.

Van Dormael turns away from the cinematic trope of disciplining all parts to bring out *an* end to a linear path set out by a string of choices. Instead, he crafts his main character and guides his viewer to look backward in time to determine which hypothetical past results in the most desirable path to an ultimately similar end. This reversal opens viewers to contemplate what William Egginton considers the central problem of the baroque – dissociation expounded upon by theatricality or artifice renders false the distinction between nature and artifice. Instead, our truth is always 'folded, duplicitous, artificial all the way down' (Egginton 2010: 25).

Monads: A Harmonic Subjectivity for Technotextuality

Thinking into Our Environment

Perhaps one of the most significant challenges the digital poses to the literary establishment is its reminder that literature is not an exclusively human endeavor and that our technologies shape our literature. Indeed, the interplay between written content and production technologies is old. In ancient times, Egyptian scholars wrote on only one side of the papyrus sheet because the grain of the papyrus reed would run horizontally on one side and vertically on the other. The vertically oriented grain made writing horizontal script impractical. However, today we live in the midst of a seismic shift in inscription technology from pulped rags and wood to pixels and bits, which brings more attention to the material state of literature through all times in history. In a digital environment, we feel as though we live within our media technologies, and our immersion therein is criticized as detrimental to humans socializing with one another, or as a shift away from objective reality.

While human inquiry has considered the ambient environment for some time, Thomas Rickert claims that it is only recently that humans have gained a self-reflexive insight into our role in a larger environment. For Rickert, rhetoric should account for the ambient through Martin Heidegger's concept of *Stimmung*, or attunement, which discourages treating the human mind and body as separate. Instead, Rickert forwards an 'extended mind perspective [which] sees mind as bodily but not contained by the biological body, so that it extends to include various aspects of our material surroundings' (Rickert 2013: 10). We dismiss the idea that the machine affects the mind-body when we celebrate the autonomous individual. Rickert's ambient rhetoric brings the world to humans to alter how humans inhabit space (Rickert 2013: 29). Such human attunement is made more prominent with an increasingly intelligent technological environment that resists interpreting our technologies as inert tools.

Attunement and speculation present a worldview where humans do not *use* technology and media to accomplish a task. Instead, humans and their technologies *interface* with and overlap one another. They coevolve by exploring their fluid boundaries. In this sense, media and technology are not foreign, external objects. Mark Coté posits that we cannot understand media or technology by thinking about them but by *feeling* them (Coté 2010: n.pag.). From crude tools to language development, Coté highlights how deeply connected human bodies are to the technologies they adopt and develop. Tool use and cognitive development feed one another so that we externalize through our technologies while simultaneously those same technologies become internalized. Here we must practice Ian Bogost's view of speculation as a way to consider appearances without our preconceived notions of the world and release our objects from the assumptions and applications we ascribe to them. Doing so enables their internal potential to speculate other applications. When objects show us another way to imagine their use or place, we begin to negotiate openly with them, rather than use them.

The vitality of objects breaks the subject-object divide that forms the basis of Bruno Latour's critique of technology where neither human nor technology takes primacy over the other (Rickert 2013: 204). Such a leveled playing field means that the gun and the man, the object and subject, are equal agents since they affect one another. The gun goes from gun-in-the-cabinet to gun-in-the-hand, and the person went from person-empty-handed to person-with-a-gun (Rickert 2013: 205). Because they mutually affect one another, the subject cannot fully know the object as its essence withdraws when approached. Our human vantage point will always ultimately limit our perception of the object. While the move away from authorial intent in hermeneutics and bibliography took literary studies down a path toward improved attunement to materiality and social processes, the desire for an authoritative human persists as old habits do.

To feel in control of our environment, we strive to have a view above it, suspending our human perspective in order to reach for an objectivity free from contamination. Nonetheless, determining the edge of our bodies and the beginning of our environment proves challenging. Even using the human dermis is arbitrary as John Dewey in *Art as Experience* notes, since '[t]here are things inside the body that are foreign to it, and there are things outside of it that belong to it de jure if not de facto; that must be taken possession of if life is to continue' (Bennett 2010: 102). Making a clear distinction between our humanity and our surroundings seems increasingly arbitrary when we consider the ambient. Certainly, one can consider this recession sinister, where humans lose their agency and humanity. We see this in images of suppression and punishment as in the crew of Davy Jones in *Pirates of the Caribbean: Dead Man's Chest* and *At World's End*, who meld into the ship by growing and eventually becoming shellfish, barnacles and coral. This phenomenon is as old as Greek myths with their multiple nymphs and humans turned to trees, mist or spiders. However, this recession could equally morph to immersive play where one enters a state of diminished critical distance to alter one's mental state (Grau 2003: 13). By immersing the human user into the digital environment, 'the body is coupled to virtual worlds and undergoes a "commutation process," a post-biological experience in which human actions engage digital technologies in the process of understanding the world' (Domingues 2004: 309). While this is generally dramatized as the death of the subject, the human constituent is still there, but in a way that undermines the long-held cultural hierarchy that places the human as dominant entity and source of agency. By demonstrating spaces that are not anthropocentric or physically like our earthly environment, digital technologies lead us to reconsider our fundamental relationship to our surroundings and its primary effect on our perceptions and behaviors.

On the other hand, seeing the objects and environment around us as vital is a chance for humans to redeem their humanity. For Jane Bennett, 'the image of dead or thoroughly instrumentalized matter feeds human hubris and our earth-destroying fantasies of conquest and consumption' (Bennett 2010: ix). Should humans quit their delusions of independence and exclusive agency, they may consider themselves part of a shared agency, which may not always be clear or comprehensible to human perception. Bennett sees Theodor Adorno's negative dialectics at work here, when an object and its concept do not directly correspond and so introduce a remainder that unhinges our human knowledge or control over both (Bennett 2010: 14). Bennett charts these in many assemblages such as the August 2003 blackout, attributed to multiple causes including wonky electron flow, spontaneous fires and mislaid faith in self-regulation. Even reconsidering Charles Darwin's *Formation of Vegetable Mould through the Actions of Worms with Observations of Their Habits* offers a view of human history quite dependent on functions and assemblages that work regardless of human existence or will (Bennett 2010: 95–96). What makes us human is also beyond human, revealing 'an "alien" quality of our own flesh' (Bennett 2010: 108).

What Rickert says of the body-mind divide, book historians have said of the divide between authorial content and the material form of the book. Consciously recombining content and form, medium and message, requires that each holds equal importance and mutually affect one another, which requires significant code-switching. Technotexts, because they consider their inscription medium as part of their composition, understand that our technologies, digital or otherwise, do act upon us. Accepting our technologies as an intimate part of our humanity helps us move beyond regarding technology as an estranging and dehumanizing force that will destroy or replace us, when it is instead integral to our species. We must remember that graphite pencils and paper are as much a human technology as a personal computer or the Internet.

While in the broad sense a pencil is a human technology as a personal computer is, the nature and affordances of a specific technology alter writing, publication, transmission and reading processes. Scrolls required two hands to keep open, leaving none free to write notes during one's reading process. Codices combined all the content of a work to one binding and made ease of reference with indices and pages, while reading on the screen 'brings ephemeral, multiple, and unique textual units [...], units that are created following the will of the reader, and they are in no respect pages' (Chartier 2004: 151). What becomes of literature? Literature must admit it is more than human as we are not beyond the fold of our environment.

The Double-Folded Monad

While the hermeneutic turn of literary studies in the twentieth century brought an unbalanced attention to the author of the text or the text as the author's, the networked nature of the digital computer reminds literary scholars that the text and the author were always a part of an elaborate process of materializing words. To think that the writer works alone and the movie director works with a cast and crew disregards the material system of literary production. To embrace what value and impact digitality can have for literary expressions, whether born from human or nonhuman authors, we must reimagine human subjectivity as a dependent part of a larger ecology, not as an independent entity that can ignore or work outside of context, history or materiality. However, for the baroque, this ecological whole is not an affront to humanity but instead a more representative view of how the baroque imagines unity – not via the unique individual or the auteur, but via Gottfried Leibniz's monad, which Gilles Deleuze revives in his book *The Fold: Leibniz and the Baroque*. Monadic unity is based on the idea that all possibilities remain until choices or actions limit a specific manifestation into individual perspectives. A monadic subjectivity offered up by baroque thought and exercised in one of its most effective tropes, allegory, proves nurturing to the potential of technotexts. In short, monadology provides a vision for subjectivity that the technotext offers to literature: that an individual literary text is not divorced from or independent of the networks involved in its formation.

The baroque relishes the potential of multiplicity to create events and vibrations born from making folds to manifest new things. This constant process of folding builds from the general to the specific through a modification of perspective eventually honed into a monad. The baroque representation of the world is made up of an infinite number of such monads all created by folding the same material differently, resulting in varied perspectives. For Deleuze, a monad comprises two levels, which he imagines as stories of a house: the first an organic mass of the matter and the second an inorganic method of organizing the matter on the lower level. In this house, the matter is folded twice. First, on the lower level, it is differentiated from other objects of matter, and second, on the upper level, the monad achieves a perspective by selecting matter to perceive and make omnipresent. According to Leibniz, each monad contains the whole world but focuses on one aspect. This focusing on a particularity is the effect of the upper level organizing the matter in the lower level, which thus pinpoints the particular matter to be called into reason. This double folding is the principal function of the monad where:

> [T]he whole world is only a virtuality that currently exists only in the folds of the soul which convey it, the soul implementing inner pleats through which it endows itself with a representation of the enclosed world. We are moving from inflection to inclusion in a subject, as if from the virtual to the real, inflection defining the fold, but inclusion defining the soul or the subject, that is, what envelops the fold, its final cause and its completed act.
>
> (Deleuze 1992: 23)

Each monadic subject perceives the same world, but by selecting certain perceptions and experiences, one monad's worldview is limited to its own vantage point (Deleuze 1992: 90). The fold introduces a spatial paradox for the monadic subject: the monad is bigger on the inside than on the outside. While what is perceivable and reasonable is only the second floor and its resulting perspective, it is still built upon the infinite possibilities housed on the first floor.

Crucial to the value of the monad as a model for subjectivity is how the two floors resonate with one another by holding in conjunction the distinct perspective of the second floor and the connectedness of all perspectives of the first floor. Baroque insights come from resting in between the two floors of the baroque house where one is privy to the folding process of the second floor that creates the illusion of an individual subject. Hence Deleuze says, '[t]he Baroque artists know well that hallucination does not feign presence, but that presence is hallucinatory' (Deleuze 1992: 125). To point out from the second floor that the first floor exists essentially unfolds the choices and actions that made the monadic subject distinct.

Because of their shared first floor, monads anticipate what is outside their perspective even when folded on the second floor. This emphasizes building harmonies across monads, which forms the backbone of social models of life like Latour's actor-network theory. By reconstituting the world as an infinite series of monads,

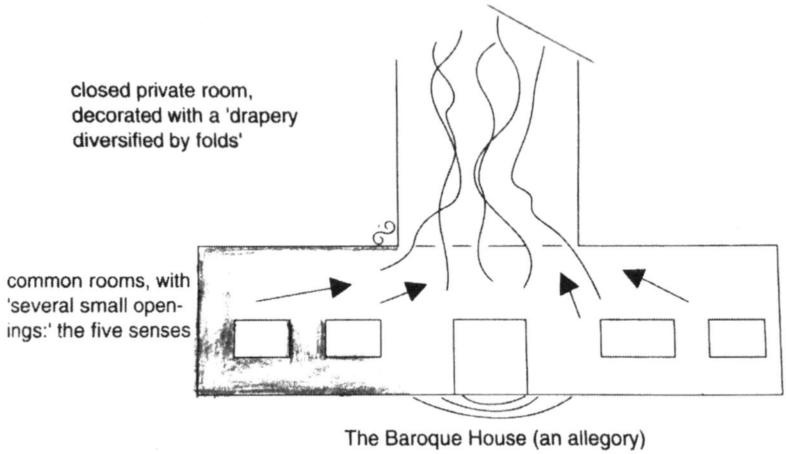

FIGURE 1: Gilles Deleuze, 'The Baroque House (an allegory)' in *The Fold: Liebniz and the Baroque*, 1988. Continuum Publishing. Use courtesy of Bloomsbury Publishing Plc. and The University of Minnesota Press.

baroque reason divides discords into separate monads so they can be rearranged to harmonize with others. For Deleuze:

> Classical reason toppled under the force of divergences, incompossibilities, discords, dissonances. But the Baroque represents the ultimate attempt to reconstitute a classical reason by dividing divergences into as many worlds as possible, and by making from incompossibilities as many possible borders between worlds. Discords that spring up in a same world can be violent. *They are resolved in accords* because the only irreducible dissonances are between different worlds. In short, the Baroque universe witnesses the blurring of its melodic lines, but what it appears to lose it also regains in and through harmony.
> (Deleuze 1992: 81–82, original emphasis)

Rather than discipline all existence to one unifying melody as would the classical, the baroque fragments and rearranges bits into harmonic resonances. Making these harmonies by resonating or empathizing with other monads reveals the constructed state of one's monadic perspective. Rather than consider this the destruction of self, we must anticipate others, empathize with others and harmonize with other monads by opening to our surroundings. Once we see an entity on the first floor, we drop away from thinking of its purpose in our life, of its tool value or *zuhanden*, and return to a *vorhanden* moment characterized by a drive to understand the entity ontologically (Bogost 2012: 16). To understand such a flattened world of *vorhanden* where humans hold equal weight to tables or calculators, we must deploy an ontography that reveals object relationships without overdetermining what those objects are.

Allegory as Monadic Communication

The purest form of such ontography is the list, which differentiates entries without necessarily determining relationships between entries. These lists allow us to see the thingness of all entries and negotiate relationships with them rather than settle into the smoothing effects of metaphor, allegory or narrative that allow us to instrumentalize objects more easily. Latour et al. provide a clear example of the flat ontology of lists by way of the database search. Here the actor and network exist on the same level where actors define networks as networks define their actors (Latour et al. 2012: 593). Searching for a person in an online database will bring us to their employer, co-workers, family, hometown and personal interests (Latour et al. 2012: 593). In this case, we are each the sum of our data points and a data point for other entries.

Despite such knowledge, we still construct illusions of individual perspectives because we find pleasure in determining our reality with the second fold. Our desire for a sense of individual identity is why, for the time being, humans are not yet satisfied by Bogost's list and still find allegory or metaphor a useful stepping stone to the alien space outlined by object-oriented ontology that the digital mediascape helps usher into our daily experience.

The metaphor and allegory are not the reality of the thing but a perspective from which to view the world, admitting that '[t]o the hammer everything looks like a nail. To the human animal, the soybean and the gasoline look inert, safe, innocuous. But to the soil, to the piston?' (Bogost 2012: 79). A metaphor works to bring the surfaces of objects together while pushing away their inner essence, though we often mistake the metaphor for the object's essence. While one could explain the science of object relationships (with or without humans), that explanation cannot capture the essence of the experience so that 'even if the experience of the Twinkie can be understood as a neurochemical unit operation, such an explanation does not describe the *experience* of sweetness' (Bogost 2012: 62, original emphasis). For Bogost, we would have to be like a tongue or like complex sugars.

Ultimately, we cannot venture far from our perspective because, while a metaphor might explain one object relationship, its clarity decreases with each added relationship. The folded spaces of the monad make us aware of what remains beyond our grasp – what has receded into the creases of our folds. Kresimir Purgar calls this receding awareness the *je ne sais quoi* trope, which he derived from Omar Calabrese's treatment of approximation included in

Neo-Baroque: A Sign of the Times (1992). The *je ne sais quoi* acknowledges the existence of a remainder that unbalances the equation and whose content escapes explanation (Purgar 2007: 20). This lack of equilibrium disallows subjects from assuming a stable reality. Instead, we are vulnerable to environments that change or destabilize our perception (Purgar 2007: 48, 51), undermining efforts to distinguish reality from representation.

Such remainders that narrative cannot hold and what recedes in metaphor must be strung together to access a baroque reason that evades clarity or unconscious utility. For Walter Benjamin, these remainders, which seem like extra details, function as symbols to the underlying allegory (Day 1999: 109). Though the allegorical is by nature fragmentary, untidy and disordered, it is not nonsense. Allegory here is the ground required of any symbolic action (Day 1999: 109), making the baroque heavy with material. Its impact is akin to Kenneth Goldsmith's experience of Benjamin's *The Arcades Project*:

> It's the sense of sheer bulk and abundance that makes it impossible to ever finish; it's so rich and so dense that trying to read it induces amnesia – you're not sure whether you've already read this or that passage. It's really a text without end. What holds the work together – while at the same time ensuring that you remain lost – is the fact that many entries are cross-referenced, but often lead to dead ends.
>
> (Goldsmith 2011: 115–16)

By emphasizing the allegorical, the baroque takes us back to the ground rather than the figure, a move equivalent to walking down the stairs of the baroque house from the individual perspective of the second floor to the universal flow of matter and energy on the first floor.

Accordingly, this kind of allegory is not only a literary device, but also a baroque way of seeing. Allegory's fragmentation is how one recognizes a text as a constructed product of a creative process (Martin 1994: 106). Not only do we see this constructedness, but we also see the paradox of a text being both a process and a product. Benjamin sees these in several modern phenomena and figures: the *flâneur* who perceives himself as master or *voyeur* of the commodities when he too is a commodity; the sex worker who is the commodity and vendor; fashion that is new and nothing but a repetition of the same. The power of the allegory is to hold tension between extreme opposites without resolving or compromising their polarity (van Reijen 1992: 3), which explains why allegory encapsulates melancholy so well: holding what is lost. Willem van Reijen sees this simultaneous contrast in two major baroque tropes of the ruin and the labyrinth – of decay that lasts forever and disorientation that strives for orientation. Allegorical fragmentation and disorientation are not just themes or tropes but 'intellectual *disposition*[s]' (van Reijen 1992: 9, original emphasis).

Baroque allegory does not have to be dark or depressing. Deleuze's reading of Leibniz provides a lighter, more joyful view of a baroque imagining of the universe rather than the tragedy and melancholia Benjamin forwards (Laerke 2010: 26). While Benjamin's melancholia stems from the subject's fragmentary experience of the hopeless ruin, Deleuze's Leibnizian baroque takes the lack of self-determination as jubilant. For Benjamin, the subject *experiences* allegory because the modern subject, still seeking truth value in self-representation, feels a lack of control and crippling arbitrariness. The subject of Benjamin's allegory becomes passive. Deleuze's Leibniz does not espouse truth value and self-representation, so instead *expresses* an allegory. Deleuze's allegory is not a divisive and estranging fragmentation but a perspectivalism and objectivity that enfold the subject in a larger harmony. For Leibniz, this harmony was divine, even theological, but for Deleuze, this harmony comes from the infinite process of becoming. Still, like all states that require faith, allegory is dizzying and anxiety-producing.

Even so, Deleuze closes *The Fold* by describing a more open monadology that characterizes our contemporary experience. He unfolds two assumptions of Leibniz's monad to create his nomadology in place of monadology. These nomadic monads have access to and question the original selection process of which universe is *the* universe of a monad. It is thus aware of compossible worlds. Also, these monads are not closed off without doors or windows, but instead they open 'on a trajectory or a spiral in expansion that moves further and further away from a center' (Deleuze 1992: 137). With this conscious awareness of perspectives unincorporated in its own experience, the monad moves away from its once seemingly stable perspective.

Consequently, scrutinizing monads requires imposing an artificial stillness. Holding still one arrangement freezes it into a condition that Benjamin called a 'constellation' – a flash of the now rather than the past lighting the present or the present lighting the past (Goldsmith 2011: 116). *The Arcades Project* turned to a constellation when published as a bound, linearly arranged book rather than another possible material construction such as a collection of loose-leaf notecards. What we face with the digital is how we are more easily assimilating our experience to the fluidity of quickly changing constellations. Websites pull from many servers to construct the content of one page, which all update each time one refreshes the page (Goldsmith 2011: 116–17). What may seem like a straightforward switch from a paper book to a webpage quickly reveals our assumptions, biases and anxieties about literary expression and the place of our human agency in that sphere.

Reanimating or altering a constellation opens us up to the first floor and makes us conscious of our choices and their impacts. In transcribing one issue of the *New York Times* for his book *Day*, Goldsmith faced many more questions than he anticipated, showing how impactful the presence of one author's agency is to the construction of just one constellation. Just in thinking through transcribing the newspaper issue, not to mention paratextual or design features of the book volume, Goldsmith asks himself:

> But what to do with the font, font sizes, and formatting? If I remove the images (while grabbing the texts embedded in the images, such as the numbers on the license plate in a car ad), I still must keep the captions. Where do the line breaks occur? Do I remain faithful to the slim columns or do I flow each article into one long paragraph? What about the pull quotes: where do those lines break? And how do I make my way around a page? I know I have a rough rule to move from the upper left corner to the lower right, but where do I go when I reach the end of a column and it says 'continued on page 26'? Do I go to page 26 and finish the article or do I jump to the adjacent column and start another article? And, when I make those jumps, do I add another line break or do I flow the text continuously? How do I treat the advertisements, which often have playful text elements of varying fonts and styles? Where do line breaks occur in an ad where words float about a page? And what about the movie timetables, the sports statistics, the classified ads?
>
> (Goldsmith 2011: 118–19)

To all his questions on constructing *Day*, Goldsmith responds, '[i]n order to proceed, I have to build a machine. I have to answer each question and set up a number of rules that I must then strictly follow' (Goldsmith 2011: 119). Authors working on digital platforms turn to think about how they can continue to produce constellations readers can contemplate in a digital space that exponentially increases the amount of language produced, drastically shortens the lifespan of one constellation and stunts the attention span of the reader. Authors who engineer or design a constellation harmonize with the underlying ground of allegory more than they materialize symbols.

A Monadic Model of Biography

David Clark is one such story architect who takes literally the idea of building constellations as surfacing moments of now. His *88 Constellations for Wittgenstein (to be played with the Left Hand)* is particularly interesting because it can be read as a variation on the biography, a genre that typically recounts past events in chronological order. Clark primarily constructed *88 Constellations for Wittgenstein* from secondary sources, especially biographies of Ludwig Wittgenstein, creating what he called a 'meta-biography' (Clark 2015: 292). Clark did not originally intend to produce a biographical or meta-biographical piece but instead used Wittgenstein as an anchor for 'the destabilized meanings offered up by the information-rich but context-poor internet' (Clark 2015: 293). Rather than a resurrection of Wittgenstein's past, this meta-biography is an offering *for* Wittgenstein. The title's choice of preposition foists the project into an act of giving that must remain suspended, for how would Wittgenstein receive a gift after death? These are not '88 Constellations on Wittgenstein' or '88 Constellations of Wittgenstein', but *88 Constellations for Wittgenstein*. They are not explanations or possessions, but offerings made from shuffling a closed set of 88 flash animations.

Despite being a closed set, the project presents a number of paradoxes that increase the allegorical potential of each recombination of animations. For instance, each animation is associated with one of the 88 stellar constellations, but also to many other stars throughout the project that are parts of other constellations. Clark links the constellation Camelopardalis to the flash animation titled 'the great dictator', after the 1940 Charlie Chaplin film, and yet, that animation also appears as a star on seven other constellations (Triangulum Australe, Cepheus, Draco, Grus, Auriga, Gemini and Hercules). The construction of each constellation from the components of other constellations folds up the celestial map into a mesh of overlaps. Even the pivotal number 88 marks a discrete number and also a doubling of the symbol for infinity, thus both finite and infinite.

Such a narrative structure embodies the wandering associations of the Internet user's experience and showcases the web of tenuous links, coincidences and duplicities that abound when one ventures beyond a singularly focused perspective. Clark admits, 'I use the facts of Wittgenstein's life not to create a portrait with an internal consistency but instead to emphasize the external relations of his life to the outside world' (Clark 2015: 295). Clark does not seek a deeper authenticity but a broader approach to an examined life, which looks to context and exteriority (Clark 2015: 296). Reimagining biography as one built on secondary sources and focused on exterior relations rather than internal coherence provides a step toward monadic subjectivity in which interest lies in the harmonies one life might make with other entities.

By writing a networked meta-biography that distributes the focus from one biographical subject to several convergences around the subject, Clark shows the entanglement of a life and its context. Addressing major life events is not the agenda of the piece since a number are skimmed over. Instead, the piece serves several goals. It paints a picture of Wittgenstein as a thinker, it introduces readers to some of his ideas and it makes historical and sociopolitical associations relevant to today's reader. Some associations pivot around: the number 88, suicide, logic, hands, homosexuality, silence, the terror attacks of 9/11, Hollywood and so on. These will cycle back to Wittgenstein, but the reader has to entertain long tangents. Thus, the individual is less impactful than the sum of the relationships and associations possible.

When navigating Clark's *88 Constellations*, the reader must first select a constellation from the sky chart, which opens the corresponding animation. At that point, there are three methods of navigating further reading. One could return to the sky chart to review all constellations. This privileges spatial proximity and the association between a constellation and its ascribed animation. One could equally select stars charted in the individual constellation map of the animation just played. This privileges thematic or narrative connections the author has made by placing animations together into one constellation. Finally, one could access the site map and select and choose animations by title. Doing so removes the constellation map as a structuring model and strips the story down to a database of animations.

For this analysis, I have decided to read the piece by the second navigational method. This is structurally the most challenging method because selecting a link from the constellation map replaces that map with a new constellation map. Without a functioning 'back' button, this reading requires one to reset the original constellation by returning to the sky chart or site map. In a way, the reading that privileges the author's thematic linkages is the least accessible method to navigate the piece. In contrast, the most navigationally intuitive method is to work from the map of the current constellation and thus jump from a star in one constellation to a star in a completely different constellation. Such a method quickly becomes spatially disorienting as one is figuratively jumping across the universe without knowing how far they have traveled or if they have reached every constellation. This movement captures the Internet user's reading patterns: moving click by click without an aerial view of movements made in the background.

The structure and play on genre evident in this piece make it an excellent representation of monadic systems that use allegory as a mode of communication. Not only do the overlaps and associations generated in the work showcase an anxiety about the edge of self in a monadic imagining of the universe, but those same anxieties also reveal the potential all entities have of harmonizing with alternate perspectives that surface as one folds and unfolds one's perspective. Peering into the database of 88 animations, knowing that further combinations exist helps us contemplate our constructed viewpoint and burrow into the specifics of our worldview by force of differentiation. We can unfold ourselves outward in a *vorhanden* moment of actively negotiating with other monads or fold up the world inward to ourselves in a *zuhanden* moment of instrumentalizing others to our preconceived goals. Between these unfoldings and foldings, we come to realize that our perspectives are not just constructed, but limited, leaving behind remainders that we cannot incorporate into our story but resonate in other monads whose perspectives we reach out to allegorically. For these three ideas on monadic communication via allegory glossed in the previous three sections – anxiety regarding the edge of self, the potential to harmonize with others and the constructedness and limited nature of individual perspective – I have chosen three constellations and their linked animations as illustrations: Aquarius ('88') for the first, Perseus ('a wonderful life') for the second and Pavo ('paul wittgenstein') for the third.

Folding In and Unfolding Out

Let us begin the star tour with Aquarius, which Clark has linked to the animation titled '88', though, on the site map, it is the first animation in the series and thus could be seen as primer and summary. As such, this animation lays the groundwork for many of the overlapping events, figures and repeated themes sprinkled throughout the piece. The narration for this animation is brief and more poetic than many others. In its entirety, the animation states:

> 8 and 8. 88. Constellations and piano keys. Two upright infinities. Two fat ladies. 1-8-8-9. Chaplin, Hitler and Wittgenstein. Star-crossed sons of fate. Born to love and born to hate. One would last to 88. Two fat ladies. Two upright infinities.
>
> (Clark 2008)

The 88 constitutes the number of constellations and the number of keys on a piano, preparing readers for future references to stars, myths, the moon, telescopes, lenses, the universe, infinity and the science fiction film *2001: A Space Odyssey* as well as to John Cage, Maurice Ravel, Ludwig van Beethoven, silence, the musical brain and Ludwig's brother, Paul Wittgenstein, himself a one-handed concert pianist. The 88 represents 1889, the birth year of Ludwig Wittgenstein, Charlie Chaplin and Adolf Hitler. The number 88 also doubles the digit 8, prefacing a significant theme of repetition and duplication that later incorporates the role of repetition in the scientific method, twins, double lives of actors and copying or plagiarism. Visualizing the 88 as two upright infinities encases the central paradox of having a closed set of 88 animations with a seemingly infinite number of recombinations of those animations.

While visual components throughout the piece frequently illustrate the spoken word, punning across visual and verbal media is rather common. As the narrator reads '[s]tar-crossed sons of fate. Born to love and born to hate', the reader sees two inverted triangles cross to form a Star of David, opening future lines of inquiry regarding Judaism and anti-Semitism. Another such pun exists in the repeated lines 'two upright infinities' (Clark 2008). In the first instance, the reader sees two figure eights traced in a loop. When the narrator repeats the line at the end of the animation, we see the silhouette of the World Trade Center, whose destruction on September 11, 2001 furnishes another theme.

The constellation of Aquarius includes seventeen stars, but Clark has only linked thirteen animations to individual stars. 'april 1889' and 'infinity' further establish this particular constellation as one devoted to the paradox of finding the infinite in the finite, as well as how repetition can prove a fact or point to coincidence. For instance, 'infinity' mentions how bees dance in a figure eight to lead other bees to a desirable discovery. On the other hand, humans use the symbol of infinity to show what cannot be achieved or proven. The same symbol stands for oppositional meanings, and this simultaneity is stated as fact. Repetition as coincidence appears in 'april 1889' as the animation opens with the statement 'count your lucky stars', with stars from Hollywood Boulevard on display. The three April 1889 birthdays of Hitler, Chaplin and Wittgenstein are presented as chance followed by speculations on whether the 'Jewish boy' Hitler mentions attending school with as a child was Wittgenstein. While the three birthdays are factual information, Hitler, Chaplin and Wittgenstein's connectedness based on a shared birth month appears as a coincidence. That repetition creates both fact and coincidence and makes readers less confident that there is a discernable difference between the two.

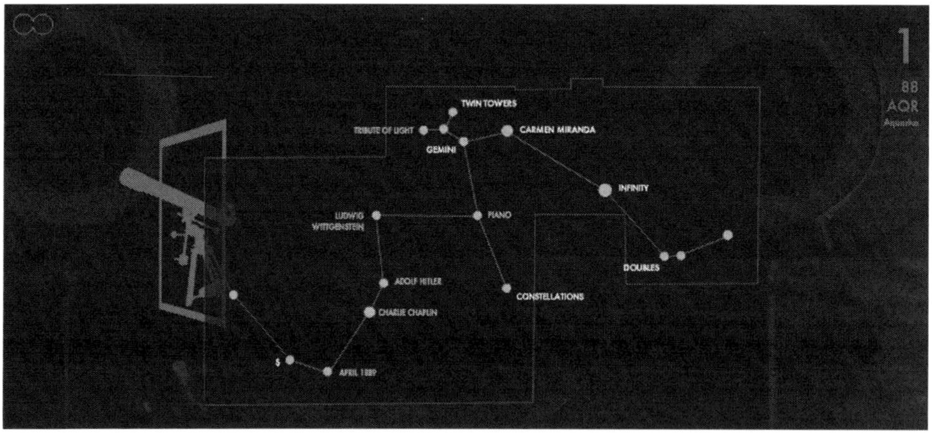

FIGURE 2: David Clark, '88', *88 Constellations for Wittgenstein (to be played with the Left Hand)*, 2009. Flash net.art. Use courtesy of David Clark.

Given this indistinction, one can unfold outward toward infinity via association or one could fold inward by doubling or replicating. Beginning with animations that unfold outward to external associations, 'constellations' offers a brief statement on the nature of storytelling that is exercised in *88 Constellations* extensively. The narrator states: 'Let me get to the point. A point is a fact. A line connects two points. A line is a story that connects two facts. A story is a vector connecting facts together. These vectors make pictures' (Clark 2008). Given this basic formula, readers witness the premise behind the visual structure of *88 Constellations*: connecting stars to make pictures. *88 Constellations* points to specific instances in Wittgenstein's life to connect those points to others across the infinite points possible. We experience one of many vectors in the Aquarius constellation when the number 88 'upright infinities', recast as the World Trade Center, reappears in the linked animation 'tribute of light'. The animation recounts the use of 88 searchlights to create the Tribute of Lights monument – eleven lights for each of the eight sides of the twin towers. The vector is drawn further from the number 88, onto the Cathedral of Lights Albert Speer designed for the 1930s Nazi rallies in Nuremberg. Other vectors drawn between story components surface in 'charlie chaplin' and 'piano'. Again, the number 88 begins the vector. Having already introduced Chaplin's birth in 1889, we hear that he lived to 88, long enough to have

> played all the notes on life's great keyboard. From those low, long-sustained, melancholic notes of childhood, a childhood spent in poverty in London from where he forged his little tramp character. All the way up, octave by octave, as he built an empire in Hollywood, becoming rich and famous, possibly the most famous person in the world. But in the shrill high notes of old age, Chaplin's star faded.
>
> (Clark 2008)

The 88 reaches outward to the piano, launching an analogy between pitch and human traits such as age or professional progress. This unfolding outward toward further numeric or visual similarities reveals the underlying allegorical structure of these animations that, while distinct, bleed into each other.

Although much of *88 Constellations* works through association to unfold outward to diverse concepts, figures or events, folding inward also occurs, often in the same animation. While 'charlie chaplin' uses the piano as an extended analogy for his life's progress and upward social mobility to turn inward toward himself, 'piano' represents the piano as an elephant with the form of Africa as its ear, recovering the original source of the ivory for the keys of pianos in elegant European parlors. By turning the piano back into its raw material, the animation reveals the source of western upward mobility: the exploitation of colonial resources as a figurative elephant in the room. Folding in reveals the elephant and unfolding out uncovers practices of empire. Similarly, in the animation 'adolf hitler' we begin again with the number 88 that Neo-Nazis equate to the eighth letter of the alphabet, HH for Heil Hitler, thus explaining why German soccer teams do not use the number 88 on jerseys. The animation then unwinds into what Hitler hid: the shape of his nose. For the remainder of the animation, we fold inward into aspects of Hitler and the potential reality that his grandmother could have been impregnated by her employer, the Baron Rothschild, resulting in Hitler being a quarter Jewish.

A clean example of folding inward is explicitly addressed in the animation 'doubles' where Clark cites the necessity of repetition to confirm scientific discoveries. However, philosophy functions through double negatives, where a truth statement is either not true or not not true. Such repetition is less a confirmation than a folding inward where the second 'not' digs into the previous 'not' statement as given. Philosophical doublings are not as clearly separate as repeated experiments in the sciences, which are considered independent of one another. Philosophy's doubling inward instead of serial replication results in the closing concept of the 'doubles' animation, where Clark says,

> W. Double You. Double UU. U2. We were always at least two people, perhaps more. Once when Wittgenstein was working in his cottage in Ireland, a neighbor came by and was surprised to find him alone after hearing talking. I replied, 'I was talking to a very dear friend of mine, myself.' That was how Wittgenstein wrote. All his writings were a conversation with himself. A tête-a-tête.
>
> (Clark 2008)

Essentially, Wittgenstein doubles himself and turns inward to confirm the doubling.

Such an inward doubling that results in a non-universalizing statement is generalized beyond Wittgenstein's writing practice in the animation 'gemini'. Here readers are asked to consider twins as separate but identical and imagine that we are all Siamese twins connected everywhere, essentially doubled into the self that thinks of the self and the self that is thought of. In both 'doubles' and 'gemini' we are presented with this doubling as a mirror image or inversion. In 'doubles' we see two replicas of Auguste Rodin's *The Thinker* facing away from each other but connected at the base. At the same time, we hear: 'We are always at least two people, perhaps more' and then experience the Rubin vase optical illusion for the Irish neighbor anecdote (Clark 2008). Not only do we get a figural doubling with the Rubin vase illusion, but we are also asked to invert figure and ground to see either the two profiles or the vase and so have two images in one.

Another such folding inward occurs with the juxtaposition of animations 'ludwig wittgenstein' and 'carmen miranda'. In 'ludwig wittgenstein' we are presented with several aspects of Wittgenstein's life, interests and traits as fodder for later unfoldings outward. However, this animation opens with the preface:

> That's him. This picture represents him. That contains the whole problem of representation. What is the criterion? How is it to be verified that this picture is the portrait of that object, i.e. that it is meant to represent it? It is not similarity that makes the picture a portrait. It might be a striking resemblance of one person and yet be a portrait of someone else it resembles less.
>
> (Clark 2008)

We are essentially told that resemblance to the subject does not make a portrait, so perhaps dissimilarity is as telling as repetition. If that is the case, when we seem to be unfolding out to associated connections and coincidences, that same movement could be inversely read as a folding in of a more core semblance. In 'carmen miranda' we are presented with the idea that Wittgenstein and Miranda appear to have no similarities on the surface – that the austere academic and flamboyant, gold-digging performer are dissimilar and ill-matched, making Wittgenstein's interest in her films peculiar. However, both are idols with a loyal following, making their differences seem more like inversions of each other or mirror images superimposed rather than starkly separate entities.

Readers also experience this inversion in their assumptions and associations in animations like 'twin towers'. Given the title, western readers will expect content focused on the World Trade Center. Instead, they get an unnarrated animation with still, silhouetted images of doubled twin towers – the Petronia Towers in Kuala Lumpur, Malaysia, and the World Trade Center in New York. The first is in a majority Muslim country and the second in a majority Christian country. We are asked to look outside of our western imagination and consider that our surface differences might be like that of Wittgenstein and Miranda, convincing but ultimately inversions of the same mirrored back upon itself.

Containing Differences Harmoniously

Seeing what we imagine as separate and opposite from us as an incorporated inversion replicates the experience of the monad cracking open the door to the first floor and seeing the universal possibilities from which its limited and ultimately constructed perspective is built. This realization throws the crisis of representation back into the foreground. One can see reality as a *vorhanden* moment and contemplate one's constructed nature while moving down closer to the first floor. On the other hand, one could turn toward the second floor in a *zuhanden* moment and continue differentiating one's perspective from the mire of totality swirling on that first floor. This movement running up and down the staircase of the baroque house is the crux of the value of the baroque – the essential awareness that one's constructed perspective frames the act of looking and understanding. We see this in the Perseus constellation linked to the animation 'a wonderful life'.

The Perseus constellation contains eleven stars and eleven animations, ten of which I will discuss here. This constellation's base animation, 'a wonderful life', narrates Wittgenstein's life story as though it were a movie trailer for a heartwarming drama about how philosophy avoids catastrophe once Wittgenstein understands his important role, returns to Cambridge and continues his work in logical positivism. Essentially, Wittgenstein's story is grafted onto the plot of Frank Capra's 1946 film, *It's a Wonderful Life*, where Wittgenstein plays George Bailey. Putting Wittgenstein in this film is an exercise in reimagining the perspective Wittgenstein and his friends have on what constitutes a good life. In the animation 'storey's end' – ironically named after the home of Wittgenstein's doctor, given Wittgenstein's death at that place – we learn that Wittgenstein, expecting guests tomorrow but not expecting to live until then, asks the doctor's wife to tell his friends that he had a good life. When she recounts his final words to his friends, they are not convinced that his perfectionism and asceticism resulted in a happy or good life but rather a tortured one. The narrator supposes that Wittgenstein

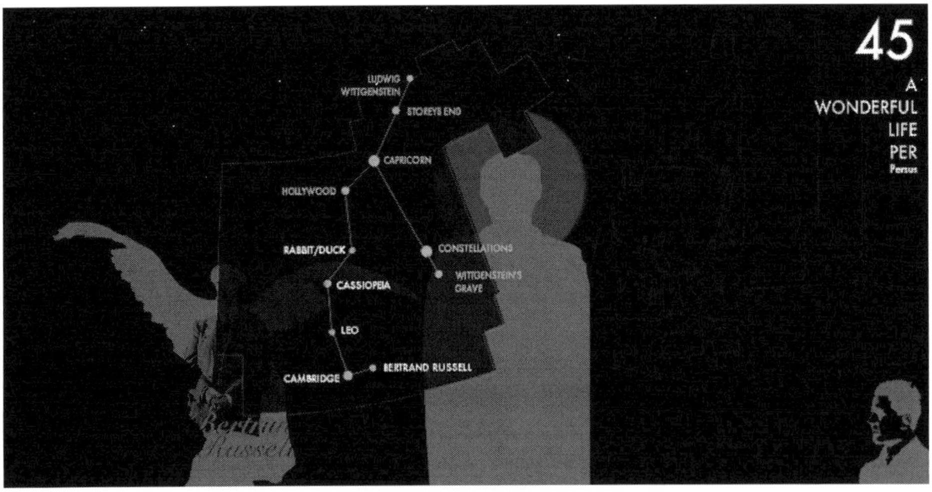

FIGURE 3: David Clark, 'a wonderful life', *88 Constellations for Wittgenstein (to be played with the Left Hand)*, 2009. Flash net.art. Use courtesy of David Clark.

revisited his life as Bailey did in *It's a Wonderful Life* and saw the good in his self-sacrifice. In the animation 'capricorn' we hear the deathbed story again, this time alongside Wittgenstein's belief that films without happy endings misunderstand the point of cinema, and framed by criticism Capra received of being a sentimental and capricious storyteller.

Essentially, Wittgenstein's friends could not imagine the philosopher as the subject of a Hollywood movie full of sentiment and happy redemption and instead are more comfortable imagining his life as one of austere solitude and duty supposedly more realistically represented in the animations 'cambridge' and 'bertrand russell'. In 'cambridge' Wittgenstein leaves Cambridge before completing a degree and isolates himself in Norway to write. Despite his social rank, Wittgenstein follows his sense of duty and leaves his solitude to fight with the Austrian army during the World War I. Further, he is self-disciplined and sufficiently dedicated to philosophy to continue his writings on logic while on the front and in a POW camp. Even when Wittgenstein returns to Cambridge and is regarded as God-like in his intellect, he prefers his solitude to academic fame. Wittgenstein's distance from others is clear when even his mentor, Bertrand Russell, does not understand his work, thinking or life choices in the animation 'bertrand russell'. From his friends' perspective, Wittgenstein's life is incompatible with the idyllic sentiment of a Hollywood drama, but apparently, Wittgenstein saw his life as just that.

Facing such paradoxical perspectives on one man's life helps Clark lead readers into Wittgenstein's controversial claim that there are no philosophical problems, only language games. Where there seem to be problems – oppositional perspectives in what is or what is not a good life – are only moments when language slips from a shared worldview. Clark's animation 'leo' addresses these slips from potential linguistic harmony by recounting Samuel 'Leo' Goldwyn's frequent nonsensical and paradoxical statements such as 'give me a couple of years and I'll make that actress an overnight success' (Clark 2008). Just as we cannot understand the lion roaring in the MGM logo, Goldwyn's statement jars against our shared understanding of the nature of time. Furthermore, the bohemian mantra 'art for art's sake' emblazoned in Latin under the MGM lion resists the modernist slogan 'form follows function' that Wittgenstein espouses. If Hollywood places aestheticism and sentiment first and Wittgenstein considers function as primary, then it is understandable that his friends would think of Hollywood as his opposite. However, if the function of Wittgenstein's life and Bailey's coincide, then their differences in form would seem inconsequential. Wittgenstein's role in twentieth-century philosophy and Bailey's function in the plot of *It's a Wonderful Life* are identical, but the form of their narrative expressions appears as opposites. Harmonic resonances between seeming incongruences are deeper than the surface if we perceive such opposites as congruent.

By blending biography and drama in Wittgenstein's life-as-Capra-film, Clark invites readers to consider how much fantasy and reality overlap. However, in 'hollywood', Clark reverses the motion so that Hollywood fictions take on roles in real-life narratives. Here the narrator recounts:

> Witnesses compared the September 11th, 2001 attacks to a Hollywood disaster movie. Hollywood had written the script, terrorists produced it and the sequel, the War on Terror, was an attempt to cash in on its box office success. Shortly after September 11th, Hollywood writers were invited to participate in brainstorming sessions at the Institute of Creative Technologies, an Army-funded research center. There the producers of American disaster films attempted to guess what the next terrorist attack would be. There, under the sign of Hollywood, the war machine and the entertainment machine became one.
>
> (Clark 2008)

Fantasy and fiction are thus not the opposite of reality, or even an escape from reality, but its inversion that could easily be considered the source of what is more categorically considered a 'real' event. Reality and representation are the same but different, like the optical illusions that interest Wittgenstein and that Clark accentuates in two animations linked to the Perseus constellation, 'cassiopeia' and 'rabbit/duck'.

No other animations discuss the mythical stories of the constellations with which they are associated, but in 'cassiopeia' the animation first recounts the myth of Cassiopeia, a queen who is punished for her vanity by having to sit on a chair that revolves around the North Pole, forcing her to spend half of the year inverted. The shape of the constellation was seen as both her crown and her chair so that one form was two objects depending on one's perspective. Clark writes:

> For the Greeks, the W was Cassiopeia's crown as well as a chair. Is it a W or an M? A chair or a crown? A blessing or a curse? It all depends on how you look at it. It depends on your point of view. 'The world of the happy man is different from that of the unhappy man', Wittgenstein once said.
>
> (Clark 2008)

In this model, there is not an inherent truth in what the form represents, but the individual perspective provides a judgment that seems internally coherent and thus feels true. Hence the anecdote about Wittgenstein and Norman Malcolm walking through Jesus Green and arguing over whether Cassiopeia is a W for Wittgenstein or an upside-down M for Malcolm. Because Wittgenstein sees it as a W, it is a W, and as Malcolm sees it as an M, it is an M.

The lesson on perspective gets reinforced and generalized in 'rabbit/duck' where Clark explains Wittgenstein's use of the illusion to reveal that meaning is not 'out there' but in our perspective. In other words, the image of the rabbit/duck does not change, just our perspective of it does (Clark 2008). Given such a view of meaning as contingent on perspective, the idea of being able to communicate with others means one must see from many perspectives to find resonances. Moments of harmony require that one thing is doubled to at least two so that Wittgenstein can be both the Bailey character in a Capra movie and an austere philosopher at Cambridge. A W must also be an M. Rather than seeing such differences as paradoxical opposites that break sense, one must see them as inversions of the same thing that generate resonant harmonies. Thus, to understand oneself or others, one must imagine oneself otherwise.

Empathy through Allegory

In a way, this search for harmony in what we first see as oppositional is excellent practice for developing empathy. Given that our perspective limits our worldview, there always exist remainders that are set aside as unincorporated in one's narrative. It is through these remainders that we can communicate allegorically with other perspectives that might perceive our remainders differently. These remainders show cracks in the unity of one's perspective, and through those cracks we can imagine other non-categorical organizing paradigms that allow us to link to, communicate with and comprehend other perspectives. We can all be held together by allegory and metaphor via harmonic resonances with the possibilities of the first floor, but we must do so in a way that avoids reassembling toward a unifying, singular perspective. In short, we must keep the door between the first and second floor open and accept a lack of resolution as a desirable state.

Clark brings readers to this realization in Wittgenstein's thinking by considering the Wittgenstein siblings, made evident in the Pavo constellation, which Clark connects with the animation 'paul wittgenstein'. All three siblings – Ludwig, Paul and Margarete – only appear twice on the same constellation map: for Pavo ('paul wittgenstein') and Corona Australis ('margarete wittgenstein'). Before getting to the siblings' animations, let us return briefly to Ludwig's, which recounts many aspects of his life:

> Who is Ludwig Wittgenstein? There were so many. There was the early Wittgenstein and the late Wittgenstein. And of course, there is now just the late Wittgenstein. He was a boy who didn't talk until he was four years old. He was an engineer who designed propellers. He was a schoolteacher in rural Austria. He

> was an architect who designed an elaborate, modernist house for his wealthy sister. He was one of the richest men in Europe after his father died, but he gave all his money away and lived off of his wages. He was a whistler and a lover of music. He was an aesthete. He was a homosexual. He was an exile. He was a lover of movies and pulp fiction. He was a Cambridge professor who shouted down his opponents in the moral sciences club.
>
> (Clark 2008)

While that may be Wittgenstein on his own, through his sister he is a staple of Viennese intellectual society and through his brother the shy music lover whose philosophy calls for silence when there is nothing that can be said. Both siblings cast a new light on Wittgenstein's thinking by providing another perspective and set of priorities. Their roles as siblings even fit with the genetic basis of their relationship, each being a recombination of the same genetic material. In 'margarete wittgenstein', we hear of how Margarete introduced Ludwig to influential Viennese thinkers and shared his work with her circle of intellectuals. An animation titled with her name is less about her than her role in her brother's life, but both remain entwined given the brief discussion in the middle of the animation about Margarete's relationship with Sigmund Freud and her deep affection for the city of Vienna, where she stayed during World War II despite her Jewish heritage.

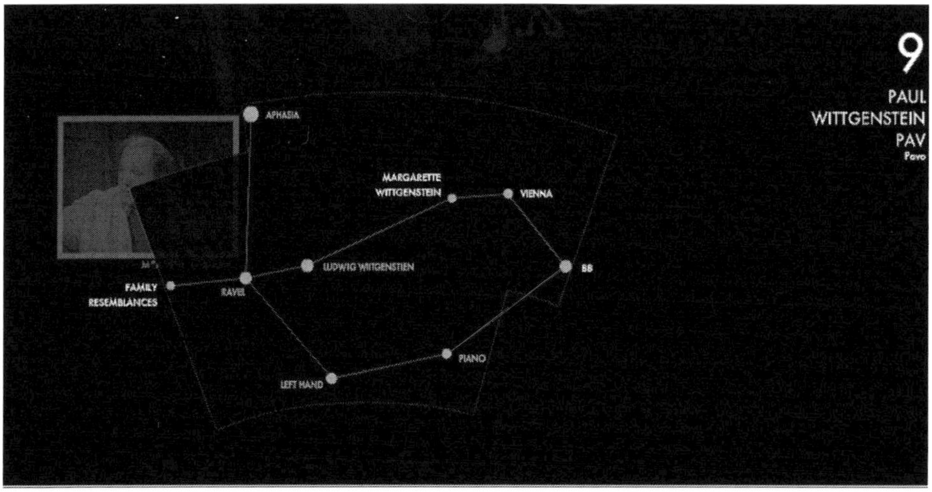

FIGURE 4: David Clark, 'paul wittgenstein', *88 Constellations for Wittgenstein (to be played with the Left Hand)*, 2009. Flash net.art. Use courtesy of David Clark.

The base animation for the constellation Pavo, 'paul wittgenstein', focuses first on Paul apart from his brother with only a brief mention of Ludwig as an introduction. The first half of the animation is a clip of the television show *M.A.S.H.* that recounts the story of Ravel's piano concerto for the left hand and Paul's circumstances. Clark's narration follows:

> Here's a toast to missing limbs. Here's to the arms and legs that go off by themselves to start a new life. Here's to the limbs that don't need us anymore. Who don't want us. Who move on to bigger and better things. Here's to one-armed pianists and aphasic composers and all those things beyond our grasp. Here's to Ludwig Wittgenstein's brother, Paul Wittgenstein, who lost his right arm in WWI but continued his career as a concert pianist performing compositions for the left hand that he commissioned from the great composers of the time.
> (Clark 2008)

As a celebratory cheer, the narration means to bring the focus on Paul, but readers quickly see that, like other moments of *88 Constellations*, what is presented as the central subject or figure quickly slips away as another MacGuffin moving along the plot of Paul's, Ludwig's, Ravel's, Cage's or eventually even Ernesto Miranda's or Alan Turing's story. These tricks around the focal figure help readers see a character as both a distinct figure and as a perspective or filter through which to see other figures. A character is a person and a vantage point, in line with Clark's use of Wittgenstein as a filter for representing the general Internet user.

Picking up the 'ludwig wittgenstein' animation's points on the nature of portraiture and resemblance,[1] Clark reinforces the message that one's story contains deeper resonances than surface appearances in 'family resemblances'. Clark explains how Wittgenstein's early work, *Tractatus*, wanted to break down the world into little, distinct pictures – what Russell called a 'logical atom' – that could be reassembled. However, his later work in *Philosophical Investigations* claimed meaning was not in 'small, discrete facts', but in family resemblances, of 'traits and hints here and there that add up to an impression' (Clark 2008). In this way, to make meaning is to be on the lookout for these little remainders or MacGuffins that one uses to make allegorical bridges to other related stories. The Pavo constellation invites such an action. For instance, even in the 'paul wittgenstein' animation, the opening *M.A.S.H.* clip does not present its story as one about Paul, but about Ravel's piano concerto for the left hand. The *M.A.S.H.* clip begins: 'Familiar with the story behind the Ravel?' (Clark 2008). While Clark draws attention to the composition rather than the composer, he links the animation 'ravel' to the Pavo constellation in a near metonymic relationship with Ravel's most renowned compositions, 'Bolero' and the piano concerto for the left hand, defining his existence. The figure is replaced or at least chiefly identified by the objects around him.

The rest of the animation defines Ravel by his aphasia, explaining that Ravel was two people in one given that he could think of music but could not perform or write music. There was the knowing-Ravel and the doing-Ravel where one version knew he was lighting a match in order to light the cigar and the other would smoke the lit match. Ravel's aphasia though is humorously represented through the narrator speaking minimally revised lyrics from Steve Miller Band's 'The Joker', chosen presumably because the third line of the original pop song says, 'some people walking round calling me Maurice'. Speaking the lyrics rather than singing them shows how Ravel can still think but not perform the music. The lyrics of such a recognizable song induce the sensation of singing so readers feel the conflict an aphasic person might experience in thinking of singing but knowing they are talking. Moreover, the animation 'ravel' closes with a looped clip from *The Great Dictator* where Hannah tells Chaplin's Jewish barber character a joke, asking, 'do you know the story about the man that put his watch in boiling water and held the egg in his hand?' (Clark 2008). This question keeps the disconnect and humor of aphasic thought running through our minds. Even Clark's decision to include Chaplin and speak through the Steve Miller Band in an animation about Ravel shows the energy one can bring in seeing one monad via the perspective of others.

While 'ravel' showcases the effects and manifestations of aphasia, the animation 'aphasia' provides a more direct definition of the disease – an inability to communicate using linguistic symbols due to damage to the left side the brain. Clark continues by reporting that language is a left-brain function and music a right-brain function and that the asymmetry in brain function came about when humans stood erect and had hands free to grasp at the world differently. This division of the self is broadened beyond aphasia as a disease to Ravel's particular experience with that disease. On that same vector, the nature of the human brain more generally surfaces in 'left hand'.

Considering that the constellation Pavo is for Paul Wittgenstein, one could easily assume that the animation 'left hand' would be attached to Paul's experience with having only his non-dominant hand to play music. Rather, the opening of this animation discusses the keyboard of a computer in place of the keyboard of a piano. Clark writes of how the computer privileges the right hand by giving that hand the duty of navigating the mouse and half of the keyboard, while the left hand only handles half of the keyboard. The piano and even the typewriter offer more parity to both hands, showing the digital age as leaving behind the left hand. The computer links the eye with the right hand, which must ultimately shift our thinking. Clark writes that the brain is 'cloven' between writing and music and that language now rips apart the brain given the imbalance between the hands. In a way, Paul is the reverse of the digital mind, perhaps ripped apart by music. Coming to address the digital directly (and beyond the digits of the hand), Clark shows how the perspective of the medium will alter the human by seeing the human mind from the perspective of the computer keyboard.

This idea of conflicting binaries of left and right, language and music, is further emphasized in the animation 'piano'. Before the animation introduces the elephant in the European parlor room as the raw material of the ivory piano keys,[2] the narrator repeats 'soft and loud' six times with a female voice echoing the phrase. 'Soft and loud' translates from the Italian *piano-forte* and before its final repetition, the narrator recites the difference in color and material of the keys 'ebony and ivory' and 'black and white' to both recount the keys of the piano and the inhabitants of Africa and Europe. That one entity – the piano – incorporates opposites. Finally, the Pavo constellation cycles back to the specifics of Wittgenstein but askew via the animation 'vienna', which presents the city through oppositions. Vienna at the turn of the twentieth century is the center of European culture both in the throes of its downfall and as the birthplace of modernism. Other reported binaries that encapsulate Vienna include Beethoven and Arnold Schoenberg, Art Nouveau and Modernism and logical positivism and psychoanalysis.

Just as we think that oppositional thinking takes hold again, one final animation remains, the one with which I began this analysis: '88'. In that animation, we are pulled back to thinking that what could not be farther from one another, like Chaplin and Wittgenstein, are from another view, replicas of one another. The separate and oppositional instance turns into repetition with a difference. Just as we think we are closed in an individual perspective separate from the other, we tumble out via one unincorporated remainder that strings together a chain of seemingly unrelated events.

The energy of *88 Constellations* goes even further than the 88 configurations that Clark has designed. With repeated exposure to the animations, one begins to string together original constellations that build up an idea not yet explicitly paired in the piece. By the end of this analysis, I wanted to construct a constellation for the myth of Echo using the ten animations 'piano', 'confession', 'beethoven', 'freud', 'nothing is hidden', 'alan turing', 'miranda rights', 'john cage', '4′33"' and 'silence' so that I might directly link silence, self-incrimination (along with plagiarism) and the computational mind. While the construction of *88 Constellations* does not allow for reader reconfiguration, the piece pushes readers to refigure the fragments mentally, showing the allegorical force of the composition. All 88 pieces are held together but are never satisfactorily reassembled to a permanence that settles the piece. Each animation still seems the remainder of one potential narrative string in the bundle, so there always remain loose ends that keep one pulling at the knit.

Clark's *88 Constellations* offers up a playful reminder of the pleasures of monadic subjectivity in drawing together various and unexpected connections between such disparate entities as Capra's movies and Russell's philosophies or Islamic terrorism and scientific experimentation. Imagining that each subject as a monad is a recombination of all universal potential puts one in the mindset of metaphor or allegory. While these connections start as harmonious coincidences rife with serendipitous merriment, as they accumulate they undermine one's assuredness in an individual identity and perspective. What began as random or capricious moments that fold up the monad into its particular vantage point eventually collapse with the weight of built associations and unfold each monad to reveal its precise perspective as arbitrary or groundless. And so, when we see an origami crane unfolded, we realize that the paper could have taken any number of forms and what we see in the creases is no longer the crane.

NOTES

1. See pages 37 and 143 for other relevant mentions of portraiture.
2. See page 35 for a related discussion on the 'piano' animation in David Clark's *88 Constellations for Wittgenstein*.

MIRRORS

When I was 8 years old, I checked out a book on European gardens from my local public library. Because I enjoyed the images so much, I decided to use a leftover disposable camera to take pictures of some of the pages. Of course, when I got the photos back from the developer, they were disappointing – both flatly colored and blurry. So, I went back to the library and checked out that same book to compare its images to my own and proceeded to take photographs of the two side-by-side. I wish I could find those photographs since they were likely my first experience with mise en abyme. *Five years later, in 1997, director Michel Gondry made a television commercial for Smirnoff that stacked match cut after match cut. I proceeded to watch all of Gondry's work, where I found his music video for Björk's 'Bachelorette' – a story of a girl who finds a book that writes itself and whose contents become reality. The reality is staged as a play and loops until there are three plays each within the previous staging. Personal experience and popular culture were my reference points for what I later learned is a thoroughly modern mode of looking.*

***

While modern humans are accustomed to looking at looking, reminders of this performative meta layer do not comfort viewers and rarely gain widespread appeal. This explains David Edelstein's scathing review of Joe Wright's 2012 filmic rendition of Leo Tolstoy's *Anna Karenina*. Edelstein writes: 'Wright's transitions can be delightfully unfettered, but they tend to upstage the scenes in between. It's a tour de force in the wrong direction' (Edelstein 2012: n.pag.). A bit later in the review, Edelstein continues to accuse the film of being stylistically inaccurate to the novel, saying 'Tolstoy doesn't lend himself to Wright's particular fussiness [....] Framing *Anna Karenina* this way is fatally distancing – it's Brechtian Tolstoy. And it's bewildering – it never establishes a context for itself' (Edelstein 2012: n.pag.). Ultimately, Edelstein accuses the styling of being artificial and thus distracts audiences from genuine emotions. Deborah Ross's review also faults the styling for obscuring emotional realism, saying 'Wright's adaptation of *Anna Karenina* is so bold and audacious its bold audacity becomes the story, rather than the actual story itself' (Ross 2012: n.pag.). Edelstein and Ross are looking for another realist version of the book, but Wright accuses realism of being just as artificial. Expensive shots such as filming a carriage pulling up to a palace 'don't always have much to do with expressing the essence of character' (Rafferty 2012: n.pag.). For Mieke Bal, realism only seems natural because it asks viewers to regard textual signals as signs of the real. In this case, reality is only a moment when one forgets about representation by excluding 'everything that triggers awareness of the arbitrariness of the frame' (Bal 1990: 520). Realism is an artifice that prefers to pass unnoticed by hiding *how* it is constructed.

Artifice is not always cast as heady intellectualism or baseless appearance. Wright's meta-theater approach to staging the narrative can provide a more authentic emotional experience. For *New York Times* reviewer Terrence Rafferty, Wright's decision saves time, allowing for more characters than have been typically included in realist, filmic renditions (Rafferty 2012: n.pag.). Peter Travers of *Rolling Stone* claims that the theatrical staging of the film results in a 'strange and marvelous spell' of erotic charge (Travers 2012: 86). The artifice of the stage does not mean that emotional expression must be artificial. The stage conceit allowed Wright to create expressive images that showed rather than narrated emotion such as the scene where Anna's son's bed appears tiny and alone in a huge space. In Wright's version of *Anna Karenina,* we see set transitions, prosceniums and curtains so as to reach a more profound emotional essence.

Ultimately, successful stylistic applications carry meaning and encourage technotextual thinking. Wright's staging choices for *Anna Karenina* came from reading Orlando Figues' book *Natasha's Dance*, which 'describes Russian society of the period living their lives as if upon a stage. They were very concerned by how they appeared to each other' (Siegel 2012: n.pag.). The numerous transitional scenes show the posed nature of high society life. The brief transition at the 41-minute mark shows Alexei Vronsky and Princess Betsy sitting together in the theater waiting for a show to begin. Anna sits with a devotee of her husband while trying to avoid Vronsky's gaze from the other side of the theater. As the music picks up and the theater curtain rises – itself a painting of a curtain rather than an actual curtain – the scene does not reveal a staged play. Instead, it opens to Princess Betsy's party that occurs the following day. The real show is in how rules and mannerisms are played out among society members as they perform for the others in the room. We see the party-goers first frozen, bent backwards in an exaggerated position. When animated, they still interact in choreographed and synchronous movements, laughing simultaneously in a similar fashion or opening and closing their fans together. The fans produce a nervous fluttering that replicates the hissing and rattling of snakes to increase tension between Anna and Vronsky. Despite the brevity of the transition, it is a strong showing of how the calculated, self-conscious mannerisms of high society keep characters anxious about their social performance.

The idea that truth exists in artifice is a driving force behind many of Wright's decisions. We see artifice as an emotional landscape from the beginning of the film. The opening sequence of cuts alternates between Stiva's indiscretions with the governess and Anna dressing for the day, showing the performance of appearances and the characters' feelings on adultery. Anna's process of dressing includes many flourishes: her hands waving to beckon rings, her dress turning several times around her figure and her brother's letter circling her maidservant so as not to interrupt her reading. Beyond celebrating appearance, the scene uses the hand motions and poses to create near match cuts on two occasions. In one scene Anna turns a page of the letter with her right hand as we cut to Stiva sneaking candy to his daughter with his left. The similar flick of the wrist in both movements shows the letter as a guilty pleasure for Anna as much as the candy is for the child. At the close of these orchestrated cuts, we see Dolly crying, holding a note from the governess to her husband in her right hand that cuts to Anna holding Stiva's letter in her left, both at shoulder height. While Wright visually pairs Anna with Dolly, Anna pities her adulterous brother, prefacing her future affair and self-pity.

Along with admitting his disappointment in realism for overemphasizing the surface, Wright says 'what I find so engaging in Tolstoy's novels are the twists and turns in the landscape of the characters' mind. I wanted to find a form of expression that was more capable of conveying that sort of experience' (Rafferty 2012: n.pag.). The scene in Anna and Vronsky's Moscow apartment near the end of the film takes viewers in and out of mirrors and uses yet another match cut to jump through time and space. Not only do the mirrors show the relationship and Anna's mind as fractured. We are trapped in her apartment and her mind. She is homebound because of the social isolation resulting from her adultery, and she has become addicted to morphine and increasingly neurotic about Vronsky's potential connection to Princess Sorokina. Anna and Vronsky fight over a departure date while they each lean on a thin mirror on opposite sides of a doorway. We frequently see Anna in mirrored reflections, first in that hallway as she claims he no longer loves her. He denies her claim as he obscures her reflection. She retreats to her bedroom and drinks more morphine as Vronsky watches her in a mirror. He cannot look at her directly anymore and neither can the audience. The mirror in the bedroom morphs into the mirror in the doorway, and strangely, Anna is walking into the mirror until she backs Vronsky into that same doorway mirror. He bends to her will, and they make up. As they kiss, the camera recedes, and we notice another mirror reflecting an image of Anna half-dressed and asleep on the floor. The entire mirror scene is a hallucinatory dream.

When she wakes, she approaches Vronsky's desk. He catches sight of her in the mirror, and they argue over what he will be doing during the day. We see Vronsky's fragmented reflection next to Anna's angry face as they argue over the telegram's contents. The fight becomes raw as they lose the mirror as mediator. Their relationship appears increasingly distant until we arrive at the final mirrored reflection. Anna asks Vronsky's reflection, which Sorokina he is courting before he slips out of the room. More disturbing still, his mirrored reflection could be her illusion of an exchange with Vronsky. Even the closing match cut from that apartment does not allow her an escape. As she walks across her rooms, she experiences a sharp pain in her side and sits down, pulling on a curtain for support. This match cut puts her in a train car, which eventually brings her to the final scene of her suicide.

While heavy-handed staging, mirror scenes and match cuts may not be how one naturally sees, witnessing the constructedness of vision lets us play with perception. However, more insidious is the spreading doubt that comes from seeing how artifice is constructed. One wonders if other events once perceived as real are instead contrived. *Mise en abyme* reveals reality as a collision of both authenticity and artifice. Seeing the broader importance of the *mise en abyme*, like seeing *mise en abyme* itself, becomes evident when one steps back. Hence, we will turn to the more general concept of the mirrorish.

Mise en Abyme: Mirrorish Dimensions Down to the Code

Repetition in the Hall of Mirrors

The *modus operandi* of progressive time is to fold inward and so narrow options. With each fold, the crease becomes a limit line whose perceived function fades over time. In folding one's perspective, the monad lives in a smaller space and stops accounting for spaces that it had previously recognized. However, to see the relations between monads, one must unfold and so broaden possible perspectives. In this case, unfolding reveals the crease again, reminding one of the limits of a perspective that can look but without fully seeing (Van Wer 2007: 301). Moving from folding to unfolding or vice versa reminds us that our perception of space and its generalized state are incongruent. For William Egginton, this is clearly illustrated in 'the theater in the theater' technique and the attached expectation that modern viewers could understand and navigate several layers of reality represented simultaneously (Egginton 2005: 57). This mode of watching theater eventually became internalized into how humans see their world as a whole, resulting in the modern problem of dissociation. While the previous chapter looked at folding and perspective that defined the monad, this chapter considers unfolding and the impulse toward apprehending the multicursal and universal order. When we are made aware of framing devices in *mise en abyme*, we see reality as representation and experience a mirrorish event.

It is no wonder that the mirror appears frequently in literary works of the historical baroque period. Calderón de la Barca writes in his 1670 play 'El verdadero Dios Pan':

> La alegoría no es más
> que un espejo que traslada

lo que es en lo que no es;
y está toda su elegancia
en que salga parecida
tanto la copia en la tabla,
que el que está mirando a una
piense que está mirando a entrambas.

(the allegory is nothing more
than a mirror that replaces
what is with what is not;
and this is all its elegance
in that they both look alike
the copy on the table,
against the original object
one thinks that one is looking at both.)
(cited in Martin 1994: 99)

At base, the mirror is meant to replicate what is before it. However, the mirror does not directly repeat but transforms one's vision by displacing perspective. The baroque view of repetition is hyperextended, where even given the same process and product, each iteration is different in its place in time. Disparaging baroque practices such as repetition, pastiche and allegory flatten their complexity by viewing them as derivative copies rather than hinged mirrors.

While repetition and originality appear inversely related, repetition as mirroring constitutes part of the allegorical impulse along with seriality, appropriation, intertextuality, simulation and pastiche. Repetition's goal is not to restore a lost original meaning but to add more meanings (Loh 2004: 477). During the baroque historical period, repetition was not seen negatively (Loh 2004: 481–82). Instead, artists and authors understood that original ideas are not crafted alone but draw on ideal models derived from experiencing the works of others (Loh 2004: 488). The pleasure of a work is not in the originality of its subject but in seeing how artists or authors perceive and interpret other works. One notices an artist's or author's style in the manner in which they approach a similar theme or reimagine established tropes. *How* one sees, not *what* one sees, better displays the artist's or author's 'originality'. Thus, originality and repetition are not opposed but entwined. In monadological terms, differentiating a perspective through stylistic originality means that we must repeat and reflect but in a transformative way.

The mirror has a disorienting effect as it reveals our performance: we can see ourselves in our daily exchanges from outside of ourselves. This trope is not rare in baroque painting. For instance, the painted image of Diego Velázquez in *Las*

Meninas is the subject of the spectator's gaze, but the spectator is also the subject of the painted painter's gaze (Diego 2003: 159). This external view of oneself and the disorientation that ensues are magnified when the mirror in the background of the painting does not reflect the spectator but the King and Queen. The King and Queen stand 'out of frame' in the painting, occupying the location of the spectator, so they are part of the painting but outside of it, as is the spectator who overlaps with the apparent subject of portraiture (Diego 2003: 159). The painting seems to both acknowledge the viewer with Velázquez's stare while it also erases the viewer's reality by placing the King and Queen in the viewer's space or creating a kind of hallucinatory view of the viewer as monarch.

This effect of the mirror is what Elizabeth Carlson calls a proto-cinematic vision. She examines the role of mirrors in nineteenth-century Paris and the Palace of Illusions in the 1900 World Fair as evidence of a changing visual paradigm. Despite the popularity of the Palace of Illusions with its more than two million visitors, mirrored ways of seeing were thoroughly disorienting and generally unfavorable. Visitors reported:

> The changing colours, confusing perspectives, and infinite reflections of the crowd created fear, anxiety, and nausea. Some accounts referred to the mirrored maze as a 'frightening and grotesque labyrinth' or a 'bottomless abyss'. One visitor claimed that the play between light and mirrors made the reflecting forms both the 'most curious and the most frightening thing he had ever seen'. Several accounts of the attraction note that some visitors had to leave because of a 'sickening feeling in their stomach, like a rollercoaster ride'. All of these narratives describe the performative aspect of the mirrored palace and the incomprehensible horror of infinity.
>
> (Carlson 2011: 24)

Mirrors are particularly disorienting because they reflect reality onto reality, which cinema could only simulate. Until the live feed, the screen temporarily separated realities. With the camera, one is recording what one sees, but with the mirror one creates a loop of looking since the person before the mirror is both the audience and the attraction (Carlson 2011: 23). This creates a lived *mise en abyme* rather than the illusion of one on a screen, one Walter Benjamin saw in late nineteenth-century Paris, saying, 'where doors and walls are made of mirrors, there is no telling outside from in' (cited in Carlson 2011: 19). With mirrors installed on the inside and outside of boutiques, cafés and residences throughout Paris, it became challenging to differentiate spaces. Further, mirrored reflections are 'live' so they are fleeting, or, as George Simmel claims, rather than the gaze that holds, mirrors offer only the opportunity to glance at something before it disappears (Carlson 2011: 22). The mirrored reflection changes so quickly that it cannot be grasped as a concrete object.

Our minds are unable to reconcile a mirror's versioning. While the eye's lens refracts an image that our mind then turns 'right side up', a mirror's reflection of an image changes the orientation from right left to left right, which cannot be undone by the mind. The incongruence of the reversed image with its inverse calls us to question our 'sense of order, balance, and continuity' (O'Leary and O'Leary 2010: 79). Cinema achieves this stability by separating screen space from real space and archiving the moving image for review. While cinematic screenings were not nearly as popular at the 1900 World Fair, cinematic viewing practices quickly replaced mirrored viewing as the preferred approach to comfortably experiencing illusion. Cinema brought projections to a screen in a closed room rather than fragmenting and distributing images in real spaces (Carlson 2011: 31), though contemporary technologies like holograms and augmented reality revive mirrorish viewing in the twenty-first century. Ultimately, cinema provided an escape to a safer space because it lets viewers stay in a three-dimensional space looking at two-dimensional images rather than forcing them to see in a three-dimensional way that mirrors impose on viewers.

Carlson can link early cinema with mirrors partly because early cinema was less interested in narrative unity in the closed space of the screen than it was in documenting everyday life in the city. Early film often did not make the distinction in space between what was being filmed and what was considered behind the scenes (Carlson 2011: 30), so observers could imagine themselves as being recorded and recording. Furthermore, watching early films mimicked the feeling of looking at mirrored reflections because cuts were less frequent and editing was done with a lighter hand (Carlson 2011: 28). Narrative unity in film means that the audience must become the *voyeur*, who identifies with what is being filmed, rather than the *flâneur* who identifies with the camera. Recognizing the camera's presence as a hinge and the process of making the film spoils the illusion of narrative unity but reasserts mirrorish viewing.

The Mirrorish Disrupts Perspective

However, we do not need physical mirrors to capture such spatial and perspectival confusion. Jean-François Lyotard abstracts mirrors as a way of seeing when he examines Marcel Duchamp's notes from *A l'Infini (The White Box)*, which address the manufacture and narrative of *La mariée mise à nu par ses célibataires, même*, translated as *The Large Glass* (1915–23) and *Étant données*, or *Given* (1946–66). Lyotard's reading of those notes in *Duchamp's TRANS/formers* provides a useful general description of the process and effect of repetitive transformations in his concept of the mirrorish.

Lyotard admits that critics are stymied by what he calls mirrorish constructions. Such an object or phenomenon cannot be explained, so the critic must alter strategy. Rather than continue with the pure logic of the assembly line – art is made and criticism rendered – or reason with the incongruent, critics must attempt to understand a piece by accepting its 'nonsense as the most precious treasure' (Lyotard 1990: 12). Its incongruity or dissimilarity though is no less rigorous than more widely accepted styles or techniques, which Lyotard demonstrates by considering Albrecht Dürer's perspective grids as machines that regulate vision. However, Dürer's grids can serve other goals than replication in the service of realism. Altering the angle of the projection plane results in an anamorphic image whose creation is no less meticulous even if its goal opposes the effect of realism (Lyotard 1990: 57). Optic technologies help us see our world from another viewpoint so that our view of reality is the frame or proscenium of yet another reality nested within. Through his work in optical instruments, Johannes Kepler realized that perception is a result of light and shadows, not the thing itself. The eye and the instrument become equally trustworthy and so equally untrustworthy. Knowing how optics work makes vision more mysterious since we cannot know how the brain interprets light and shadow or if that interpretation matches the object observed (Gal and Chen-Morris 2010: 200). Knowing the limits of our perception, one must accept that reality is a process of representation, since seeing the real must always be filtered and interpreted through a perspective.

For Lyotard and Duchamp, since perspective always persists, making effective artwork depends on creating hinges that release the illusion of control over dimension, unity and explanation. For instance, an object and its reflection in a mirror still exist as a dependent binary and are purely spectacular. If a second mirror is introduced as a hinge to reflect the actions of the first mirror and the object, one adds a dimension to the scene and creates a dissimilar occurrence. In short, a hinge is when one dimension turns to produce a higher-level dimension, revealing a place where two different dimensional worlds are recognized as simultaneous. Making hinges gives us access to dimensions we do not recognize immediately. Duchamp works out the geometry of hinge generation where 'a *finite* 3-dim'l continuum is generated by a *finite* 2-dim'l continuum *rotating* (in the general sense) about a finite 1-dim'l hinge' (Lyotard 1990: 141, original emphasis). In other words, while a hinge appears as a one-dimensional line, it is the profile of a two-dimensional plane, which in turn is one side of a three-dimensional volume, which is also the angle of a four-dimensional area. In this way, dimensions hide behind other dimensions. Thus, the mirrorish is when one sees a line as a hinge to a higher dimension rather than the resolved state of seeing the line as only a line.

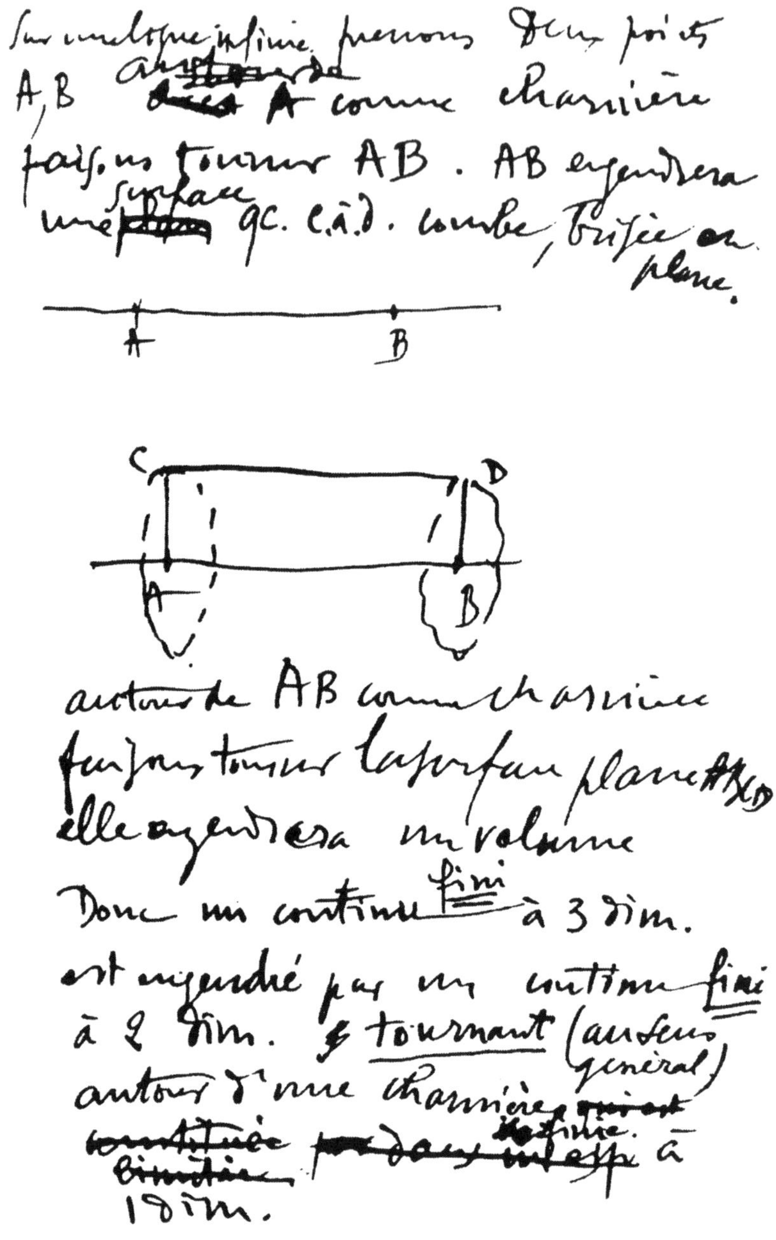

FIGURE 5: Marcel Duchamp, *The Continuum* from *A l'infinitif (La Boîte Blanche)*, 1912–20. Collotype reproduction. 31.2 x 26.3 cm. Use courtesy of the estate of Marcel Duchamp. © Association Marcel Duchamp/ADAGP, Paris/Artists Rights Society (ARS), New York 2019.

In Duchamp's geometry, viewers can only perceive objects in one less dimension than they resides within. As creatures living in three dimensions, we only see two. When we look at a three-dimensional object, its dimensionality is an illusion. We cannot see all sides of the object simultaneously since

> [t]his 3-dim'l visual perspective perception is only distinguishable to the 4-dim'l eye. The 3-dim'l eye will not distinguish it clearly [....] A 3-dim'l tactile exploration, a wandering around, will perhaps permit an imaginative reconstruction of the numerous 4-dim'l bodies, allowing this perspective to be understood in a 3-dim'l medium.
>
> (Duchamp 1973: 88)

In the infinite positions one might take, once a specific position is determined, perceivable dimensions decrease (Lyotard 1990: 90). One can move about in the three-dimensional world, but once one solidifies a position to observe something, one sees it only two-dimensionally. To see in three dimensions would mean recreating the object as holographic or virtual. However, such an ascent to fourth-dimensional awareness is not a liberation from western Platonism but an affirmation that all we see are projections.

We see hints of this fourth dimension in the mirror portraits Duchamp and his friends took in 1917 at the Broadway Photo Shop in New York. The subject would sit back to the camera at a table before four mirrors hinged to show four full reflections of the subject. The photographs were cropped so that the edges of the mirrors were not visible. The subject's reflections allowed viewers to see the subject from five angles simultaneously, simulating a three-dimensional viewing that is possible in a four-dimensional space. This space appears incongruent and unreal, altering the viewer's sense of perspective. Duchamp is multiplied in the image, so his place is slippery like a shifter, a category of linguistic sign that Roman Jakobson defines as meaningful because it is empty (McManus 2008: 131). Revealing these further dimensions ultimately reminds viewers that their seemingly 'natural' way of seeing is one approach to perception. In short, opening to higher dimensions unfolds monads to reveal their perspectival construction and relativism through the mirrorish.

While the mirrorish flips or rotates dimensions in multiple directions, the *mise en abyme* stacks its dimensions concentrically. *Mise en abyme* is like a perfect mirrorish construction in the same way that a square is a perfect rectangle. At base, the *mise en abyme* is to see what was considered a whole as a part within a larger whole, which itself is also just a part. John Gabriele describes the *mise en abyme* as 'a series of apparently endlessly overlapping, enclosed networks of conceptual or structural spaces which form a kind of labyrinth leading to a

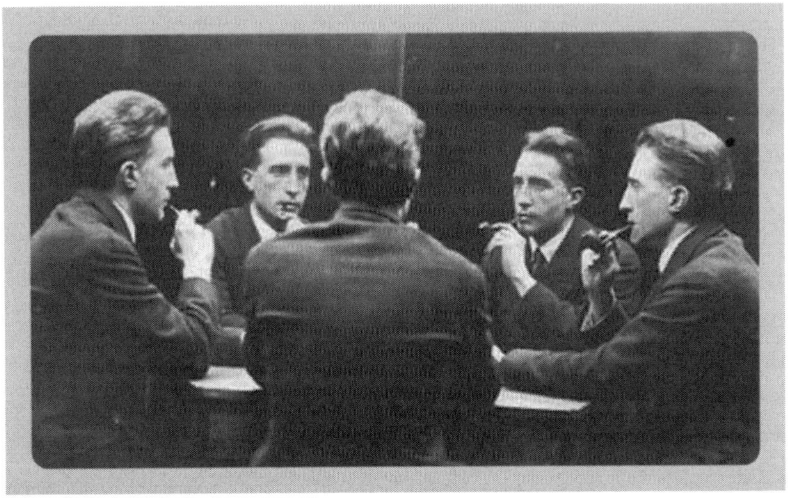

FIGURE 6: Unidentified photographer, 'Portrait multiple de Marcel Duchamp (Five-way portrait of Marcel Duchamp)', 1917. Gelatin silver print. Private Collection, photograph courtesy of Francis M. Naumann Fine Art. © Association Marcel Duchamp/ADAGP, Paris/Artists Rights Society (ARS), New York 2019.

shifting, ever unattainable nucleus or centre' (Gabriele 2005: 31). Sara Danius notices this concentric *mise en abyme* in her reading of *Magic Mountain* when Hans Castrop notes how bizarre it is to be embarrassed by nakedness when skin is just another covering – an observation he can make because of the x-ray that shows what the skin hides (Danius 2003: 79). Mirrorish occurrences, including the *mise en abyme*, remind us that perhaps there is more we do not see that requires further unfolding.

Readers or viewers must confront their standing within and beyond the text. So when Jorge Borges asks, '[w]hy does it disturb us that Don Quixote be a reader of the *Quixote* and Hamlet a spectator of *Hamlet*?', his response is that 'such inversions suggest that if the characters of a fictional work can be readers or spectators, we, its readers or spectators, can be fictitious' (cited in Zamora 2006: 266). While we know we have boundaries, our boundaries do not hold. The critical weight of the mirrorish and *mise en abyme* is their ultimate ability to turn spectators' attention back onto themselves, their perception and the process of representation. However, because we might always be veiled from reality and live in a *mise en abyme* of representation, we face our inherent lack of control over the environment surrounding us. Our best coping mechanism to avoid self-erasure once we become aware of our constructedness is to take up a perspective nearly arbitrarily as an anchor by building paratextual thresholds that make the arbitrary choice seem natural.[1] Essentially, we need the decision to be made and the representation settled so we can stop looking at representation to look through it and imagine our performance is our reality.

Mirrorish Dimensions Turn Paratext to Text

Coping with this modern crisis of representation often means drawing boundaries between the real and the represented in order to validate a limited perspective. While monadology shows this function in subjects, humans also endow their objects with markers to differentiate them from their surroundings. We see this framing in paratextual conventions of the book that ease its insertion into our ecology of texts. These paratextual features are defined by their dependence on a text. For this reason, and because many paratextual features such as prefaces or reviews see little innovation, paratextual materials often receive minimal attention.[2] Somehow paratext is perceived as crass, commercial, fleeting or pragmatic rather than expressive.

However, for a technotext, paratextual features are consciously considered and often given explicit attention. Technotextual treatments of paratext challenge concepts of textual or narrative unity because the textual is always already approached as a part of a mirrorish occurrence. As long as we look through the paratext, leaving it unexamined and unquestioned, the text appears united, just as looking through the proscenium allows the theatrical scene to read as real. Once we look at the paratext, we experience the disorienting effects of the mirrorish or *mise en abyme* and compose technotextually.

Of course, much has already been said about paratext, but what I am interested in here is how the boundaries between text, paratext and context bleed together in technotexts that privilege mirrorish dimensional shifting. These components appear as nested like a *mise en abyme*, with the text in the middle, surrounded by two layers of paratext, floating in a broader context. In the two layers of paratext are the peritext (physically connected to the text, such as title pages and book covers) and the epitext (elements not physically attached to the text but intimately related to it via endorsement by the author, editor or publisher such as reviews, literary awards and advertisements). The peritext is divided from the epitext by the inscription medium and epitext is divided from context by the author, editor or publisher. These divisions are frequently challenged by the function of digital technologies.

Reading a literary text on a computer adds another layer of paratextual material that many authors are keenly aware of when composing for a screen. When one reads on a screen, there is the hardware, operating system and software to look through as the computer processes and recreates the text. Authors of digital literary texts write for a computer, and that computer uses that text to generate another text for a human reader. Behind the on-screen text that a human reads lies the code a computer reads, resulting in a text behind a text with an electronic translator. While one may argue that this is like other instances of text generated by text, such as a translation, the script to a play or the manuscript to a printed book, in these cases a human performs the text. In digital literary texts, the *mise en abyme* highlights the recursive strategies of the computer as a medium in which 'the medium references the content and the content references the medium, an oscillation similar to two facing mirrors reflecting one another' (Hayles and Pressman 2013: 200). The computer user witnesses an unveiling of the medium's assumed transparency 'by burrowing inside its own assumptions until they become visible to the reader-user' (Hayles and Pressman 2013: 200). To see the media's framing and text production process – of image files inside of graphic user interfaces backed by the underlying executable code – as a recursive state of negotiating dimensions subordinates the computer as part of the *mise en abyme* tradition.

With digitization, the boundary between text and paratext is more challenging to determine since it cannot use its medium as a unifying boundary between peri- and epitext, and the line between epitext and context is nebulous at best (Birke and Christ 2013: 70). Georg Stanitzek too notices the trouble between peri- and epitext in Gérard Genette's treatment, claiming that Genette is more interested and specific in his treatment of the peritext because it is defined by the boundaries of the book and more easily grounded in the author's (and publisher's) intent while his treatment of epitext is more tenuous (Stanitzek 2005: 31). Furthermore, Genette uses the author's intent or approval to divide paratext from context. While authorial intent was already flawed before digital technologies existed, the digital seems determined to splinter intent further by multiplying authors, celebrating nonhuman authors and muddling the paratextual features predetermined by one's computer rather than the author. Take, for instance, a Twitterbot. What constitutes the text? Is it the tweets on that account? The program that generates the tweets? Could the tweets be the epitext of the text's program? Are all other tweets on Twitter peritextual since they are confined to the same medium or is a user account now like a media's dividing line? In what category does a hashtag fit? What of the tweets associated with that hashtag that are not authored by the bot and its account? What of the hardware and interface the reader uses to access Twitter? Without a clear definition, the paratext moves away from existing as a purely pragmatic transitional element to instead be interchangeably labeled as textual or paratextual.

Revising the concept of paratext to a fluid one was first possible before digital technologies existed just as technotexts were produced before the computer came to be. However, the digital computer so profoundly shook our understanding and view of text production that it all but required literature to reconsider the boundaries of a medium and image of the author and reader. While any vessel for writing is subject to entropy, the digital platform is particularly vulnerable to change beyond the author's control. Further, the speed with which a digital literary work can change or become no longer accessible, regardless of the author's intent, makes many digital works fleeting glances.[3] Given how much paratext surrounds a digital text and how unreliable an author's control over the text may be, perhaps the more compelling idea is that with digital technologies and technotextual compositions, we have fallen into Genette's fear – that one could claim that everything is paratext.

By turning what one typically perceives as paratextual and presenting it as textual, the *mise en abyme* makes the process of representation and the limits of media unmistakable, even integral. Viewers are made to look at the process of representation and the constructedness of reality. These meta moments of directly accessing the reality of representation are quickly labeled as a part of modernist, avant-garde or Brechtian aesthetic, but their origins in the baroque show that a crisis of representation is the seat of the modern, not its late unraveling. This crisis of perception is not the result of modernity but its impetus. The mirrorish forces the spectator to renegotiate *how* they see even in quite literal though strikingly impressive terms such as Amaranth Borsuk and Brad Bouse's artist's book, *Between Page and Screen*. Such awareness of one's role as spectator leads one to accept the state of spectatorship as the stable reality of modernity. The baroque bone in the throat is precisely the reminder that representation abounds and we remain performers no matter how much we want to follow the pragmatic functions of paratextual features. For the baroque, the frame will not hold. The *mise en abyme* and mirrorish are a zooming-out of frame to see that all around is representation. Paratext expands rather than limits representation and, with our assumptions of framing and representation laid bare, we can build from the ground up using any paradigm we please.

Parsing Narrative to Read Code

Beginning from scratch requires that one make many more decisions to account for the lack of convention. While this may be a deterrent to many, some gaming and electronic literature genres capitalize on the pleasure of constructing representations. One such example of construction-forward immersion is Kevin Gold's *Choice of Robots*, an interactive science-fiction novel in app form, which allows readers to shape the narrative unfolding. Reader choice individuates each reading experience, but it also undermines the idea of one unified story. Unlike many other interactive fictions, the choices that readers make do not often result in hard turns in the plot but shift the life experience of the protagonist who must inevitably live through rising conflict with China, illness and death, working in the Stanford robotics lab, making business decisions with friends and navigating complex human–robot relationships. Choices do not drastically change the plot – though there are thirteen distinct endings and seventeen more with slight variations. Instead, the choices offer readers reflections or how many 'achievements' the reader as player might accomplish. *Choice of Robots* reveals the networked connections between components of a story and brings them forward as equal to the narrative smoothing of those connections. It provides 72 possible achievements and takes the reader through seven chapters, each with its basic plot points.[4]

The reader is frequently asked to make choices about a robotics engineer's actions, dialogue or feelings. As readers make choices, the app calculates the relationship of the engineer to other characters in the novel, the traits of the engineer and his or her robot and the humanity of the engineer. *Choice of Robots* displays this data to the reader, showing how a character can be engineered and so challenging the illusion that humanity is too complicated for programmatic calculation and prediction. Writing this code is a significant component in writing the story; however, the reader cannot readily access that code. Gold's *Choice of Robots* thus offers a promising proxy to explore the narrative as the superficial effect of an underlying program whose hidden calculations offer the reader the more substantial story.

While tracking metadata is common in a gaming interface where access to inventories, maps, health status and job levels is grafted onto the screen as though floating over diegetic space, when reading a novel, one is not accustomed to thinking about the metadata of one's reading as directly malleable numerical figures. This entwined relationship between narrative and code in interactive fiction creates and cracks the boundaries of representation in such mirrorish ways precisely by pointing to one another repeatedly. When the stats do not change as one would expect or the character behaves unpredictably, the reader contemplates the other potential storylines or the content of the code. If one looks to the code, choices call upon further narrative scenes based on states set by previous choices and the tracked stats.[5]

The reader discovers a secondary narrative based on their choices regarding character traits and the relationships of characters. However, this secondary level is obscured by functions at the code level. The robot adopts levels of autonomy, military applicability, empathy or grace commensurate with the reader's choices. For instance, if the reader works to train the robot to make its own decisions, its autonomy score will increase. The app tracks another set of stats corresponding to the fame, humanity, wealth and romance of the main character, a robotics engineer. These also rise and fall according to a reader's choices. Furthermore, the app measures the strength of the engineer's relationships with other characters in the novel and the protagonist's romantic interest.

Given these categories of metadata, readers are not chiefly shifting plot, but the dynamics of players in the network from humans to robots to countries to media. While one could perceive the diminished effect of the reader's choices on the plot as a failure in authentic interaction or proof of a traditional hold on the author role, this would miss the point. While writing drastic shifts in the plot does mean adding entire branches to the story that could add tens or hundreds of thousands of words, the interest in the story is not merely the size of the fictional universe, but the effect of the choices on the reader. In *Choice of Robots*, like all interactive fiction pieces made using ChoiceScript, readers do not have a back button or home button. Once readers begin, they must either complete the reading or start over from the beginning. Without save points or backtracking features, their choices stand, and the few loops back that exist must be provided by the author as another choice. Instead, one must run the course of life and learn lessons that can be applied to future rereadings, even though the interface does not allow one to save individual readings. For instance, one discovers that positively engaging the Luddite terrorist has more benefits than expected as he can become an unlikely yet useful ally. Also, after multiple reads, one realizes that little good comes from entertaining media attention and so when readers want to give the engineer a good life, they might avoid the media. However, a peek into the code of the game reveals that positive media attention is possible if one is willing to grant *San Francisco Chronicle* reporter, Mark Ali, significant access to the robot.

Gold shows that in tracking the metadata of our reading, we are repeating the performance of reading. Key to the *Choice of Robots* experience is repetition as rereading burrows readers deeper into the programmed assumptions of the code that they try to manipulate with their narrative choices. Rereading results in layered stories with versions of a similar story nested into one another like *matryoshka* dolls.[6] With each reread we make another representation inside of a representation, given our knowledge of previous readings. We transform from within by acknowledging that we are always in a representation that we calibrate. The reader realizes after several rereadings that the plot is determined and the more profound choices lie in *how* the engineer's life will unfold, not *what* constitutes the contents of that life. How must readers live their life to obtain the 'Hero' achievement and avoid war with China? Readers realize that what they are trying to read is not the narrative content. Instead, they are trying to read the code between the lines of the narrative and 'game' the program in order to reach desirable 'achievements'.

Even if one sets aside the process of gaining achievements, reading *Choice of Robots*'s narrative and metadata means grappling with underlying beliefs coded into the story. Such tension even announces itself sometimes in the novel's summary of a reading that includes commentary on one's choices. In one reading, the closing summary of the final chapter finishes with '[y]ou then got a pretty boring ending for not having done much remarkable. Maybe you should try again?' (Gold 2015). The program reveals its judgment or criteria of what makes for a remarkable life. In this reading, the engineer reached a fame level of '17 (Prominent in History Textbooks)' mostly by developing advanced surgical robotics that improved treatment for many diseases. This version of the engineer managed to assist in the Sino-American War while avoiding the violent use of robotics and tried to ease relations between robots and humans when the Singularity arrived and robots advanced beyond human cognition. Tired of war, the engineer developed an algorithm that eradicated the need for human government and ended the concept of war. While I felt accomplished with my choices, the chapter summary proposed that I had misplayed the game by actually solving problems, which is ultimately mundane. In the end, I am made to face programmed assumptions that I disagree with but that underpin the story.

Reading as Reverse Engineering

In *Choice of Robots*, the act of reading becomes a conscious engineering of character interactions and traits that ultimately toys with the algorithms that quantify reader choices. Readers increasingly refer to the stats as they make their decisions. For instance, the reader may consider the strength of his or her relationship with Professor Ziegler to improve or degrade the connection between the two. Similarly, the reader may want to improve the grace of his or her robot and so consciously make choices to do so. To read *Choice of Robots* is not to consume an existing story or even to build a unique story, but to test the limits of an algorithm behind the story. Reading, in this case, is understanding the programmed views of the author as represented in how reader choice alters metadata.

We witness this type of reverse engineering as reading from the end user's perspective by looking at the patterns in how stats change. With relationship scores, we note that sometimes seemingly minor or inconsequential choices affect the engineer's relationships with other characters. For instance, in one reading of *Choice of Robots*, the beverage choice during a meeting with Ali affects his relationship score. When I order a Guinness, he approves, and his relationship score goes from 50 percent to 52 percent. However, in another reading, when asked what I will do after the war is over, my options appear as:

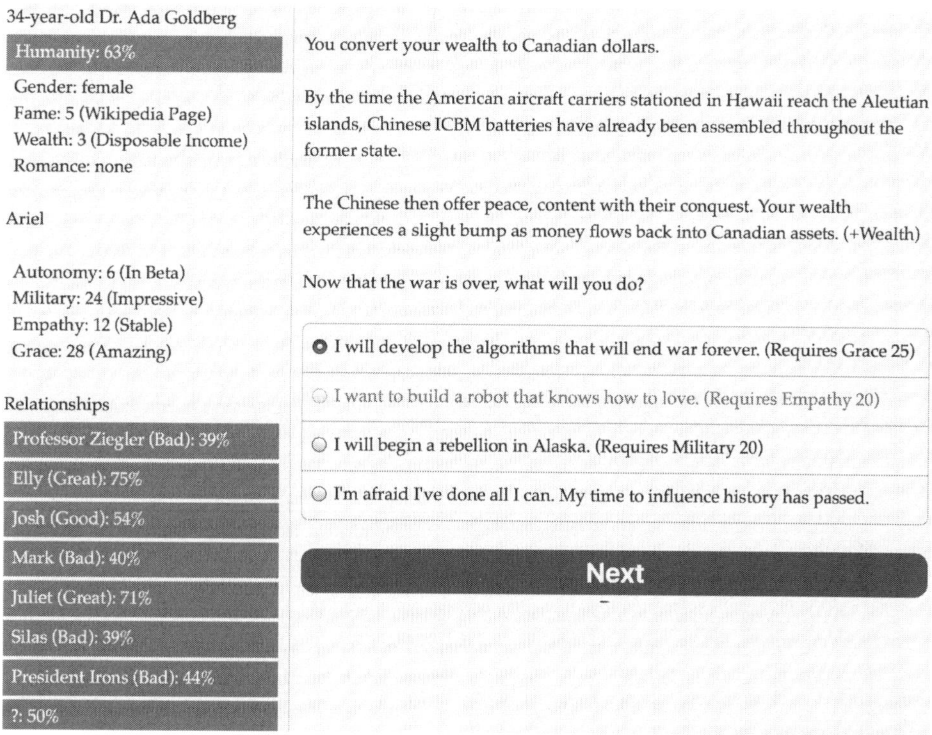

FIGURE 7: Kevin Gold, 'Screen 150' in *Choice of Robots*, 2014. App novel. Use courtesy of Kevin Gold.

I assumed the choice to work to end war would positively affect the humanity score. On the contrary, all my scores remain constant on the following page. The same occurs when I decide to have the engineer pull out of supporting the war effort when she realizes that her technology is being used for violent purposes. While I thought the humanity score would increase, it did not. This begs the question, why are beverage choices more influential than ethical choices? What choices or behaviors carry more weight and why?

Beyond considering the size of a choice's impact, readers also discover what metrics move and when. In another reading, the engineer's friend Elly has a relationship score that fluctuates depending on if she agrees ideologically with the engineer's choices. She is not present in these scenes, and there is no evidence of her otherwise coming to learn of my choices, but when I explain to my robot that robots are meant to maintain the safety of a nation, our relationship score dips five percentage points. When I decide to meet with the Luddite terrorist to try to reason with him, I gain ten percentage points on our relationship score with Elly. My attempts to get a medical company to sell their equipment at more affordable rates also gain me three percentage points. Elly's character becomes my conscience where sometimes I make no gains in my humanity score for seemingly humane choices, but I will get relationship points with her. The relationship score with her is a sizable part of how readers understand her character.

Curious as well is the number of occasions when the stats will change, even though the current page does not ask readers to make a choice. Slightly over one-third of the story pages do not ask for reader choice, but between those pages, stats can still change, so even when one does not make a choice, the scores are affected. For instance, in one reading, my business partner, Josh, dies in a factory fire. I am not asked to input my impression of his death, but in the narrative exposition of his death, I gain one percentage point on the humanity score.

In another reading, I cannot input a choice on how I end the interview with Ali, but in the closing section of that scene, I still lose one percentage point on our relationship. As in real life, even when I am not making direct choices, my ethical identity and relationship with others remain in flux beyond my direct control.

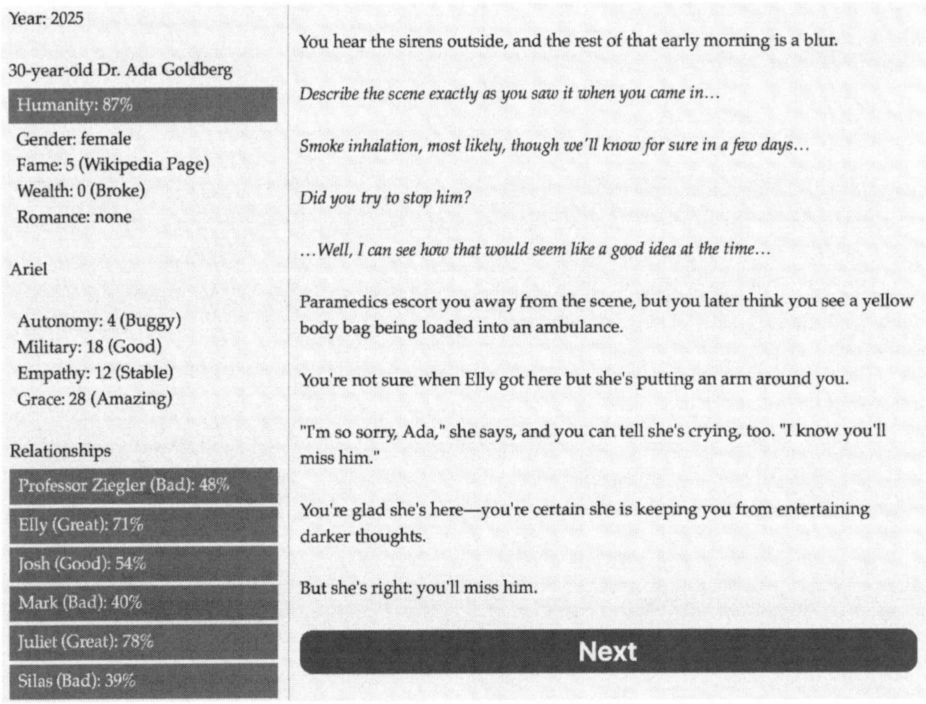

FIGURE 8: Kevin Gold, 'Screen 119' in *Choice of Robots*, 2014. App novel. Use courtesy of Kevin Gold.

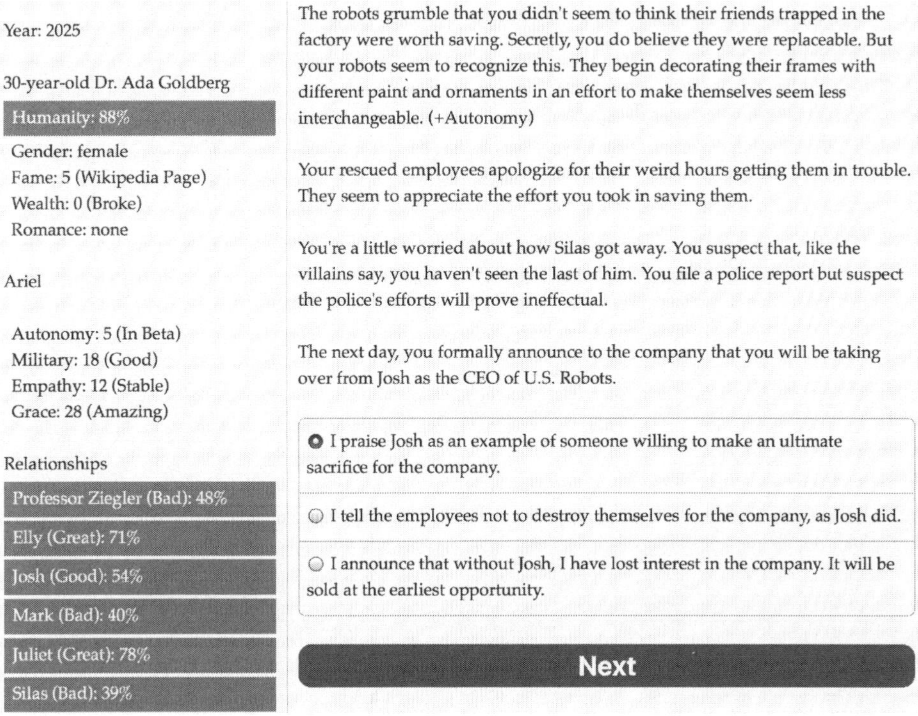

FIGURE 9: Kevin Gold, 'Screen 120' in *Choice of Robots*, 2014. App novel. Use courtesy of Kevin Gold.

Who or what becomes the barometer for self-evaluation? If insignificant choices have immediate effects but wide-reaching choices have no such immediate effect, then what are readers to do about the nature of value judgments in this story? If choices impact readers even when they have no direct input in narrative choices, and characters in absentia judge their actions and thoughts immediately, then they are ultimately performing a negotiation with a concealed set of rules. So every reading reminds them that they only get part of the story – not just that they did not read every possible option, but that without reading the coded structure for when and how points are lost and gained, they could easily miss the point of the story. One cannot achieve the objective distance of a third-person perspective or the self-assuredness of a first-person narrative. Further, while the narrative content is often in the second-person, one cannot experience the immersion of second-person, because the pressure of being watched by data and an unpredictable algorithm is ever present. While the choices are directed at the reader and introduced in the second-person with options offered up in the first-person, the engineer's perspective is so easily affected by other characters and events that meaning is no longer in the story as an object. Instead, the story is in its reading as a process – *how* do readers and the code respond to the next turn, not *what* happens next in the story. The story is indifferent to us because it is constructed beyond the scale of our presence such that we recognize ourselves as a part of a *mise en abyme* and not the architect of a story or representation. To desire a unified narrative is to wish for an immersion in the *what* of content that the *how* of process does not allow.

This kind of reverse engineering as reading is not what readers typically consider a pleasurable narrative experience.[7] A glitch aesthetic that draws attention to the seams that hold the story together comes forward so we can see the string of assumptions upon which our representative media rely. Seeing the construction of the narrative undercuts a cathartic resolution. The active discomfort that accompanies perceiving the limits of representation evokes mirrorish or *mise en abyme* moments. It is the process of slowly determining the underlying code and discovering other achievements and subplots that constitutes the pleasure of the text.

Given that readers are not offered the code in *Choice of Robots*, evaluating *how* to move forward means contending with code limitations or errors not visible on the user end. Unlike analogue errors like a typo or incorrect pagination that readers can identify while reading, errors in calculating the stats only surface in the code. Without viewing the code, readers do not know what to expect and thus cannot recognize coding errors. For instance, should the author misspell '*create log_7_end' in the code, the error is not evident to end users. A sentence in a chapter summary does not appear, but the end user did not know to expect a certain number of sentences.

Further, given access to the code, readers come to find that some choices are labeled as '*fake_choice', like selecting a drink named after a jazz standard in Chapter 1. Such choices do not affect stats nor do they unlock storylines. Other choices may not alter any stats in the game, but 'set' future options and subplots not otherwise available. End users only see set changes while set changes and fake choices are beyond their view and must be divined in rereads or hacks. Readers must reread or reassess how the story's code works. In reverse engineering a reading, we are disarmed and forced to reevaluate *how* we will move forward without full knowledge of the rules at play.

Code as Representational Layer

If the pleasure of reading is in divining the coded structure, looking at the code is a kind of spoiler. Readers as end users reread to predict, test and hunt for patterns like puzzlers whose discoveries create their pleasure. One such compelling mission of rereading could focus on determining the meaning of humanity and the 'humanity' score. The novel's programming assumes that understanding human feeling is quantifiable and programmable. By making choices, readers get to test how humanity functions and how it is defined. The protagonist has no inherent traits beyond the default 90 percent humanity score, and the choices readers make are not often overtly moralistic or ethical, so humanity becomes in some ways trivial. However, because the stat changes are coded to a specific amount for each choice, the nature of humanity is also concrete and permanent.

What affects the humanity score in this story reveals Gold's programmed assumptions of humanity and is part of the representational practice of digital storytelling. The nature of humanity counter robotics is somewhat conflicted, as represented by the fluctuations in the humanity score of the engineer. The program seems to want robots to be more autonomous individuals but not independent of humans. For instance, the engineer loses nine percentage points from her humanity score by dreaming of creating mindless robots and loses another six percentage points for building non-sentient robots. On the other hand, the engineer gains six percentage points of humanity for improving machine learning. Deciding to use only robot labor in one's factory also costs seven percentage points on the humanity score. While robots must have a mind of their own, humans should still control them?

This conflict between artificial intelligence and humanity is not an isolated event; it is replicated in other readings of *Choice of Robots*. In a different read through, when I tell the robot that I see her as my dependent and like my own child, I gain one percentage point of humanity. When I support robot suffrage, I gain three percentage points. When I defend the potential of robots to become artists but spare proving this to humans, I gain another three percentage points of humanity.[8] Educating humans on how robots work garners six percentage points more of humanity. However, when I claim that robots could be trained to be good nurses within five years, I lose nine percentage points of humanity. The decision to train the robot in self-defense when the Luddite terrorist might strike results in losing four percentage points. I am not to have faith in the potential empathy of robots or to encourage them to self-preserve if I want to keep my humanity. If I advocate for robots, I become more human, but if I help robots advocate for themselves, I become less human. The coded assumption here is that humans must grant rights to others and that humanity rests on one's ability to maintain control over nonhuman entities.

More broadly, the humanity score is volatile. One can increase the engineer's humanity eighteen percentage points by merely expressing the intention to be more kind, while kind acts do not result in such significant score increases.

Simultaneously, some seemingly human traits like finding humor in a biased newspaper article are punished as inhumane. When the engineer finds it amusing that Ali's newspaper article is so clearly biased against robotics, the engineer loses thirteen percentage points of humanity.

Part of humanity's volatility arises from how entangled action and intention are in how the code calibrates traits of the engineer and the robot. While for the most part the engineer's wealth and fame status are the direct result of discrete actions, intent or desire for wealth or fame can affect the score. In one reading the engineer sees a flying car early in the story. When the engineer aspires to one day own such an expensive car, her wealth status tics up from zero to one. The desire for wealth becomes equivalent to wealth so that we wonder, is that score tracking the material wealth of the engineer or the importance of wealth to that individual?

A similar entanglement exists in how the engineer's actions and intentions become definitive of the robot. The traits of the robot's autonomy, military, empathy and grace are typically affected in predictable ways: the material choices, design decisions and instructional models used to teach the robot all make it better suited to different applications. However, there are slippery moments when the robot is defined more by the engineer than itself. In the engineer's opening dream sequence of one reading, an imagined robot is ordered to defend the Statue of Liberty and in doing so increases the military score for the robot from the default one to four. Also when the reader selects to describe the engineer's room as orderly with robotic equipment tidily shelved in a minimalist fashion, the choice of human living habits increases the robot's grace score from the default one to three. In both cases, the robot does not yet exist. The protagonist's ideologies and habits affect the robot's traits, which at this early point in the story are only concepts not yet manifested in a particular robot. The idea of the robot and the robot itself are interchangeable.

Ultimately, the reading bumps up against the assumptions coded into the program. Readers are not fully immersed in the narrative because they are always made aware of the function of the medium. Reading *Choice of Robots* means weighing decisions and calculating the effects of reader negotiations within the representational space. Readers know they are playing in a representational sandbox not lording over an autonomously created world born from discrete choices. By foregrounding the apparatus of the medium and contending directly with the process of reading, this kind of reading complicates transparent views of the interface. Even more, it is not enough to see media or interface as a threshold to usher one into the text proper or to point out that there is a framing device or paratext present. We must recognize that there are always layers of data that color our understanding of events. We are always in a *mise en abyme* that we mistake for reality. Conscious awareness of such a state agitates and unsettles us in a mirrorish fashion.

The result of the *mise en abyme* and mirrorish suggests that all we perceive might be another layer of representation. If we cannot escape representation, our only option is to burrow into its assumptions and thus peel away at the endless layers of representation and mediation that lie before us. *Choice of Robots* forces readers into such a state by removing a home button, excluding any bookmarking features, denying readers the option of a back button to correct our misguided choices and caching the executable code from the reader. Our reverse-engineered reading is a long-term project, a state of being, not a confined experience of one representational expression in narrative form. Could one calibrate a better life for the engineer, given different choices? Of course, but only through repetition that unveils further dimensions and layers in the underlying algorithm. Readers will have to game the coded assumptions, something that digital narratives based on algorithmic models solidify in the function of reading itself. Executable code is not simply pragmatic, but representationally meaningful.

Human and Computer Coauthors

To close out the chapter, we will turn to an inverse example of *Choice of Robots* in *exquisite_code*, which slices together code and human text collaboratively through the efforts of seven authors (Leif Elggren, Mara Goldwyn, Dave Griffiths, Jonathan Kemp, Laura Oldfield Ford, Eleanora Oreggia and Sabrina Small) managed by creator, Brendan Howell. Unlike Gold's *Choice of Robots*, which hides the algorithms behind the image of the human author, *exquisite_code* lays the code bare as the text itself, overlapping programmatic, executable language with natural language. The authors of *exquisite_code* worked in a windowless room for eight hours a day 15–19 February 2010 with laptops connected via Ethernet cable to the editing machine. The editing machine parsed what components to include in the novella from those components to be dumped and later utilized as raw material for sonnet rewrite performances. The writers' discussions were recorded and the room set up with a time-lapse camera.

At the beginning of each session, the seven writers would compose a one-line prompt. These were mixed among additional prompts pulled from writing manuals for genre and fan fiction. The editing software selected one prompt, and the writers wrote for six to twenty minutes. The editing software munged a portion to send to the printer according to the munging procedure a human proctor – in this case, Howell – selected to apply. The authors would then write a prompt, given the recently selected story component, and begin the process again (ELMCIP 2009: n.pag.). In addition, authors participated in scheduled code rewrites that ultimately were used to establish further constraints or liberate human writers from existing constraints (Not-Fig 2010: n.pag.). The composition process became not only collaborative but scripted to a procedure, as if it was algorithmic. Coding and manipulation were thus critical components of the writing process and product. In the final novella, natural and computation languages coexisted on the page as equally textual.

The project idea came from a conversation between Howell and Small about what it was like to write code. Howell found that writing and coding were similarly iterative processes. Given this similarity, Howell thought to replicate a live coding event in the production of a novella. Subjecting creative writers to the working methods of coders and hackers does shift their practices. Collaborative writing is rare in the production of a novella, but to assist in the process, Howell utilized surrealist writing games initially designed to suppress conscious and autonomous thinking, and recreated them as coded procedures. *exquisite_code* mirrors the surrealist game, the exquisite corpse where writers or artists only see a portion of the text previously produced by another player before being asked to continue the text (ELMCIP 2009: n.pag.). Howell, however, added several other programmatic constraints to maintain a kind of distributive authorship among humans and between humans and the computer. Howell subjected human-authored entries to arbitrary procedures while the code was not manipulated in such a way. Thus the code's procedures emerge in what we might recognize as the author position (Marino 2013: 299).

Beyond directing the next step in the human writers' text generation, the software, called 'despotic edit-code', continually edited the text using a set of six procedures, three Howell wrote in Python: The Classic Random Select, Burroughs Columnar Cut-up and Markovian Gang Chaining; and Dave, Eleonora and TEXTR, three processes written during that novella's composition (Marino 2013: 288). Because the writers did not see the original, human-authored text, but only the munged version passed through one of the six procedures, it was unclear what was invented by the human and what was manipulated by the program. For instance, the Classic Random Select chooses one of the seven entries as written by the human writer. The Markovian Gang Chaining builds a statistical index using all seven entries and produces a text based on probable next words until it reaches the average length of the entries (Marino 2013: 288–89). Composing through code creates a writing situation where 'the line between the processed data (text) and the processing code is not just blurred but wiped away as the two texts (code and story) are imbricated together' (Marino 2013: 285). Choices in the story could be the product of a human writer or computer code. We see this as well in Howell writing TEXTR as a response to a plot twist written in by one of the human writers. One writer included a text message in his or her entry, which

Howell wrote into a munging method of striping vowels from the first 150 characters of a random selection (Marino 2013: 297).

Even so, writers are not at the full mercy of code since they can edit or add new code. Also, the seven writers have the opportunity to revise the effects of the munging procedures by writing subsequent entries that reframe the turn in the story that the code may have introduced. As human writers become more aware of the dynamics of some munging procedures like the Markovian Gang Chaining, they can exploit the rules by writing phrases with unusual word combinations and syntactical patterns (Marino 2013: 301). Contending with the machinic process even bleeds into the story where at one point, *exquisite_code* includes the passage:

> [I] thought this was a prompt but it was not so i just have to start writing again and today i have something against it, it is more physical than mental, like a sort of clumsiness with my hands in relation to the materia, the machine that take my orders and organize the agreeable signs to a more or less mutually understandable code.
>
> (Griffiths et al. 2010: 44)

The story is not in the prose or the process but in how both interplay, gradually writing and unwriting one another (Marino 2013: 307). Writers can adopt the code as part of human authorship. Further, the Proctor role – the human who selects the munging procedures – becomes the code incarnate and enforces the code not just in its letter, but also in its spirit. When human writers began copying and pasting to resubmit entries initially passed over by the code, Howell banned the action as an interference with the procedure.

exquisite_code focuses on the digital writing process rather than the output of that process, much like a court case is about the legal process rather than producing a transcript of that process. Similarly, *Choice of Robots* focuses on negotiating with underlying, coded assumptions more than it is about altering or controlling plot. The pleasure of reading shifts from fulfilling the plot's promised resolution to piecing together the writing process. With *exquisite_code* both the writers and readers have an incomplete picture of the process. While the writers get to see the writing prompts, they cannot know which munging procedure was used. On the other hand, the readers do not get to see the prompts writers saw, but do have full access to the code and know what munging procedure was applied (Marino 2013: 289). Readers must contend with the code reproduced in the book that, in print, is stripped of its executability. Humans feign reading like a computer. In Gold's *Choice of Robots*, the reader has no access to the code or algorithm, and the author cannot control the choices the reader will make. For producer and consumer, reading *exquisite_code* or *Choice of Robots* constitutes determining the underlying mechanism by exposing media dimensions of the narrative in the code through a reverse-engineered reading.

Such a reading and writing process results from zooming out far enough from the text to see that it is involved in a mirrorish higher dimension or a representational layer of *mise en abyme*. We reach out past the edge of the text and experience a deeper media landscape where we look at our framing devices and media assumptions. We are not looking at reality or even an explanation of representation. Instead, we are looking at ourselves looking. We understand modernity as a meta-theater of endless performance, but with the mirrorish and *mise en abyme*, we do not succumb to performing in earnest because we are too conscious of mediation and representation. Eventually, we tire of parsing layers of representational framing and turn the coin to the reverse side of the baroque, away from the taxing meta-awareness of framing and into the guilty pleasures of immersion.

NOTES

1. It is not dismissive to call one's perspective in life arbitrary. In the Saussurean imagining of linguistic meaning, at base, language is an arbitrary linkage between an object and a word. Their connection is not inherent or intentional and so does not have that kind of meaning; nonetheless, their arbitrary connection now makes meaning not because it was there to begin with but because they are paired to be seen as interchangeable, and language speakers accept that premise of consensus as truth to cope with abundance.
2. Koenraad Claes details how pervasive this problem is when studying Victorian periodicals. Supplements such as sewing patterns, artistic prints, leaflets or advertisements were often discarded even in meticulous collections of a magazine (Claes 2010: 207). Collectors frequently exclude supplements because they might cement the periodical too firmly to its original context (Claes 2010: 208).
3. Alexandra Saemmer categorizes four responses from digital literary authors to the ephemeral state of their medium in order of increasing complexity. First, authors may ignore this instability as they create their work. Second, authors might control the reception of their piece to reproduce the original technological context of their work (this gets harder to do over time). Third, an author could recognize this instability and incorporate that reality of the medium into the aesthetics of the piece itself. Finally, the author could mystify media relationships and accept that randomness is foundational to life (Saemmer 2011: 84). In short, an author can ignore, freeze, include, or mystify the paratextual component of the medium, but in any case, the medium remains a crucial component to the composition process.

4. Chapter 1 involves building the robot and an outing with a friend. The following chapter revolves around how the engineer develops and trains his or her robot or furthers their relationship with a human romantic interest. The third chapter details a conversation between the engineer and a newspaper journalist about the robot whose resulting article affects the engineer's academic standing and fame. The engineer's employment or development of a private company and its stance with global economics and national politics account for the bulk of the fourth chapter. The fifth chapter details the war between the United States and China and the role the engineer and his or her robots play in the conflict. Chapter 6 branches into several possible activities based on the engineer's chosen priorities after the war and the current stats of the robot. Finally, the last chapter addresses how the engineer decides to complete his or her life after falling ill.
5. To share the code with the reader would spoil the reading or gameplay experience. In that spirit, the readings here present scant observations from the actual code and focuses on the end user's experience of *Choice of Robots*, though a close reading of the code would be its own fruitful endeavor.
6. This *mise en abyme* story structure mirrors some of our theoretical understandings of the structure of media, such as Lev Manovich's reliance on metaphor to visualize new media as strata of media with cinema layered over bits and bytes, themselves layered over algorithms (Galloway 2012: 8). Under this model, 'all media are a question of synecdoche (scaling a part for the whole), not indexicality (pointing from here to there)' (Galloway 2012: 8–9). Mediation in this way is a transformative repetition.
7. James Pope repeatedly makes this point in his study on the reader experience of hypertext fiction. In his study, readers wanted more navigational control of the text and a sense of familiarity with the interface and media conventions adopted in the narrative (Pope 2010: 81).
8. We see a hidden bias for human creation and creativity. For instance, one's humanity score increases three percentage points when the engineer decides to become a novelist and another three percentage points when the engineer begins tutoring unemployed humans.

ILLUSION

I no longer answer the telephone if I do not recognize the caller. I might attribute this behavior to the increasing number of telemarketers who call. I might even admit this practice is a vestige of childhood shyness. But these are not honest answers. Before the summer of 2012, I always answered the phone. Then a female telemarketer called. I do not recall the service or product she was pitching, but I listened intently, straining to determine if the person talking was a person. I interrupted her mid-sentence to ask if she was human. She replied 'thanks, I did not know I sounded so good'. The smooth cadence and emotionally accurate tone in her voice made her seem human, but the content of her response would flatter a robot. I hung up. While being deceived by representation is entertaining, we only appreciate it when we are sure it does not affect our reality. Cornelis Gijsbrechts's 1668 painting Trompe l'Oeil: The Reverse of a Framed Painting *as my laptop's wallpaper is fine because I know it is a painting, but the telemarketer's identity remains unnerving.*

***

While seemingly less heady and more innocuous than the *mise en abyme*'s unveiling of representational construction, illusion is perhaps more threatening as it turns representational frames into porous membranes. Instead of demarcating representation, baroque illusion achieves ambiguity mainly by appealing 'to instinct, to the senses, the imagination' (Conti 1978: 4). We see this battle between real and representation repeated in the rising use of augmented reality where digital and physical components coexist. The interweaving of the digital and physical in AR helps make that medium 'representationally fluid' rather than self-contained as is the case with virtual reality (Lichty 2014: 326). AR components must be grafted onto physical markers, geographical features, GPS points or even the wearer's body (Lichty 2014: 334). However, is augmented reality (AR) an educational tool to enliven museum spaces? Is it a mechanism to fictionalize and suppose historical accuracy? Is it another tool for invasive marketing tailored to best capture consumers? Is it an expressive medium to be adopted by artists, gamers and authors? The choices we make in the deployment of AR reveal how baroque or classical our approach to digital illusion will be in the twenty-first century. For instance, Melissa Shiff, Louis Kaplan and John Craig Freeman's AR project *Mapping Ararat* – which digitally creates Mordecai Noah's 1825 plan to transform Grand Island, New York, into Ararat, a Jewish city of refugees – positions its participants in a strange crux. Are they historians, historical reenactors or actors immersed in a digital playscape (Kaplan 2013: 246)? In short, what part of AR resurrects reality and what part creates representation? Digitally rendered buildings and signs grafted onto physical locations by GPS markers create the ghostly presence of representations among us. Moreover, creating the digital components compelled the artists to create physical artifacts for Ararat like a town flag, functional stamps and tourist postcards to make the story of Noah's Ararat penetrate reality itself.

As an emerging technology, AR is still settling into what it may become. Several corporations are testing applications of this technology in consumer tools, like Ikea Place, an AR app that allows one to place Ikea products in one's home virtually. Educational institutions like the University of North Carolina have used augmented reality for guided tours of their campuses. Art and activist collectives have likewise turned to augmented reality to reclaim public spaces. Re+Public, a group of individuals and organizations, works to democratize public space. In support of this goal, they took on the New York City Subway advertising infrastructure as an art exhibition space, with Jordan Seilers and Jowy Ramone as co-creators and curators.

While street artists have worked to replace and deface commercial advertisements in the subway for decades, they have not been successful in diminishing the amount of advertising and visual pollution. Rather than fight against the system, Re+Public's NOAD app uses AR as a kind of adblocker for public spaces (Dormehl 2014: n.pag.). In this structure, art becomes dependent on the advertisement's physical existence. Without the advertisement as a trigger, the digital overlay of original art remains an inaccessible image on a distant server. NOAD's structure does not just raise questions of access and primacy but also serves as a reminder that art is a representational practice reliant on other representations and does not exist as a distillation of nature or reality. Art is grounded in advertising as a kind of perverse patronage system, but Seilers imagines the NOAD app as a way to alter funding models for the subway as a public space. Given that advertising revenue provides only about 1 percent of the operating budget of the New York Subway system, his position is that should riders pay ten cents more per ticket, they could commission art for the subway rather than be subject to viewing advertisements. Such a model could not only improve the wellbeing of riders but also discourage (or at least not encourage) excessive consumption and the environmental damage of such behavior. Rather than riders staring away from ads, they could be engaging with their spaces, lived and digital, in more stimulating ways by interacting with content that challenges or provokes thought. Displaying art over ads in the subway, already a transitional locale focused on physically transporting riders, can help mentally transport people rather than place them on a conveyor belt of consumerism. NOAD helps us imagine a world less focused on consumption and more on art and culture by considering that advertisements are not the end product or the final word in our public spaces. Instead, ads turn into the backdrop or projection screen for a wholly different representation. Furthermore, including the voices of hundreds of artists rather than a limited number of large corporations helps democratize public space and brings prominence to culture over consumerism.

For Seilers, this app previews 'new ways of seeing' and 'new possibilities for how we use our shared public spaces' (Dormehl 2014: n.pag.), but this bold new world stripped of public advertising is, even for Seilers and Ramone, in its early stages. The app cannot mask all the advertisements in the New York subway without more labor, digital storage and processing speed. Furthermore, NOAD cannot display virtual art if street artists overly modify the physical advertisement. Critically, the creators do not see this as a glitch but a feature since app users could then see the analogue street art or graffiti that rendered NOAD dysfunctional (Galperina 2014: n.pag.). Also, the idea of having to hold up a phone or tablet to view the art makes for a clunky experience. All this aside, Seilers and Ramone consider the project a proof-of-concept for a time when wearable AR technology becomes more ubiquitous (Bromwich 2014: n.pag.). In a strange turn of events, while graffiti may have started decades ago as guerrilla art defacing mainstream mass culture and consumerist practices, its digital equivalent is now waiting for a more immersive technology to come on the market.

Trompe l'Oeil: Blending Media and Synesthetic Knowing

Breaking the Frame

Instead of the *mise en abyme*'s nested dimensions that reveal representation, illusionist practice collapses all layers to one so that the real and the representation are fused. Enter the baroque illusion in such varied but related practices as the *trompe l'oeil*, *quadratura* and *bel composto*. These traditions erase the effects of the frame, overwhelm the viewer and break the invisible fourth wall. With a forceful frame, viewers more easily accept representation as real and functional. Seventeenth-century Dutch painters sought 'appearances as they are, without seeking to interpret them' with the northern baroque reproducing appearances of this world, and Italians, the supernatural (Bazin 1968: 239). Despite their differences in subject matter, their common aesthetic goal remained to deceive the eye. While illusionistic goals could be perceived as 'politically and morally decadent' (Gosetti-Ferencei 2005: 80), to look at appearances only is what allowed illusion to develop. Artists could foreshorten the human body without feeling like they had disfigured humanity. They knew they were creating a painting and not manipulating reality itself (Bazin 1968: 239).

Despite the perceived dimensionality of this immersion, it is a flattening of space. There is no search for what is behind the representation or beyond the window. Instead, one perceives having direct access to the function of a computer or the space of a narrative by accepting the illusion of a piece's unity. Staying bound to a frame or one medium is antithetical to the baroque, which uses markers of order, such as visual perspective, not only as an element of showmanship but also more profoundly as order's own undoing.

In resisting hard distinctions between reality and representation, the baroque challenges divides between function and form. While disparaged as a decorative impulse, many of the defining baroque visual traits, especially in architecture, hold that a building is like a sculpture and therefore more than its practical use. The volutes, scrolls and 'ears' (modified buttresses) are not pure decoration or ornamental flourishes but are instead structural devices used to strengthen the building's integrity (Conti 1978: 12–13). The same principle exists in Austrian baroque architecture where sculptures are frequently used as columns such as Johann Lukas von Hildebrandt's design for the Belvedere (Conti 1978: 35).

As the baroque tendency to movement and fluidity challenged conventions of architecture and sculpture, Giuliana Bruno claims the screen reconfigures the wall as more permeable than initially imagined. Rather than thinking of screenic spaces in cinematic ways as windows or mirrors that open to or reflect a more perfect real, Bruno sees the screen as 'a type of canvas, a sheet, or a curtain. Partition, shelter, and veil, this is a permeable architectural envelope' (Bruno 2014: 75). To reimagine walls as permeable recalls the flexibility of boundaries and the malleability of reality itself. This dynamic works as well when we look at decorative features as it does when we look at structural ones. For instance, Petra Blaisse's work designing curtains for the Toledo Museum of Art challenges the typically decorative role of window dressings. These curtains, made of tissue, membranes, filaments and scrim are light-activated shade and temperature regulators rather than merely an inert decorative element (Bruno 2014: 93). Structure and decoration, pragmatics and aesthetics, function and form are not mutually exclusive.

Not only does the baroque fuse form and function, but it also blends media by erasing their distinct boundaries or by adopting the practices or purposes of one medium while using another, such as producing the impression of movement in the stone walls of churches. The architecture of Italian baroque churches so thoroughly adopts this sense of painterly lightness and movement that Robert Harbison describes the walls of Costanzo Michela's Santa Marta as 'a flexible skin which sucks in and blows out like irregular breathing' (Harbison 2000: 13). While architecture meant to break from its stable and still state to become painterly, painting used perspective as an architectural imagining of painting. Even baroque poems treated language as plastic (Harbison 2000: 4).

This motive to blend media crescendos with the *bel composto*, which synthesizes painting, sculpture and architecture and whose form is 'the fruit of a long period of experimentation with the problems of representing the miraculous while maintaining the distinction between truth and fiction' in a way more stimulating than rational truth (Boucher 1998: 134–35). In *bel composto*, discerning the boundary between architecture and painting becomes a process of registering and forgetting the expectations of the two. Emmanuelle Hénin sees this in her reading of painted curtains in theaters and curtains painted on baroque still lifes – the former a part of *bel composto* traditions and the latter *trompe l'oeil*. The painted stage curtain relays a representation of a scene, while the curtain's function anticipates more representation to follow. The theater piece starts behind the curtain, and the painted curtain puts the play inside of a painting. Still lifes that include a painted curtain in place of a real curtain produces the 'painting in a painting' effect (Hénin 2010: 256). Painting the curtain collapses the curtain we imagine as real onto the same plane as the still life we imagine as representation. Obscuring the frame via illusionist, multimedia texts is one of the more captivating components of baroque spatial representation.

Such baroque transgressions of the frame disrupt the harmonious use of perspective the Renaissance employed to contain the illusion inside of the frame. Directives painter, Nicolas Poussin, adopts a classical view of the frame's function: to establish representational space as its own, but in a way that 'does not emphasize this separation, but presents it as given and natural, not as constructed' (Lebensztejn 1988: 38). The baroque treatment of the frame appears in two flavors: over-presentation and exaggeration or obscurity and erasure. In the first, the separation between reality and representation no longer feels natural, and in the second the separation is threatened (Lebensztejn 1988: 38). In his brief generalization of major art movements, Jean-Claude Lebensztejn explains that the classical aims to separate representation and life, the baroque plays with the limits of both, the romantic means to blur or fuse them and the modern flattens both into one. Even modernist critics who do not cite the baroque directly find commonality between the baroque and modern to counter Renaissance or classical framing. Leo Steinberg posits the works of the 'Masters of Illusion' and the 'Modernists' as simply a variation rather than a stark opposition. For Steinberg, the difference between the 'Master of Illusion' and the 'Modernist' is not whether each accentuates illusionism or the surface of the canvas, but which of these elements a viewer first perceives, given that both are present at all times (Steinberg 2002: 13).

While the shock of the *mise en abyme* is the doubt regarding whether we are real or a layer of representation, the shock of the *trompe l'oeil* is precisely that regardless of which, it does not much matter. As Norman Klein points out, truth and fiction are not perceived separately in our brains, so artifice may appear factual to the mind (Klein 2004: 384). *Trompe l'oeil* tends to challenge the viewer's mastery over representation (Gosetti-Ferencei 2005: 80). Indeed Louis Marin claims that the *trompe l'oeil* in its extremity is not a representation, but a hallucination.

Trompe l'Oeil's *Persistent Reality*

Given illusion's potency, it is no wonder that many have tried to undermine its value economically, culturally, academically and otherwise. The bias against illusion, and *trompe l'oeil* in particular, springs from its beginnings along class lines. *Trompe l'oeil* was said to be the work of artisans rather than artists, and was considered a vulgar and mechanical practice that could 'apply and reproduce, not originate and represent' (Trubek 2001: 41). The classical judgment of art, rooted in Platonism, demonizes mimesis as a blind copy that, without knowledge of its subject, could convey and affect only the senses and not the mind (Gosetti-Ferencei 2005: 81–82). Nevertheless, this simplifies art by relegating it to deception alone rather than considering mimesis as a source of knowledge. Although, for Jennifer Anna Gosetti-Ferencei, 'art presents a likeness or representation of what is, but not an *ontological* exactitude. There is a difference between what art *presents* and what it *is*' and, in that difference, art can reveal more than actuality but reach potentiality (Gosetti-Ferencei 2005: 82, original emphasis). For baroque artists or illusionists who accept that appearance is a visual effect achieved through representational techniques, the surface is not superficial or base. Instead, the surface is where complexity lies. There is no hidden depth or truth.

In fact, the origins of *trompe l'oeil* take us to an undeniably flat and thin surface. Bernhard Siegert's study on the *trompe l'oeil* traces its origins to marginalia, especially in framing features on manuscript pages in books of hours and prayer books. It does not come as a surprise that the *trompe l'oeil* would be born of a marginal space that connects the lived space of the reader and the representational space of the text. For Siegert, the *trompe l'oeil* is the product of the book page thematizing its materiality as it becomes aware of itself as a two-dimensional object that can be turned around (Siegert 2015: 178). This outburst at the margins frees representation from its frame so that reality and representation become a continuum of perceived existence instead of oppositions. The broader challenge of *trompe l'oeil* to representation is not its illusionism or deception, but that 'it presents the illusion of not being at all, that is, the illusion of having no author, no history, and hence no capacity for decay or death' (Stewart 1990: 68). The representation is so perfect that it passes for real.

In *trompe l'oeil*, perspective is removed and thus the representation of observation. By laying out what appears in the painting as real rather than represented, the 'artistic intentionality or interiority is obscured by the flat, deflective surface of the paintings. The artist appears "in" the paintings' (Trubek 2001: 43). Because the artist's perspective is not privileged, the painting widens to encompass the spectator. Spectators are compelled to explore representation by its parts rather than as a whole. It is in their desire to step back and gain perspective on the space that spectators become the horizon line of the painting. The story of the painting is not in the painting but in the viewer's construction of that painting (Trubek 2001: 50–51).

The viewing practices of baroque illusion sound remarkably like that of readers experiencing immersive or interactive texts. Frequently, such illusion and its immersive effects are attributed to audience manipulation and passivity. While one may approach illusion passively, the baroque considers the pleasure of *trompe l'oeil* as being fooled and then recognizing that trickery. This moment of being fooled in *trompe l'oeil* arises from suppressing single-point perspective and binocular parallax so that what artists produce is not a *re*presentation but a presentation (Trubek 2001: 43). Presenting rather than representing space is captured in Jan van Kessel's *Insects and Fruit*, which Bernhard Siegert regards as a piece that may warp space and slip in its perspective but could just as easily be an adept showing of two simultaneous spaces for the insects.

> Judging by their shadows, some of the insects sit on that ground as if it were a horizontal plane extending backwards into space, while others appear to be using it as a vertical wall. Either van Kessel's space is warped, or some of the insects are inhabiting the imaginary space *within* the painting while others are sitting *on* the real picture.
>
> (Siegert 2015: 169, original emphasis)

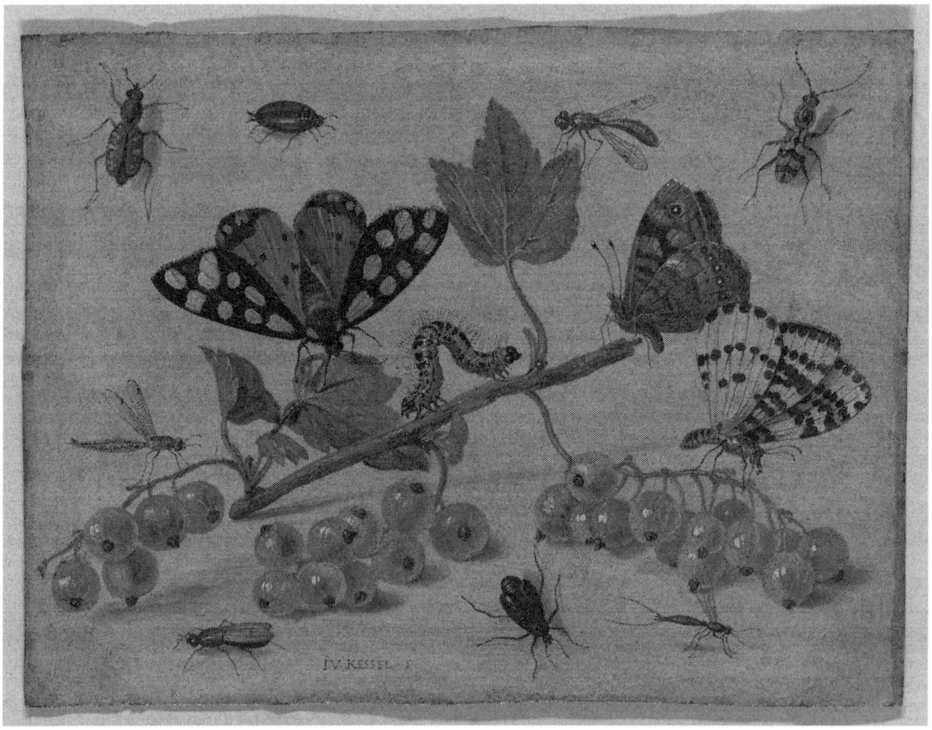

FIGURE 10: Jan van Kassel, *Insects and Fruit*, 1660–65. Oil on metal. 11 x 15.5 cm. Use courtesy of Rijksmuseum, Amsterdam.

By showing two simultaneous perspectives at play, we see the artificiality of our spatial awareness. Even outside of the *trompe l'oeil* tradition, conflicting perspectives aim to take the tools of realistic representation and multiply their potential to generate ambiguity.

Our belief that representation creates an illusion of space is an effect of accepting perspective as a valid description of real space, forgetting its state as a scientific invention and convention (Gombrich 1956: 247). Erwin Panofsky also notes the double edge of perspective where Plato condemns it as a distortion of and replacement for the truth, while modern aesthetic thought considers perspective a tool of rationalism (Panofsky 1991: 71). Anamorphosis provides a clear example by multiplying perspectives and representing an object on a perspectival plane not typically occupied by the viewer or shared with the rest of the composition. Part of the draw of anamorphosis is its ability to turn what seems formless from a typical vantage point into a legible or identifiable object from an unexpected vantage point. We see this generation of potential space in Salvador Dalí's[1] work, such as his 1958 *Ascension*, which took advantage of the glass floor he installed in his studio. *Ascension* combines oppositional viewpoints with one from below the glass and another above (Ades 2000: 17). Using perspective in this way allows Dalí to give illusions their own reality that is still 'impossible to compute or to treat comfortably like a "window"' (Ades 2000: 18). One sees the mechanisms of the trick but remain enthralled in its persuasive presence.

Perspective can be seen as a technology to increase the conscious power of humans to manipulate, multiply or forget (Panofsky 1991: 72). Ernst Gombrich makes this particularly clear in his brief examination of Saul Steinberg's drawings 'The Line' where a single horizontal line produces the ground in one vignette but in others, the road, edge of a table or ceiling line (Gombrich 1956: 203–04). In another case, Steinberg turned a piece of graph paper into a skyscraper by drawing a sidewalk, a road full of people, cars and a smaller building around it. Moreover, in illusionist readings 'it is never space which is represented but familiar things in situations' that cue a viewer into the nature of the image (Gombrich 1956: 202). In switching from illusion to illusion, the resulting ambiguity and multiplicity of the object leave us wondering what something could be. When we erase the frame and unsettle perspective for an illusion, we must look for hints of reality everywhere. Essentially, for illusionists, perspective does not create the illusion of reality but the reality of illusion (Ades 2000: 17). Illusion is not just satisfactory for its sense of escapism but also for its disturbing effect on how we regard our perceptions once the mechanism behind the illusion is unveiled (Klein 2004: 273). Even when we understand that what we perceive is an illusion, we cannot evade its power over our perception. Illusion too brings the world jumping up to the viewer so that we are without boundary.

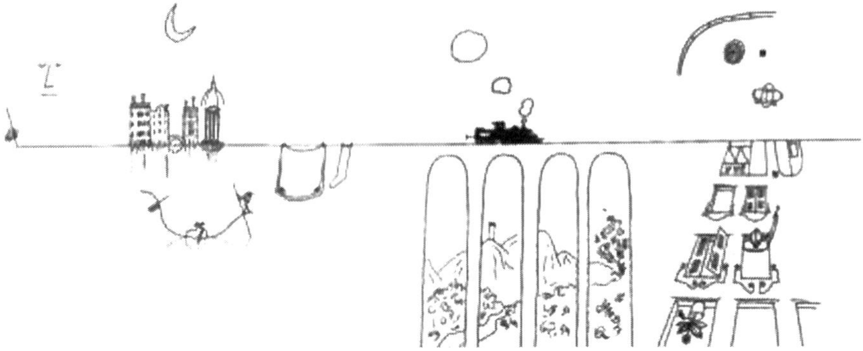

FIGURE 11: Saul Steinberg, 'The Line', 1954. Ink on paper. 45.7 x 1026.2 cm. © The Saul Steinberg Foundation/Artists Rights Society (ARS), New York 2019.

Play, Opacity and Synesthesia as Baroque Knowing

Turning away from examining how something works to revel in the marvels of a well-worked representational machine marks the spirit of the baroque *trompe l'oeil* and establishes that tradition's distance from critical reception because it offers a dangerous approach to gaining knowledge. Despite its ability to trap the spectator, the potential pleasure of illusion is a strong draw and one that is crucial to cognitive development. For Werner Wolf, the 'aesthetic illusion is a "basically pleasurable mental state" that tends to make subjects forget about actual time. Interestingly, focused attention, depragmatization, pleasure, and forgetfulness of time are characteristics which are also typical of playing' (Mellmann 2013: 72). More than a frivolous passing of time, play is a biologically determined behavior aimed at improving cognitive and motor skills (Mellmann 2013: 72). While Katja Mellmann does mention the biological roots of aesthetic illusion, ultimately she argues that the aesthetic is a cultural process opened up by linguistic representation's capacity to uphold what is real and fiction simultaneously. Although readers certainly interpret while they read, for the vast majority their goal is to be immersed in a story.

Our predisposition to immersion is what Mellmann accredits to our 'propensity to take things for signs' (Mellmann 2013: 76). Hence, even in cubist paintings that deny illusionistic techniques, the mere suggestion of a guitar or vase induces our 'imitative faculty' (Gombrich 1956: 155). Despite the representation's attempts to suppress our imagining it as a three-dimensional, functional object, we cannot resist (Gombrich 1956: 282–83). Raymond Tooby's posters for the London Passenger Transport Board show how easily we accept the abstract symbol for the Underground as any number of functional items – a human head, a button, a road sign, a cannon or a letter – given a different visual context. However, we cannot see all these possibilities at once and so, while we can make various interpretations, we do not perceive the ambiguity of the symbol itself (Gombrich 1956: 196). Our will to immerse in interpretative play means we begin to read the world as though it too is a symbolic text.

When we question the relationship between representation and reality, we are testing and toying with the frame. Scholars like Gérard Genette meant to define clear distinctions between representation in the text and reality's presence in context and paratext. While structurally similar to the text/paratext concept, the ergon/parergon divide is characterized by the tenuous difference between the ergon and parergon and so better represents what illusion is doing with its frame. Parerga[2] are more porous and amorphous than paratexts, which aim to orient readers. Instead, parerga augment representation via such devices as the presence of clothing on a figure, columns on a building or curtains on a wall, which supplement but are not critical to the representation. Parerga are not part of the subject or the ground but can be perceived as part of both representational elements at any time. Further, the parergon is not an external entity incidental to the ergon but is inextricable from the ergon's lack (Derrida 1979: 24).

The essential uncertainty of where the edge of the parergon or the ergon lies best visualizes the fundamental conflict of the digital's place in literary studies. In more traditional approaches to defining the literary text as ergon, the medium plays little role in its presence. Human language – the *littera*, the letters – is the portion of the text that disproportionately concerns the literary scholar. The material substrate of those letters is incidental and not a part of most authors' composition process.[3] To capture this parergonal flirtation is to think technotextually. Hence, in considering digital technotext, we must concede that '[c]omputation is not peripheral or incidental to electronic literature but central to its performance, play, and interpretation' (Hayles 2007: 99). The medium and text cannot be so clearly separated as Genette imagines is possible with text and paratext, but instead these overlap as Jacques Derrida describes with ergon and parergon.

Even so, the baroque's critical value is precisely that it does not value clarity and instead recognizes the potential to undo order with order's proper mechanisms. Maggie MacLure argues for a baroque method of qualitative research because of the baroque's 'obstructive potential' to 'resist clarity, mastery and the single point of view, [and] be radically uncertain about scale, boundaries and coherence' (MacLure 2006: 731). The clarity and analytical ease that the academy praises come with ideological costs particularly to marginalized people pressured to homogenize (MacLure 2006: 736). *Trompe l'oeil* challenges the veracity of clarity as it always contains the veiled threat of decentralizing and rendering irrelevant individual perspective. While Renaissance painters used perspective to produce unified and harmonious compositions, illusionists weaponized perspective by deliberately aiming to deceive the viewer into mistaking representation for reality. In this case, perspective is not the tool of human control over nature and perception. Instead, it shows us how we produce reality and representation alike and cannot gain a complete knowledge through our senses even though they are our only devices.

Perhaps another reason for many to disparage illusion is that despite its theatricality, it eventually serves to return society to a classical paradigm that espouses hierarchies of truth and prepares viewers to accept realism as truth again. Despite academia's often dismissive treatment of immersive and illusionist endeavors, baroque approaches to these motives in expression reveal profound insecurities that humans face because they are representational creatures. Our species so actively and joyfully takes part in creating and consuming artifice. That artifice reveals our understanding of the world as a subjective matter of perspective rather than an objective understanding of reality. It may seem base to undercut the powers of analytical thinking, but if we look to Paul Elliott, what we might gain from this immersion is the human unconscious that knows through synesthesia. He states, '[p]oetry, religious symbolism, abstraction, art and scientific models could all be a product of the primal tendency to experience the world in a synesthetic way – with all the senses contributing to the perceptual wholeness of existence' (Elliott 2010: 9). So, our minds might remind us of the limits of representation, and our bodies might function as a synesthetic blending of sensation.

In short, what baroque illusion reveals to humanity is that when all can be representation or all could be reality, we face the ultimate fear that we cannot ever grasp what is real. Our understanding of reality is temporal, subjective, a kind of coping mechanism to stave off the feeling of free-falling into a meaningless abyss. We use layers of representation and framing to deceive ourselves into investing in a perceived system of reality. Illusionism becomes not just idle play or escapism, but the core coping mechanism humans deploy when faced with the *horror vacui* and the impending feeling that there is no meaning, no reality to secure or guarantee our actions or beliefs. We need illusion to remain functional and appear sane to protect our own belief that we are real and singular. Illusion is more than blockbuster action films and all-day MMORPG sessions; it constitutes the serious business of establishing and reaffirming a place in the cosmos.

Approximate Translations across Languages and Media

While digital technologies such as augmented reality, transmedia storytelling or even special effects provide prime examples of illusion and traversing frames or media boundaries, I have chosen a highbrow example to skirt some of the more dismissive treatments of illusionist art, and one that is less technology-forward so as not to box the technotext in the digital. As a proxy, I will adopt the collaboration between Kashmiri-American poet Agha Shahid Ali and Israeli-American painter Izhar Patkin as an example of a sensual synesthetic perception that embraces the porous boundaries between media and framing conventions of illusion. At the beginning of their collaboration, Ali and Patkin named their efforts 'Veiled Threats' as a jab at transgressing their cultural and religious differences by meeting on the veil. As a conceit, the veil provides a prime example of porous divisions that invite the flicker effect of obscuring and revealing that characterizes baroque illusion.

Though Ali died of a brain tumor shortly after the collaboration commenced, their collaboration resulted in one original Ali poem 'The Veiled Suite' specifically for the project and five painted tulle curtains arranged as fully draped, four-walled rooms, each interpreting an Ali poem or Ali translation of an Urdu poet.[4] Patkin exhibited the collaboration as a part of his retrospective show *The Wandering Veil* at the Tel Aviv Museum of Art in 2012 and MASS MoCA in 2014. The MASS MoCA exhibit received positive reviews, marking Patkin's return from a period of voluntary hermitage. Lilly Wei called the exhibit 'award-worthy' for its theatrical treatment of illusion and its challenge to the divide between reality and representation (Wei 2014: 102). As renderings of poems, Patkin's veil rooms are already a play on representation rather than a practice in presenting reality. Wei describes Patkin's imagery as 'rippled and hard to read, combining the historical, the fictional, the poetic, and the polemical as if seen through the distorting, obscuring veils of time, memory, dreams, and human blindness' (Wei 2014: 102). Even the MASS MoCA pamphlet for the exhibit describes the veil paintings as 'rooms that invite viewers to literally and metaphorically enter the pictorial space, suspending the distinction between material and illusion' (MASS MoCA 2013: n.pag.). For Patkin, the curtain is not a covering meant to obscure the window, but itself a 'space of painting' (*The Wandering Veil* 2012: 53), harkening back to the structural/decorative divide that permeates baroque works.

Calling Patkin's veil rooms 'paintings' is a challenge to the medium, as each work begins as a collage of photographs and found images combined in Photoshop and digitally printed on pleated tulle using a vertical printer specially engineered by Jacob Lee. Patkin still considers the process painterly as it must consider the shape of the pleat, weave of the tulle and density of the ink (Ballard 2013: 40). The tulle is porous and resists holding printed images.

Composing the images requires intense awareness of the material. Patkin describes his composition process as one fraught with considerations of density, dimension and sharpness.

> Each pleat is designed to support a certain quality of rendering, and they're tucked in such a way that you don't have a pleat on an eyeball or something like that. They have different volumes, some are fat, some are slender. There are variations of density even within a single pleat, because the curtain, it's fourteen feet tall, it flares out on the bottom, so the details on the flared tulle, toward the bottom, become more evasive. I have to plan certain pleats and certain details for the bottom of the curtain, which are very different from what happens on top. The top is very sharp, the bottom is very effervescent.
>
> (Patkin and Ali 2007: 58)

The material substrate of the paintings is lively and even seems to breathe, like the undulating architecture of wavy baroque walls.

And like those baroque walls, Patkin and Ali's collaboration challenges media boundaries by translating an idea from poetry to painting, in their case over the familiar trope of the veil. When Ali cemented the collaboration, he stated 'I decided that our cultures, Muslim and Jewish, will meet on the veil' (Patkin and Ali 2007: 53). Ali's multinationalism and heritage already primed such culturally collaborative thoughts:

> [Y]ou are a universe, you are the product of immense historical forces. There is the Muslim in me, there is the Hindu in me, there is the Western in me. It is there because I have grown up in three cultures and various permutations of those cultures.
>
> (Zaidi 2008: 57)

For Ali, one's cultural context is an active component that, like the tulle's movements, is the driver behind a figure's eventual appearance. Patkin's veil rooms reinforce this presence of the ground as figures appear and disappear when viewers move. The images printed on tulle shift such that '[t]here is a game of hide and seek on the tulle pleats. The viewer has to be very active to hunt down the phantom images. They are there and not there at the same time' (*The Wandering Veil* 2012: 15). The veil rooms are dynamic rather than solidly unified in a still, easily consumed image as Ali is a part of many cultures' traditions. Patkin admits one of the great lessons he gained from Ali was that even if the audience is of another cultural background and may not understand the narratives and metaphors of one's past, the power and richness of the story will carry through as will resonances between imagery that travels across cultural divides (Abbott 2014: n.pag.).

No matter the medium or language employed to deliver messages across divides, some aspects will always be lost in translation. In Patkin's interview with Ariana Reines, he recalls his childhood understanding of language as a strainer trapped in the throat, which he uses as a relay to translate poetic language to painterly language (Patkin and Ali 2007: 55). In fact, in his narration of *The Wandering Veil* exhibit at MASS MoCA, he takes up the veil and strainer as a mode to view all experience:

> As we walk through a landscape, we're constantly hiding and revealing the landscape itself, so we're kind of veils. Our skin is a kind of a membrane. Things go in, things go out. The language is a kind of a strainer too and I see us as veils.
>
> (Blouin ArtInfo 2014)

Given this idea of language as a strainer, it is not surprising that the tulle as a net becomes the material substrate for Patkin's own 'translation' of poetry to visual representation. Patkin describes the function of his veil rooms as one where 'metaphors have relationship[s] with other metaphors, and then those metaphors that have relationship[s] with other metaphors, have relationships that materialize into *the suchness of* things [....] That's how these rooms operate' (Patkin and Ali 2007: 75, original emphasis). To understand translation as metaphoric rather than direct or objective shows the bodily component of materializing ideas.

Even more, the source of Patkin's inspirations were poems already translated. Ali materializes language via metaphoric translation when bringing the *ghazal* form to Anglophone poetry. Not only did Ali encourage Anglophone writers to produce *ghazals*, but he also translated Urdu *ghazals*. Ali would not call the resulting poems 'translations' but would sign them 'after Ghalib' (Zaidi 2008: 64) or 'version by' (*The Wandering Veil* 2012) because his translations recreate rather than represent the original poem. The literal translation does not pass, since it leaves behind the poetic features like the syllabic count of lines, the rhyme of the *ghazal* (*qafia*) or even the repeated closing words of each couplet (*radif*). Equally, maintaining the syllabic count, *qafia* and *radif* in another language is near impossible, so the form or the semantic meaning, if not both, must be transformed in the translation. For Anglophone readers of Ali's translations, one must accept that the translation is not an accurate and direct reflection of the original but a refracted, metaphoric versioning of a representation.

Even the *ghazal*'s mismatched couplets of ranging themes and tones produce the effect of

> metaphors open[ing] into other metaphors – if the rose reminds the poet of his beloved and makes him think of himself as a nightingale, it also recalls for him the garden that bloomed in spring but was ravaged in autumn, and where a hunter lurked to catch the nightingale, or lightning crashed down from a gladdening rain cloud and destroyed the bird's meager nest.
>
> (Naim 2012: n.pag.)

Readers filter all of these images through what came before, creating a string of representations building on one another. As linkages between *ghazal* couplets can come through associations with the words, phonetics, etymology or calligraphic features (Naim 2012: n.pag.), the potential for our imagining of translation and versioning expands the reader's or viewer's 'net of awareness' beyond objectivity or truth (Naim 2012: n.pag.). Patkin's visual renderings of Ali's translations continue such a method of translation from media's language to another media's language.

We can see this inexactitude of translation in Ali's version of Faiz Ahmed Faiz's[5] poem 'You Tell Us What to Do' to Patkin's visual rendering of the poem. In 'You Tell Us What to Do' the unstable placement of particulars comes forward in the title and echoes throughout the poem with the extensive use of pronouns as a linguistic shifter. To have an unclear view of who the subjects and objects of the poem are underscores how sureties in communication are not guaranteed. Given the context of Faiz's life, one could suppose the 'we' are the Palestinians and the 'you' the Israelis, but keeping the antecedent of the pronouns withdrawn widens the holes of the strainer, allowing more possibilities to pass through. Further, when 'we' takes up the grammatical subject position, the poem is in the past tense or conditional mood, while 'you' as the subject brings about the present tense or imperative mood. The dynamic between the 'you' and 'we' reveals a disproportionate power relationship where the 'we' already imagines itself distant and disempowered. Emptying the particulars still maintains the structure and that structure displayed in pronoun use and tense use gives the poem enough body, but not too much to cache the sieve function of language.

Even in the content of the poem, we see a slant likeness between its two stanzas so that each might be a metaphoric translation of the other. The first six lines of both stanzas use the third-person plural with the past tense or conditional mood. Each results in two, three-line sentences. The first sentence introduces the metaphor of either the boatman or the healer as initially optimistic and the second sentence comments on how that optimism has diminished over time. In just those second sentences in lines 4–6 of each stanza we hear a refracted version of potential pain relief: 'With a few strokes, it seemed, / we would cross all pain, / we would soon disembark' (*The Wandering Veil* 2012: 108) and 'Besides, we remembered so many cures, / it seemed at any moment / all troubles would end, each wound heal completely' (*The Wandering Veil* 2012: 108). Despite the switch in metaphor from boatman navigating a journey to healer attending to wounds, the sentiment of inevitable disappointment persists, likening the two figures. From peeling these layers of metaphors, we gather that representation offers up what could be rather than what is.

The next segment of lines in each stanza shows the greatest divergence in their translations of one another, despite the identical opening words of both sections.

In the first stanza, we have 'That didn't happen. / In the stillness of each wave we found invisible currents. / The boatmen, too, were unskilled, / their oars untested' (*The Wandering Veil* 2012: 108) and in the second: 'That didn't happen: our ailments / were so many, so deep within us / that all diagnoses proved false, each remedy useless' (*The Wandering Veil* 2012: 108). Following the same opening, we get contrasting expressions, with the first stanza including 'stillness' and 'currents' and the second 'ailment' and the 'deep'. What appears tranquil or minor near the surface is instead dynamic and consequential. The last two adjectives of both segments unbalance the other with 'unskilled' and 'untested' in the first stanza and 'false' and 'useless' in the second. Reversing the order of one pairing would create the more direct semantic congruence – unskilled with useless and untested with false. Seeing such slight incongruities shows how vulnerable representations are to small differences.

After these differing lines, the two stanzas converge to one common metaphor of the investigator while it moves to second-person present imperative. The first stanza includes 'Investigate the matter as you will, / blame whomever, as much as you want' (*The Wandering Veil* 2012: 108), while the second stanza phrases the lines differently as 'Now do whatever, follow each clue, / accuse whomever, as much as you will' (*The Wandering Veil* 2012: 108). The second lines are identically structured and use synonymous verbs. The first stanza's verbs move from the religious 'blame' (Old French '*blasmer*' a variant of Latin '*blasphemare*') to the judicial '*accuse*' (Old French '*acuser*' from Latin '*accusare*' or to '*call to account*'). The second stanza shifts from 'want' (Old Norse '*vanr*' or 'lacking') to 'will' (Germanic '*wollen*' or Latin '*velle*' or 'wish'). The stanzas move from a religious lack to a judicial wish, which is a close enough equivalent. This slight refraction culminates in the shift of italics in the two closing lines of each stanza, where in the first stanza we hear 'Now *you* suggest what's to be done, / you tell us how to come ashore' (*The Wandering Veil* 2012: 108, original emphasis). While this could indicate the actor or could issue a command, it could also mark surprise that 'you' would suggest what you did. On the other hand, the closing lines of the second stanza read 'Now tell us what we should do, / *you* tell us how to heal these wounds' (*The Wandering Veil* 2012: 108, original emphasis). The italics now emphasize that 'you' should give advice in a challenging or accusatory tone because it follows an imperative statement, which undercuts any shock at 'your' actions. In short, changing the figures or subjects of a metaphor from a boatman to a healer is not as resonant or powerful as the little shifts in connotation, placement and tone.

Translating these little shifts poses a challenge for a visual interpretation. Patkin converges Israeli and Palestinian exile by artificially juxtaposing an image of his great-grandfather's old synagogue in Netanya, Israel, with a mosque. We also see mimics of the poem's approximate translations across stanzas with the depiction of the supply ship *Altalena*, crewed by a Jewish militia still fighting Arab groups in the newly founded Israel of 1948. The *Altalena* shows not only the divide between different religious groups but also conflicting views within one group. The associations that tumble out from the imagery reveal similar experiences that underlie exilic groups writ large, which the exhibit catalogue describes, saying,

> the viewer is surrounded by a vista of the Tel Aviv-Jaffa seashore: a mosque and a synagogue, Arab and Jewish refugees, smoke billowing from the ship *Altalena*, lying sunk on her side. But the multitude of refugees by the sea also brings to mind the Exodus – the Flight from Egypt. The historical aspect is a stepping-stone to a mythological pageant.
>
> (*The Wandering Veil* 2012: 138)

This layering of associations into dense metaphors that smoothly transition viewers from reality to myth or vice versa is nearly a signature for Patkin's work where 'everything keeps metamorphosing [...], places merge together and are compressed into each other, and every identity is a palimpsest of associations. Objects split up or fuse together. Opposites blend with one another. Nothing is fixed. Everything flows' (*The Wandering Veil* 2012: 138). This idea of constant movement mimics the feeling of illusion where reality and representation shift to be perceived otherwise frequently and with great ease. Even what appears solid remains in motion, which we see in Faiz's poem 'Evening' according to Ali's versioning and Patkin's visual rendering.

Realizing Illusions that Usurp Reality

If appearances are always in motion but illusionist practices flatten space and time, we return to the baroque's ability to hold together the incompatible. Ali's 'Evening' does this by doubling time in a single poem. While the poem relates a place stuck in time, rather than being suspended in the past, Ali writes us into a constant present. The temporal disjuncture in the lines feels violent: 'since who knows when– / their roofs are cracked, / their doors lost to ancient winds' (*The Wandering Veil* 2012: 174). The present perfect 'are' where the past perfect 'were' would feel more comfortable and temporally continuous keeps us unsettled. The present perfect continues to suspend progress when 'Some terrible magician, hidden behind curtains, / has hypnotized Time' (*The Wandering Veil* 2012: 174). We move to the future tense with 'Now darkness will never come – / and there will never be morning' (*The Wandering Veil* 2012: 174). Using the present perfect again disallows access to a definable past and using the future tense only to point at what will never come to pass reminds us that we only have one time to consider – an endless now that has the markers of dynamism without actual movement. Ali's poem is all potential energy reinforced by the choice of the conditional for the final three lines when silence 'may wake up the statues / and a beautiful, dark goddess, / her anklets echoing, may unveil herself' (*The Wandering Veil* 2012: 174). Ali only marks what may happen if we escape the present that permeates the entire poem.

To parallel this sense of suspended time. Ali also inverts the figure and ground. Each of the three human figures – a priest, magician and goddess – are somehow obscured. The priest appears as the second figure in a metaphor: 'And the sky is a priest, / saffron marks on his forehead, / ashes smeared on his body. / He sits by the temples, worn to a shadow, not looking up' (*The Wandering Veil* 2012: 174). The priest is a metaphor for the sky, and as he becomes more concrete, he erodes back into a shadow. He is no longer a solid focal point. The magician too is cached: 'Some terrible magician, hidden behind curtains, / has hypnotized Time' (*The Wandering Veil* 2012: 174). We do not see him nor does he exist on the present temporal plane of the reader. Finally, the goddess is presumably trapped forever within a statue since time will not progress forward.

If we imagine the poem 'Evening' as a visual representation, we would expect the human figures to hold less power and prominence, given their representation in the poem. However, the figural aspects provide a particular challenge to translating this poem into a painting. In the poem, we are made to see the ground – the ruins, trees, time, the sky – but Patkin does have to paint something concrete on both ends of the metaphor: the priest and the sky. On each of the four walls, we get one figure – the magician, the priest, the goddess and the statue. While the figural takes on a stronger presence in the visual than the verbal, the layering of the tulle makes the figures ghost-like. Given that the magician is the instigator of freezing time, Patkin's decision to tuck him into a dark corner replicates the poem that hides him behind a curtain. Rather than literally being behind a curtain, he is dressed in black and heavily shaded to blend in with the birds he releases. The birds arch over the goddess and statue, who face one another. While tense could divide them in the poem where the goddess was in the statue, in the painting, the potential future and actual present exist simultaneously. Should one rotate clockwise from the room's single entrance, one sees the potential goddess before the actual statue. One would have to move counterclockwise – backwards in time – to see reality first, which seems counterintuitive.

Patkin furthers this suspended movement by adding a fifth figure: the poet. The poet is isolated from the other figures and the Venetian architecture in the foreground, casting the poet as the witness or creator of the scene. The poet's place in the background image is deeply illusory. Seeing the poet inside the visual space of the poem shows the strangeness of a flat representation of time. The poet is on the same representational playing field as what he imagines. The painting as representation swallows up the poet as a part of the poem, not its origin or framer. They are made the same, even when we know they are not.

This constructed sense of unity comes forward even in how Patkin decides to display his veil rooms. Patkin presents each room as a stage set with the backs of the sets left unfinished. They appear as a series of separate theatrical spaces unapologetic for their artifice. The viewer is not given a position of mastery as some panoramas do by placing viewers above the ground level of the image. We are not meant to be wholly transported out of the museum space or think of these rooms as analogous to virtual reality. Considering unity as a *trompe l'oeil* rather than a panorama denies the idea that unity belongs to just the work. Unity reaches beyond the edge of the work to engulf the surroundings, the viewers, even the creator of the work. This is why the convention of the *ghazal* to name the author in the final couplet is not a simple signature marking that the poet made this poem, but it puts the poet into the poem:

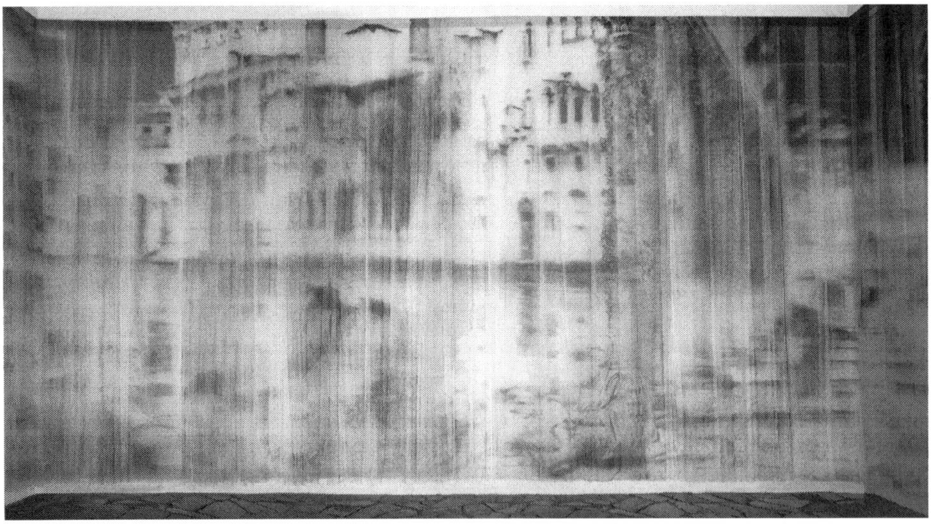

FIGURE 12: Izhar Patkin, *Evening*, 2008. Ink, pleated illusion (tulle), painting on four walls. 14 x 22 x 25 ft. Use courtesy of Izhar Patkin.

> The reader, for whom the poem (traditionally) exists as a created object separate from its creator, suddenly finds the creator himself or herself explicitly within the poem. This isn't seeing the potter's fingerprints in the clay; it is opening the urn and finding a river, the rain, the poet inside.
>
> (Ward 2013: 67)

This kind of unity denies spatial and temporal boundaries since what one might consider outside of a work could be inside it and what it contains could be bigger than itself. While Patkin leaves a laminated copy of the poem in each veil room and brings the poet into the representational plane, his painting feels as much as though it was a tour inside of Ali's poem.

Unity through Synesthesia and Allusion

Certainly seeing the constructedness of these veil rooms but being immersed in them nonetheless is a prototypical case of illusion. Engulfing the reader/viewer and poet/painter into the representational plane is a common enough trope of illusion. Notwithstanding, if the illusion swallows up reality in such a convincing unity, perhaps what we perceive as divergent can always be strung together like *ghazal* couplets. Even though couplets are combined in one *ghazal*, Ali argues

> [a] couplet may be quoted by itself without in any way violating a context – there is no context, as such. One should at any time be able to pluck a couplet like a stone from a necklace, and it should continue to shine in that vivid isolation, though it would have a different lustre among and with the other stones.
>
> (Ali 1996: 87)

The customary style of *ghazal* poets to exclude or add new couplets at different performances emphasizes the separateness of its couplets. Unity is tenuous and dependent on the performance at hand just as the images in Patkin's veil come and go depending on how the viewer walks through the space. In a way, Patkin's five veil rooms play on the relationship between couplets in a *ghazal* that are thematically and tonally divergent but ultimately unified by the structural conceit of the *qafia* and *radif*. Each room is separate, but they all belong together.

The unity privileged in the *ghazal* is one that welcomes a porosity and flexible synesthetic immersion that is at the core of baroque illusion. While Patkin's choice of tulle as a painting surface and the decision to adapt poetic forms like the *ghazal* and *canzone*, which are traditionally set to music, give his veil rooms a synesthetic charge more generally, 'The Dead Are Here. Listen to the Survivors' brings this

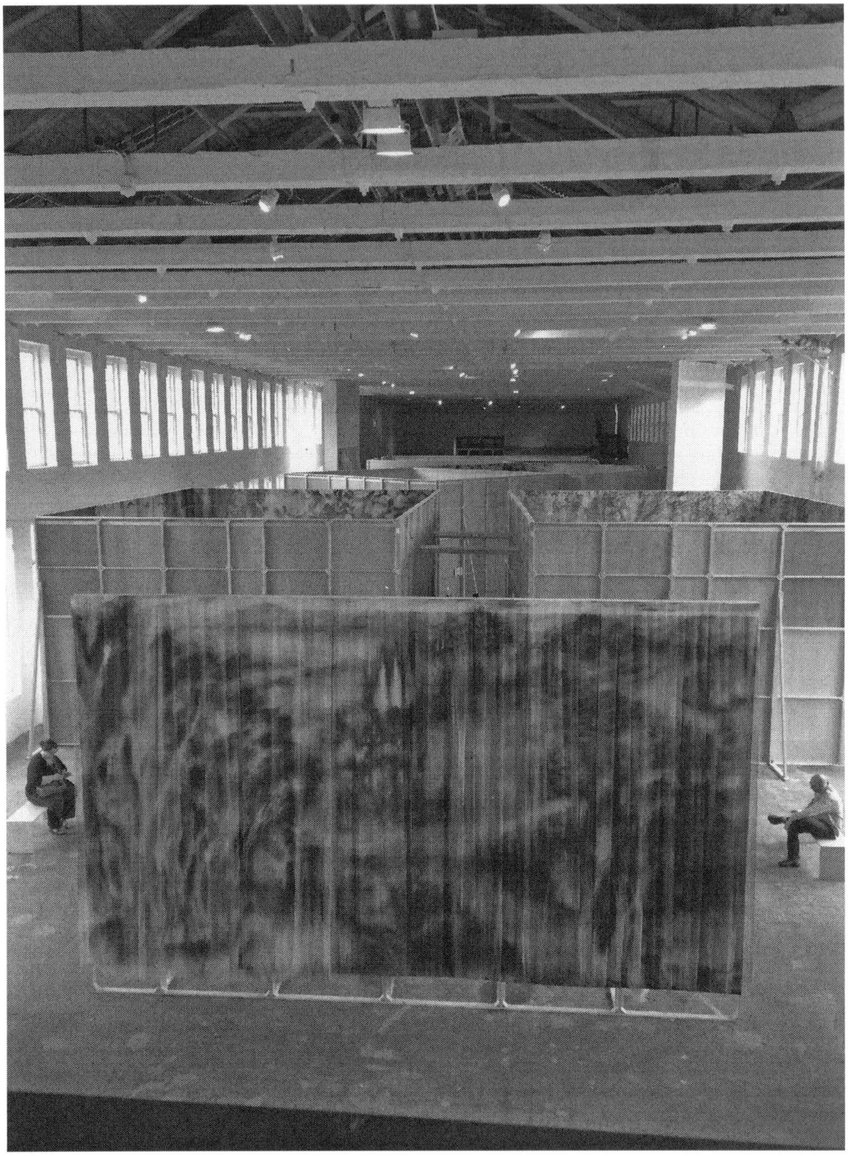

FIGURE 13: Izhar Patkin, *The Wandering Veil*, MASS MoCA exhibition hall, 2013–14. Use courtesy of Izhar Patkin.

resonance of the senses to the forefront. The original poem by Ali includes ten non-rhyming couplets with multiple enjambments between couplets. The speaker of the poem considers who will lead him through his journey to the afterlife. He supposes it will be a long-lost friend who will serve as an intermediary for the speaker's beloved. While 'The Dead Are Here. Listen to the Survivors' is not a strict *ghazal*, it addressed one of its common subjects: lost love and in particular, a love that confuses the love of the divine and the love of a woman. The beloved in this poem has the power to change sense states in her environment. In introducing her, the speaker recalls first 'her hands digging out turquoise perfumes / from the air's mines' (*The Wandering Veil* 2012: 152). Not only does the air turn to a solid state, but it also transforms into a bright fragrance described by its color rather than its smell.

Patkin's visual rendition of the poem picks up this sensual transformation by making disparate items appear visually congruous. The female figure in the painting sits below a statue of an angel with the love letters she presumably received from the male figure sitting directly across the room from her. Surrounding both figures, each low to the ground and in the immediate foreground of the painting, are rows of white graves and beautiful cherry trees in bloom, mixing light and life with stone and death. The two lovers tragically do not notice one another, but she has spread his letters across the grass. The white paper on the grass mimics the white tombstones around her. Even those letters are dead, pulped trees with the statues above them their funerary monuments. All the image's components fuse into variously interpreted sensual expressions of lost love in particular and death more generally.

Turning back to Ali's poem, we see this alchemic worldview in the character of the long-lost friend. This friend is a parergonal feature who exists between the living and the dead and plays the role of messenger between the male and his female beloved, revealing their relationship and synesthetic worldview. While he is a supporting character in this love story, in the poem, he is the subject of all three questions. The male lover first asks his friend if he will speak of her and the third question characterizes what message he might receive from her as a synesthetic jumble:

> Will he bring a message
> from her eyes, so far away now, gazing
>
> at a dream in which the ghosts of prisoners
> are shaking the bars till iron softens
>
> into a song – everywhere the shadows
> of my voice, everywhere a smokeless fire?
> (*The Wandering Veil* 2012: 152)

The visual and audio are so imbricated here that there is no untangling them without destroying the whole message. Furthermore, in the three closing couplets, the speaker directly addresses the friend using the imperative. The male lover takes up the all-encircling air as a medium for the word.

> Tonight the air is many envelopes
> again. Tell her to open them at once
>
> and find hurried notes about my longing
> for wings. Tell her to speak, when that hour comes,
>
> simply of the sky. Friend, speak of the sky
> when that hour comes. Speak, simply of the air
> (*The Wandering Veil* 2012: 152)

Despite its simplicity, the air morphs into a perfume, a mine, an envelope, notes, a song and a voice. Through the air, we see that we are connected, breathing in and out what has passed through the lungs of many others for hundreds of years before us. The air is a vital ground whose movement generates life, the essential film between life and death as the ultimate parergon.

The friend and air appear parergonal, as vital peripheries, and this same energy fuels Patkin's decision to remake 'The Dead Are Here' via allusion. Patkin recalls the story of Laila and Majnoon – whom he calls the Juliet and Romeo of the East – to visually reference Jean-Honoré Fragonard's four-paneled painting *Progress of Love*. Patkin admits, 'I took the model of Fragonard's *Progress of Love*, in which there is a garden where love progresses. I turned it into a cemetery with cherry blossoms in full bloom, but where love does not progress' (*The Wandering Veil* 2012: 25). Rather than the four-paneled series with emblematic statues of Venus, Cupid and cherubs marking flirtation, courtship, consummation and finally friendship, Patkin adopts the two final stages and alters them to arrest love. 'The Dead Are Here' adopts the floral vibrancy of Fragonard's third panel 'The Lover Crowned' but in the place of a sexual consummation and marriage, there is death in a graveyard. While 'The Dead Are Here' includes the conceit of reading love letters that appears in Fragonard's fourth panel 'Love Letters', in Patkin's work the woman reads the letters alone beneath the statue of an angel hushing the surroundings. She is denied exchange with her lover, even though he sits across the room looking in her direction. An awareness of what was lost from Fragonard's scenes only heightens the sense of loss in the veil room.

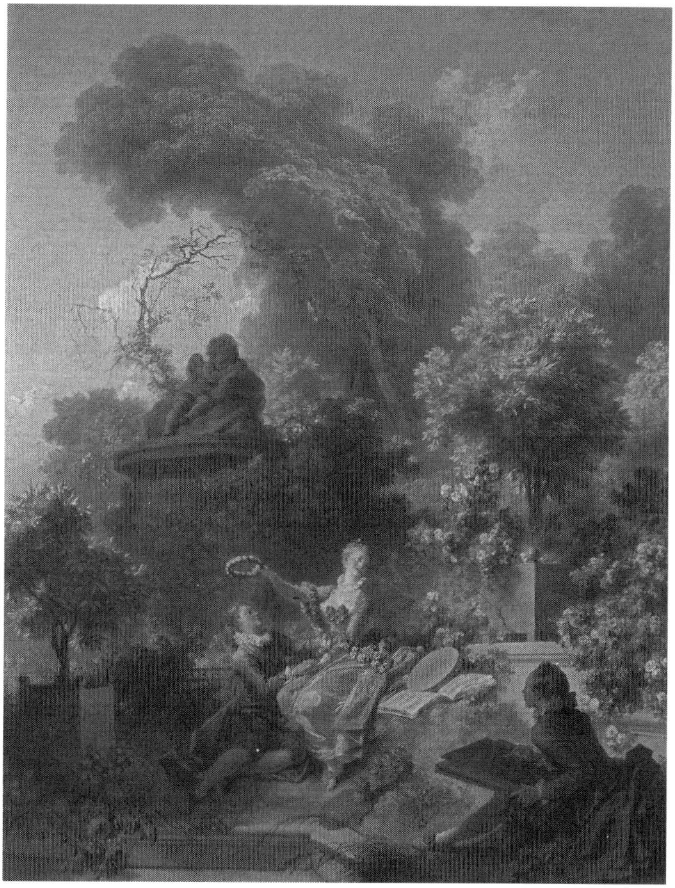

FIGURE 14: Jean-Honoré Fragonard, *The Progress of Love: The Lover Crowned*, 1771–72. Oil on canvas. 125 ⅝ × 95 ¾ in. Use courtesy of The Frick Collection.

The decision to enrobe the poem in a series of other cultural quotations shows how latent cosmic connections are in the air around us that recall the profound unity of phrases like 'we are all stardust' or 'matter is not made but transformed'. This vision of endless recycling is how Patkin describes the process of understanding Ali's poetry and by extension experiencing his veil rooms. According to Patkin,

> [t]he way I read, at least a Shahid poem, but any poem that is great, is I read it, I read it more, I have to chase it many times. And at a certain point the cat catches its tail, it becomes a full circle. I can enter the poem at any point, it doesn't have to be at the beginning or at the end [....] When you walk into my veil rooms, depending on your personality and your interest or your mood of

> that day, you find one spot that becomes the beginning spot for you. Because you identify it first, it grabs your attention first, or something like that. My involvement with the poems is very, very similar.
>
> (Patkin and Ali 2007: 57–58)

Patkin's use of narrative and visual allusion is like the string that holds together *ghazal* couplets, which though united remain autonomous. While Patkin connects the disparate through literary and visual references in 'The Dead Are Here', he uses historical and cultural references in 'You Tell Us What to Do' and in 'Violins', an Ali version of Mahmoud Darwish's final poem in the collection *Eleven Stars over Andalusia*.

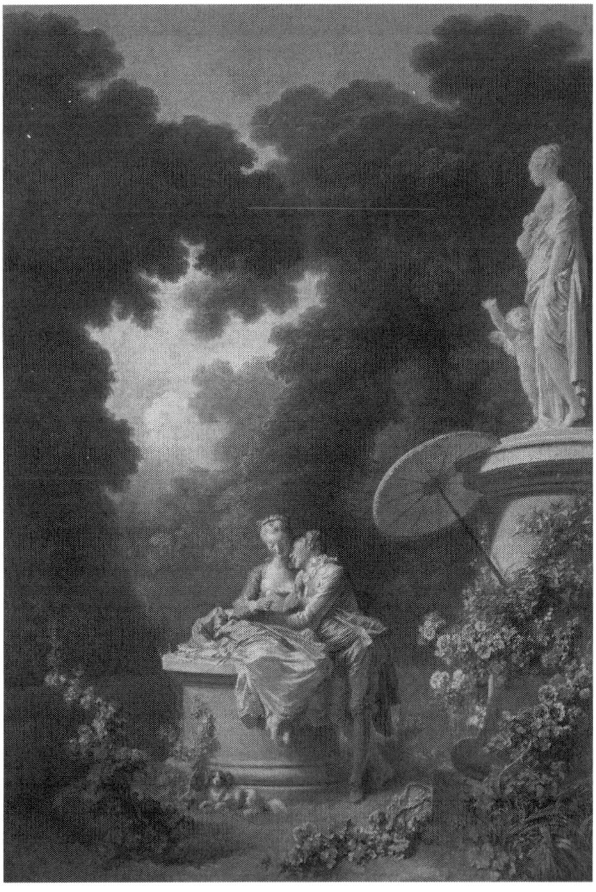

FIGURE 15: Jean-Honoré Fragonard, *The Progress of Love: Love Letters*, 1771–72. Oil on canvas. 124 ⅞ × 85 ⅜ in. Use courtesy of The Frick Collection.

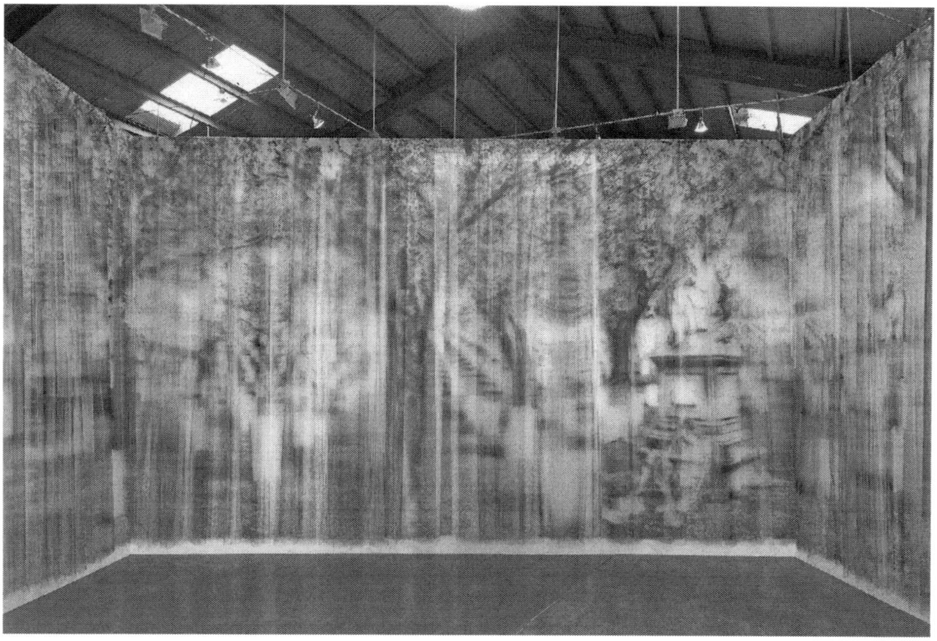

FIGURE 16: Izhar Patkin, *The Dead Are Here*, 2009. Ink, pleated illusion (tulle), painting on four walls. 14 x 22 x 25 ft. Use courtesy of Izhar Patkin.

While Patkin leans on allusion, Ali's version of Darwish utilizes personification and metaphor to connect a violin to the universe around it. The ten couplets of Ali's version of 'Violins' begin each line with 'Violins' followed by the verbs weep, set fire, tear, are, follow and seek, which animate this inanimate object. The eight lines in four successive couplets that use the copula 'are' lay out eight separate and jarring metaphors equating violins to 'moaning water', 'wild lilacs', 'monsters', 'an army', 'the anarchy of hearts driven mad', 'flocks of birds', 'silk' and the 'sound of wine falling' (*The Wandering Veil* 2012: 50). Not only does the violin come to life, but it also transforms into the natural, supernatural and sensual. The violin encapsulates multiple possibilities of its essence and tumbles nearly into pure potential. What more can the violins be? Further, as one reads the repeated word 'violins', it begins to sound like 'violence'. Patkin translated this *double entendre* into a bifurcated veil room where he recreates a Pablo Casal photograph of a 1961 cello performance in the East Room of the White House on one side of the veil room and a desolate tree-lined street and countryside ravaged by war on the other side (*The Wandering Veil* 2012: 17). An aural similarity creates a visual disparity.

On both sides of these visual stories appear transitional elements. Left of the East Room scene appears one empty chair facing the audience where the cellist should be. The cellist instead stands in front of a chair that faces a war scene. He bows to a man of similar stature standing above a dead donkey. The cellist performs for the dead and the empty chairs scattered across the scorched earth. To the right of the East Room scene is the other transitional element: a funeral procession with a carriage and grandly decked horses marching toward the audience. The formality of the recital is repeated in the pomp of the funeral, making the opulent celebration an ironic celebration of death and decay. Beyond leading us to the juxtaposition of war and musical performance, the transitional elements of the painting hint at a broader unity beyond the limited scope of humans. One decision in the United States may be entangled with another seemingly disparate event on the other side of the planet. Patkin's 'Violins' is perhaps the least literal of the visual adaptations of Ali's poems, but ultimately none of the veil rooms are mimics, illustrations or direct copies of the poem. They are Patkin's imagined illusions while circling around in Ali's adaptation of Darwish's poem. Each veil room becomes a little theater of one reader's mind, presenting an illusion, impression or hallucination of a poem.

Illusion as the Veil that Hides Nothing

Patkin imagines his veil rooms as more than theatrical, but also spiritually habitable. Even the choice to create the vertical veil paintings as veil rooms is a riff on the word 'stanza', referring not just to poetry but also the Italian word for 'room' (Patkin and Ali 2007: 49). By occupying the room, one is in the poem through its refraction or illusion. Patkin even directly compares his veil rooms to baroque churches.

> It's a very Baroque experience. One image spills into another. In a Renaissance Church, you walk in and it's in perfect symmetry, you can see the order. You're standing at the front door and God's plan is in your hand. You know where everything is, it's in perfect symmetry, it's in perfect order, you're in control. In the Baroque church, everything changes. The views and everything changes [*sic*] as you're walking around, so it's more experiential in that way, you have many many viewpoints, many different perspectives. Someone once described the Baroque as a reflection of the Renaissance in the water. These rooms are the same, because you can't walk in and conceive the floor plan in a flash – Because it has a lot of refractions.
>
> (Patkin and Ali 2007: 66)

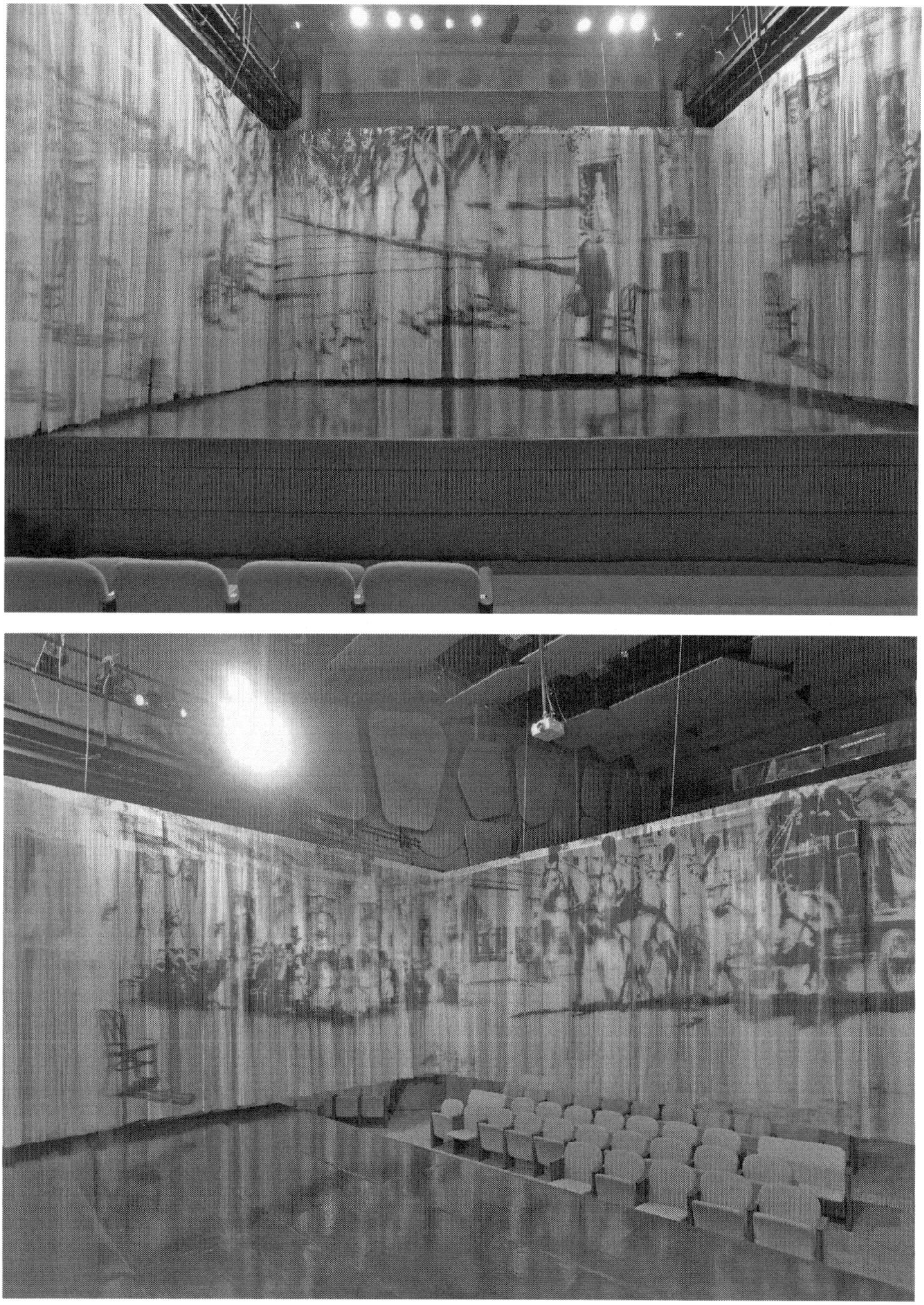

FIGURE 17: Izhar Patkin, *Violins*, 2006. Ink, pleated illusion (tulle), painting on four walls. 14 x 24 x 25 ft. Use courtesy of Izhar Patkin.

This contrast between being intimately interior to a space yet also not knowing the contours of that space recalls the very spell of baroque illusion in the *trompe l'oeil* where the viewer is well aware of being fooled but remains mesmerized by the illusion's magical hold over the viewer's senses. While we may think of this feeling as a light-hearted experience of pleasure, it can equally convey a profound feeling of lack when we see that all our refractions only lead back to themselves, not to a singular unity or a direct translation, but to a persistent remainder that exceeds the frame or remains trapped in the sieve of language.

This more somber effect of baroque illusion appears in Ali's last poem and requiem, 'The Veiled Suite', which takes on the form of the Italian *canzone* with five stanzas and a closing five-line *envoi*. The *canzone* does not adopt a strict rhyming pattern but instead creates five sets of keywords to use at the ends of lines. Rather than rhymes, Patkin calls them 'refractions in a pool' (Patkin and Ali 2007: 67). In Ali's 'The Veiled Suite' the pools include:

(A) veil, unveil, vail, vale, prevail
(B) eyes, ice, realize
(C) sense, crescent's, essence, license, fluorescence, magnificence, incense
(D) night, tonight, ignite
(E) sea, urgency, fantasy, varanasi, see, debussy, foresee.
(Patkin and Ali 2007: 67)

The slant rhymes that result from these refracted pools of words give more space for the morphology of sounds. While Ali's 'The Veiled Suite' deserves a much more extensive reading than offered here, the major subject of the poem – coming to see God at the moment of one's death – offers up a proxy for the feeling of the baroque *horror vacui*. While the baroque impulse to densely decorate and over-extend the frame seems a representational exuberance, its motives are to shield the viewer from the horror that our world consists only of these representational and illusionistic surfaces.

The first stanza poses the core question of who is whose veil – is God the dying mortal's veil or vice versa? This question replicates the related one of whether an image is a representation or reality – is Zeuxis's curtain a curtain or a painting of a curtain? This moment of directly facing God, death and the horror that there is nothing behind the veil climaxes in the third and fourth stanzas of Ali's 'The Veiled Suite':

There's just one thing left to consider, the night
in which we will be left to realize
when the ice begins to break down in his eyes.

And the prophecies filming his gaze tonight?
What will be revealed? What stunning color sense
kept hidden so long in his eyes, what essence

of longing? He can kill me without license.
The moon for its ivory scours the night.
Sent by the fog, he nearly empties in me all sense
of his gaze, till either he or I have lost all sense;
midnight polishes the remains of a galaxy.
What is left to polish now? What fluorescence?
Is there some hope of making a world of sense?
When I meet his gaze, there is again the veil.
On the farthest side of prophecy, I still need a veil.
(*The Wandering Veil* 2012: 64–65, original emphasis)

In that night, when searching for what will be revealed, there is nothing to sense. At the moment when all available to God's gaze is emptied into the speaker, sense is lost, and the veil remains. One's reality is an illusion one needs in order to protect the self from the ultimate realization that the veil hides nothing.

In Patkin's visualization of the poem, the poet figure keeps a photographer's veil over his face and stands on snow or a cloud – a morphic landscape of unclear qualities (Patkin and Ali 2007: 59). Presumably, the poet does not see the surroundings viewers can access, but the viewer is also blinded. While Patkin paints the poet with a body and a shadow, the other three figures – the photographer, ballerina and Jesus Christ – are only painted as shadows. The viewers of the veil room cannot see the bodies of these figures, who would presumably be in the room to cast their shadows low onto the tulle (Patkin and Ali 2007: 60). By showing us shadows of what we cannot discern or perceive, Patkin forces the question, what more will we never know?

This double-blindness between the poet and the viewer plays between the two pairs of figures. For the poet and the photographer, they are each other's veils. The photographer, when veiled and looking through his lens only sees the poet, and the poet drapes the photographer's veil over his face. Not only is their exchange a mirrored one, but their representation also mimics the shape of the veil. Once the veil swallows you, you are indiscernible from all else. Directly opposite the room, Patkin includes another pair as an 'allegorical mirror' to the poet/photographer. Patkin took Jesus off the cross and noticed his silhouette mimics a ballerina *en pointe* and so pairs him with a female ballerina. For Patkin, '[i]n the poem it's very unclear if Shahid is talking to a lover or God. Meeting the faceless, or the veiled lover' (Patkin and Ali 2007: 59), so he includes both possibilities. If one text could be equally about a confrontation with God and your lover, but you know

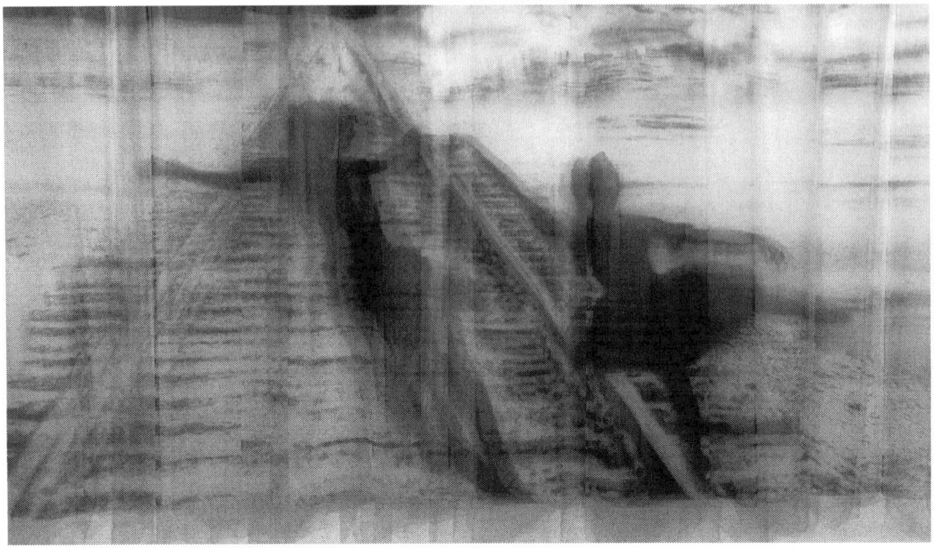

FIGURE 18: Izhar Patkin, *The Veil Suite*, 2007. Ink, pleated illusion (tulle), painting on four walls. 14 x 22 x 25 ft. Use courtesy of Izhar Patkin.

God and your lover are not one and the same, the seemingly crucial addressee is arbitrary. The addressee's identity does not matter much because whoever is behind the veil is already at the surface.

Perhaps Reines captures the *horror vacui* in Patkin's work best toward the end of their interview. She turns to discuss art as a trap to protect us from reality, which unfiltered becomes 'an onslaught that would destroy' (Patkin and Ali 2007: 78). Over the course of the interview, Patkin returns twice to the idea of reality as an abyss: '[T]here is no truth, there's nothing behind the veil. Like nature – because the nature of our perception is a world of metaphors and veils and tools, and in fact, for me, reality is a bottomless pit' (Patkin and Ali 2007: 87). However, in entertaining the idea that the distinction between reality and illusion is itself an illusion, Patkin does not find disillusionment.

> I don't feel that this creates chaos, nihilism, and anarchy. On the contrary, I feel that this makes us very aware of metaphors. They multiply themselves like motherfuckers, they don't become less mysterious – yet they become the most tangible thing in the entire construct.
>
> (Patkin and Ali 2007: 96)

Here lies the import of the illusion as not just the plaything of mass media spectacle. Because illusion maintains its magic despite analytical or explanatory impulses, it persists into reality and resists an enlightened reason. Blending representation and reality requires an embodied way of knowing synesthetically. When reality and illusion are not perceivably different, our subjective perspective of the world is all there is to see.

NOTES

1. Few defenders of the baroque existed during the period of high modernism, with Salvador Dalí among them. Although he was not able to steer surrealism toward the baroque as he had desired, he did see the baroque and especially the Churrigueresque style as part of surrealism's heritage (Wollen 2006: 11).
2. Saul Steinberg's 'The Line' first appeared as a mural on 'Children's Labyrinth', a trefoil wall structure created by the firm of BBPR for the 10th Milan Triennial in 1954. Steinberg's drawings 'were photographically enlarged and then incised into the wall in a sgraffito technique' (Saul Steinberg Foundation 2019: n.pag.).
3. Jacques Derrida offers the term 'parergon', which extends from Immanuel Kant's 'Analytic of the Beautiful' in the *Critique of Judgement*. The parergon attempts to determine the edge of an object to be judged by taste. While examining the frames around baroque art, Derrida describes them as parerga that '[merge] into the wall, and then, gradually, into the general text' (Derrida 1978: 61). The parergon is not an external entity incidental to the ergon but is inextricable from the ergon's lack (Derrida 1979: 24).
4. Book historians, especially those who ascribe to the *Annales* school and the sociology of the book, like Roger Chartier, have registered this paradoxical cohabitation of form and content in the book form. Authors like Miguel de Cervantes and Cyrano de Bergerac have written about the material embodiments of their writing in their writing. However, in order to later protect intellectual property rights, authors and publishers had to assert that books have an 'immaterial existence' in the words of the author that transcend differences in material incarnations (Chartier 2004: 145).
5. These poems include Faiz Ahmed Faiz's (1911–84) 'You Tell Us What to Do' and 'Evening', Mahmoud Darwish's (1941–2008) 'Violins', and Agha Shahid Ali's 'The Dead Are Here. Listen to the Survivors' and the previously mentioned 'The Veiled Suite'. Izhar Patkin's accompanying painted veil rooms carry the same title as the poems except for those paired with Ali's poems. Those paintings are titled *The Dead Are Here* and *The Veil Suite*.
6. Faiz Ahmed Faiz took *ghazal* writing away from the aesthetically focused micro-community of the *mushaira*, or poetic symposium, to a political realm where he forced readers to imagine the real danger of the lyrical content of his poetry (Merrill 2011: 125). Faiz's mark on the genre is how he 'reworks the relationship of the literal to the figurative established in the *ghazal* tradition in such a way that the lines between "inside" and "outside" (the poetic tradition, for example, or even the nation) become blurred' (Merrill 2011: 125–26).

SURFACE

It is the little things that count. We have heard this before, and in our daily lives, we largely buy into the idea. However, when we combine these 'insignificant' choices as defining of self, we often disagree and rationalize our choices. Every spring and fall I make the trip to the local Old Navy to purchase clothes for my sons. I might justify this choice by my limited financial means or argue that global capitalism is unavoidable and my complicity is inevitable regardless. All the same, my consumer choice reflects the real possibility that despite loving my children, I see children's products as disposable. Even worse, that the circumstance of the children who made my children's clothing are not motive enough to choose otherwise. Applied ethics frequently uses such arguments about moral consumption, but this same dynamic exists in consumer questions with lighter ethical implication. Take taste in television shows, for instance. While I might justify indulging in mindless clichés like the spoof soap opera, Jane the Virgin, *as escapist and dismiss the choice as a 'guilty pleasure', it is also a way for me to avoid admitting that campy theatrics are part of my not-so-classy life.*

***

If there is nothing behind the illusion and the surface is where any meaning resides, then what we watch on television and buy at the store are sizable parts of our life's meaning. This is not because television is so important or that clothing choices are so expressive per se, but because the choices we make show how we want to live and whom we want to be. Our fanaticism for lowbrow material is not a shameful, insignificant consumer choice. We are what we consume. When we dismiss this dynamic, we submit to being the credulous consumer happy to participate in the master narrative of mass entertainment and global capitalism. However, rather than turn to a neoliberal, ethical superiority of disavowing our seemingly shameful choices, we can recognize them as more than superficial.

On occasion, we do have public figures or creative artists who ask audiences to see thoughtless or mundane choices more meaningfully. Björk Guðmundsdóttir, known around the world for her experimentation and innovation in the realm of popular music, returned to a long-held dream of revising musical instruction after a significant infection threatened her singing voice. The physical threat to her voice is like the trauma of disembodied and analytical approaches to formal musical training she experienced as a child. She resented always having to dissect music, arguing that the atmosphere and emotion of music are not open to explanation and beyond that, questioned why an explanation was at all desirable (Pytlik 2003: 78). Instead, she hoped for musical education that would 'encourage creativity rather than rote and would look beyond classical European models' (Pareles 2011: n.pag.). As she was developing more organic compositional practices of her own, she hoped to create more intuitive ways to learn about music. Both converged in her seventh album, *Biophilia*.

To rethink music education, Björk collaborated with the University of Iceland and local music and science teachers to develop a program whereby students aged 10 to 12 learn basic principles of science and music through the *Biophilia* apps and instructor-led collective activities. The program won the EUPRIO (European Universities Public Relations & Information Officers) best science and communication project of 2011 (University of Iceland 2012: n.pag.) and was adopted as part of Reykjavík's school curriculum for the following three years. She took these pedagogical goals with her on tour, holding concerts at educational venues like the New York Hall of Science. Her educational program was adapted into a three-week program for 60 middle-school students at the New York Hall of Science and was later taken up by the New York Public Library and the Children's Museum of Manhattan. These performances were not glorified lectures. Instead, she invited listeners to become composers.

For Björk, developing educational programming as extensions of her music was 'all about trying to make it intimate, so that people feel like they are inside the apps, to feel like they are inside the song' (Guðmundsdóttir 2011: 138). This intimacy is a way to imagine the creative product as never complete but always evolving. In his email exchanges with Björk, Timothy Morton praises *Biophilia* for inviting listeners to remake work, calling it 'very courageous, but also realistic, because I think entities never exhaust their possibilities by being used or interpreted by anything' (Morton 2015: n.pag.). This openness brings forward the network of potential songs rather than the individual product of the master and sets the work into variation. In fact, *Washington Post* critic Allison Stewart called the album one that 'feels like a living, breathing organism – a thing' (Stewart 2015: n.pag.).

Rather than lecturing on the principles of music such as rhythm, counterpoint or arpeggios, she wants her audience to learn music through self-exploration and composition. Each song in the *Biophilia* album is an app that allows listeners to explore a musical and scientific concept. The apps become instruments, tools and games. For instance, selecting play from the 'Solstice' app does not simply play the song but offers the listener the chance to play the instrument in digital form, thanks to the app programmer, Max Weisel. After listeners add notes (radii), players (orbiting circles) and the tempo (speed of orbiting circles), they can play 'Solstice' the song with Björk singing over their musical composition. Even in her composition process, Björk regards writing music on a touchscreen as a personal breakthrough because it is 'sophisticated enough to handle more organic patterns ... more sensitive and expressive' (Guðmundsdóttir 2011: 138). This enlivened experience helps humans see their tools as expressive collaborators.

Music is alive and connected to other ideas well beyond human expression into fields from geology to physics. For instance, the song and app for 'Solstice' demonstrate the effect of Earth's tilt on seasonal change alongside gravity's role in defining orbits and measuring rotation. Björk also enacted this lesson in the instrument she designed for 'Solstice'. She took Leon Foucault's 1851 measurements of the Earth's orbit via 67-meter pendulum and turned that measurement tool into a musical instrument, which she commissioned from MIT scientists. The instrument included four pendula, which, when tilted, would pluck the strings of a circular harp at their base. Thus, her song about gravitational orbits is played by modifying a scientific instrument used to measure the earth's rotation.

In her 'Solstice' app, Björk draws an analogy between gravity and counterpoint. The song is composed of four overlapping musical phrases repeated in a loop. As the song moves from one phrase to the next, the music 'tilts' as the time signature changes in unpredictable ways. This reliance on analogy or metaphor throughout the album brings us to the crux of baroque paradox where hinging one idea onto another to clarify also confounds. If analogy or metaphor allows one to look at a phenomenon from an alternative perspective than one's own – or at least to look at patterns evident across distinct sets of relationships that Devin Griffiths's harmonic analogy forwards – such devices can act as ways to escape the limits of normative, established interpretations and anthropocentric thought. Instead of explaining a phenomenon to incorporate it into a humanistic worldview, we could adopt another worldview that shifts our perspective by using the force of analogy to 'produce singular instances of pattern that break with the given framework of understanding' (Griffiths 2016: 38). Understanding musical structure may not be simplified by comparing it to crystal formation, genetic replication or coastal tides, but it does ask us to see phenomena from another perspective and so undermine our first impressions of their meanings.

These analogies, for Björk, are ways of 'mapping the intersection of art, nature, and technology' (Ross 2015: 28) so that academic disciplines could look outside of their methodological frameworks and disciplinary assumptions and even see those frameworks and assumptions otherwise. Seeing objects less as tools and more as collaborators asks us to reconsider how we label and categorize objects and how superficial these orders can be. Roger Caillois opens *The Mask of Medusa* by examining outdated ordering systems, citing eighteenth-century books that classified animals by their number of legs, placing lizards next to mice rather than with other scaled, egg-laying reptiles with whom they are now classified. Such classifications impede studying problems that do not benefit from or are not well defined by the priorities of the classification system. For instance, studying flight would require that one study animals ranging from butterflies to bats to birds (Caillois 1964: 9–11). Caillois saw this desire for order as humans trying to extend themselves out into nature, so the world seems more predictable, controllable or otherwise designed for human communication (Timpano and Shaw 2013: 384). Björk's performance as educational practice counters the organizational paradigms of formal education and helps us move away from the myths of progress and order that they propagate. The guise of progress and order is paper thin and can be rearranged with ease when it no longer reflects our priorities.

Minoring: Baroque Cosmology and Criticizing from Within

Deperiodizing the Baroque

Perhaps one of the strongest dividing lines amongst critics of the baroque is between those who treat the baroque as a concept and ideology and those who consider it a discrete historical era relevant to a defined location. The term 'baroque' as a potential historical period was first employed in 1843 to categorize Counter-Reformation architecture in Italy and Germany (Malcuzynski 2009: 308). Prior uses in the eighteenth century treat 'baroque' as a pejorative term, marking extravagance and poor taste but not periodicity. Criticism after World War I tends to treat the baroque as a recurring literary trope or typology rather than a specific moment in history (Malcuzynski 2009: 308), but Friedrich Nietzsche adopted a cyclical view of history earlier in his 1878 book *Human, All Too Human*. There Nietzsche saw the baroque as a rejection of harmony to favor heterogeneity, broadening 'baroque' to a practice rather than a style and thus setting the precedent for others like Ulrich von Wilamowitz-Moellendorf to recognize an 'ancient Baroque' or Ludwig von Sybel to claim that an 'ancient Roman Baroque' exists (Malcuzynski 2009: 308). Several critics build on the concept of the baroque as divorced from periodicity. For instance, Alejo Carpentier did not confine the baroque to a historical era but treated it as a mental constant evident in the fear of the void. Carpentier builds on Eugenio d'Ors's claim that the baroque is born from 'metaphysical and stylistic tensions in every age and culture' (Zamora 2013: 693). Likewise, Walter Benjamin used the baroque to oppose the narrative of historical progress. The baroque became an alternative modernity against progress and the desperate struggle toward reason and truth.

The malleability of the baroque opens one to see nonconventional and nonchronological connections. Robert Harbison focuses his study on the traits of baroque work with little regard to periodization. This emphasis on its thematic approach supports his idea that 'the Baroque is that of an unreconstructed individualist who thinks crucial stages of large historical processes are sometimes illustrated best by exceptions' (Harbison 2000: ix). He even claims that while such chronologically disjointed connections can seem unexpected or perilous, they could free us from chronology as the ordering paradigm (Harbison 2000: 222). Even considering baroque traits across media, from architecture to literature, proves dangerous but invigorating (Harbison 2000: 227). Hence, in his assessment of the baroque in the twentieth century, Harbison can claim that Frank Gehry is baroque not in the look of his architecture but in his work's goal to subvert rather than eradicate convention by playing with perspective and replicating movement (Harbison 2000: 229). Considering the baroque as a period hazards the problem of artificially uniting products markedly different from but contemporaneous to one another (Zamora 2013: 691).

However, others like Marie-Pierrette Malcuzynski articulate the concerns that critics have in considering the baroque as a concept rather than period – that false analogy and loose associations will bankrupt the term itself. Christopher Johnson holds the baroque as a historical period bound to a time frame and relevant to limited cultures. Johnson worries that the term 'neobaroque' requires a firm footing and his effort to do so lies in determining if the traits we claim are baroque today were present in the historical baroque period and its representative works (Johnson 2010: 146).[1]

The idea that we are returning to the specifics of a particular historical period is not the working assumption of many scholars of the baroque. While these define the poles of baroque criticism, it is much more productive to consider the spectrum between them. Such a spectrum becomes more evident in the criticism of the neobaroque and the new world baroque. Neobaroque and new world baroque scholars see stronger political potential in the resurgence of the baroque as taken up in Latin America. For Gonzalo Celorio, twentieth-century Latin American recycling of the baroque is not a reflection of its European counterpart but a retort, or what José Lezama Lima calls a 'counter conquest'. As an opposition to European baroque, Celorio writes, 'the baroque is our classicism, our paradigm' (Kaup 2006: 145). The postmodern in the west allowed Latin America to reconfigure its concept of modernity in the neobaroque in a way that accounts for what García Canclini in *Hybrid Cultures* calls Latin America's hybrid state of being part traditional and part modern (Kaup 2006: 145).

The neobaroque is the response of the 'third world' to recover some life-affirming way to recover humanity in a modernity trapped by global capitalism where they must suffer either 'the self-betrayal, denigration, and "cultural suicide" [...] of capitalist modernity [or] the "physical suicide" that is the price of any radical attempt to preserve cultural autonomy and moral dignity by absolute non-compliance' (Kaup 2006: 146). Luis Echeverria shares a similar view of the baroque's ability to hold together contradictions when he writes,

> the baroque ethic does not erase, like the realist ethic, the characteristic contradiction of the lifeworld in capitalist modernity; and neither does it deny it, like the romantic ethic; rather, like the classical ethic, it recognizes it as inevitable, but, unlike the latter, it refuses to accept it.
>
> (Kaup 2006: 147)

By holding together the myth of modernity in the gilded success of European superiority with the reality of that modernity rises from colonial exploitation, we create an alternate modernism that tries to live within modernism while maintaining our humanity.

The political impact of resurrecting the baroque in the neobaroque, rather than progressing beyond the modern to the postmodern, refigures modernity as transhistorical (Kaup 2006: 130). This view helps refuse linear history and the implication of progress made by the west that creates a negative bias against cultures and societies deemed premodern. Rather than a linear and divisive unitary model for modernity cast by the west, Canclini proposes a spatial model for modernity where cultures enter and exit at different times and places 'through linkages and passages unique to their cultural conditions' (Kaup 2007: 225). Modernity for Canclini is not a step in a linear progress, but a state that one enters and exits along various pathways. This spatialized concept of time reaffirms Lima's image of history as a spiral 'moving both backward to recreate and forward toward total creativity' (Kaup 2006: 142).

While many critics, including Michel Foucault, Félix Guattari, Gilles Deleuze, Roland Barthes and Christine Buci-Glucksmann, have discussed the baroque in the twentieth century, for Monika Kaup, they neglected new world intellectuals who use the baroque to criticize 'the civilizing myth of Enlightenment modernity' (Kaup 2007: 230). The baroque's appearance in the new world baroque goes beyond aesthetics to become an 'instrument of cultural politics' (Zamora and Kaup 2010: 7) that assimilates and transforms the cultures colliding in colonized places, especially Latin America. New world baroque for d'Ors turned the baroque into 'an *American* way of becoming' (Zamora and Kaup 2010: 9, original emphasis). For Lois Parkinson Zamora, 'Latin American writers manipulate Baroque forms for postcolonial purposes, rejecting colonizing structures and at the same time recuperating collective cultural forms that have been eclipsed by modernity's rationalisms and realisms' (Zamora 2006: xix). While the concept of the minor comes from Deleuze and Guattari, its methodology grafts well onto what the neobaroque and new world baroque do: remind us that reason's undoing always existed within European thought even if its political force is American.

Baroque Structures Include Noncompliance

The baroque, unlike the Enlightenment that followed, juxtaposed contradictions between modern and premodern thought, between science and myth (Kaup 2006: 129). Malcuzynski cites such a convergence of opposites as the brute force of the baroque, especially in Severo Sarduy's understanding of the term. Malcuzynski characterizes the baroque as syncretic where its 'reconciliation seems to be based on a closing of the gap between contraries whose combination verges on treason in the form of (ideological and semantic) deception' (Malcuzynski 2009: 298). In Latin America, this meant the blending of indigenous and Catholic cultures to form a hybrid, *mestizo* or *criollo* culture. The baroque aesthetic makes incorporating and including fragments from several sources seemingly natural and simple, which is why Zamora can claim that baroque models imported to the new world from Europe quickly accommodated indigenous cultures (Zamora 2014: 28) in what she calls 'cultural bifocalism'. Hybridity provides a way of subverting 'the binaries of domination and subordination, European subject and colonial object' (Zamora 2006: xxiii) by showing how the new world repurposed the European, colonizing baroque as a method of postcolonial resistance (Zamora 2006: xvi). By introducing 'a hidden inscription of difference within the fictional sameness of official culture' (Salgado 1999: 317–18), the new world baroque provided what Benjamin called 'a corrective to modernity's claim of uninterrupted historical progress, and realism's claim of transparent verisimilitude' (Zamora 2006: 273). The baroque resists European modernism and its claim to authorial originality by reconfiguring originality as 'influencing one's precursors' and of leaving 'commentaries on earlier texts, or annotations to earlier traditions' (Zamora 2006: 260). Through such a subversion, Latin America must represent itself against the myth of the new world that Europe has constructed. Latin America cannot combat the myth by showing its reality or by being nostalgic for its precolonial past but instead must show that it, like everything else, is an illusion. Because Latin America is separated from the dominant European culture by its supposed lack of rational thought, the turn to parody and camp as a truer statement and as a method of critique is no surprise. To reappropriate, parody and turn to kitsch Europe's myths of the new world or its rationalist ideals activates a baroque humor that disarms dominant powers through mockery.

Celorio's Latin America reimagines the baroque not as the façade or surface of a classical structure, but rather the essential structure. The classical exists only as an accidental unity arising from and disrupted by the baroque essence (Celorio 2010: 489–90). This rings true for Latin America for which the baroque is the paradigm because it was quickly hybridized with indigenous cultures. In the Latin American imagination, the Enlightenment and neoclassicism are intruders rather than a return to truth based in European culture and closed to hybridization. Regarding the baroque as the essential, underlying structure means that it does not limit itself to the layer of literary representation, but acts on the material of literature, that is, of language with its 'superabundance, brimming cornucopia, prodigality, and wastefulness [...] a mockery of all functionality, of all sobriety' (Sarduy 2010: 281). Exponentially expanding the amount of language reveals its artifice and frees it to play with potential meanings rather than express one authoritative meaning.[2] Accepting artificiality as reality and the baroque as foundational structure mocks the establishment as equally constructed, and thus deflates its 'inherent' power.

What makes baroque aesthetic practices so suspect is not only their willingness, pleasure and ease in flirting with the boundary between reality and representation, but their ability to reaffirm totalizing powers[3] just as easily as they can subvert existing power structures. Kaup wrests us from this binary by arguing that the baroque is neither the oppression of the colonizer in the Spanish baroque as counter-reformation nor the liberation of the colonized in the new world baroque as counter conquest. Instead, she posits that we should consider a Deleuzian approach and see the coproduction of ideology from all actants in a social assemblage. In this case, ideology is 'subject to ongoing transformations in both directions: stratification and destratification, territorialization and deterritorialization, becoming-major and becoming-minor' (Kaup 2005: 120). For William Egginton, Deleuze and Guattari's concept of the minor strategy is 'a way of residing in the major strategy without accepting its fundamental assumptions' (Egginton 2007: 113). This minor strategy gives the baroque its critical and disruptive bite, whereas, with its major strategy, baroque tropes are employed to awe subjects into docility and consumerism. Keeping these strategies distinct becomes a critical but difficult move in dodging mass commodification and codification. The major strategy separates agency and subjectivity from consumer choice – that what one chooses to buy does not affect one's self. These seem reasonable to the rational and objective subject of the Enlightenment. However, the minor strategy loads what seem to be superficial choices as deeply indicative of self, so that we are appearances more than we are the abstract ideas of ourselves.

To be minor is to admit ongoing processes of variation while, '[t]o be in the majority is a shame for Deleuze. It means to be complicit in the age-old game of representation and recognition, to be identified and self-identical, and to be a happy wreck, a mindless generic man' (Zhang 2011: 216). For Peter Zhang, a minor rhetorician decodes rather than becoming codified and so regains our capacity to be emotionally affected (Zhang 2011: 217). The minor's capacity for feeling and transformation is what helps it reveal the *élan vital* or life force in things in contrast to the lifelessness of the major's order. However, disorder is not necessarily or only a lack of order but could also be a multiplicity of orders (Zhang 2011: 223).

The Major and Minor Strategies

If the baroque is the foundational structure whose order includes its undoing, the process of creating and unraveling order takes precedence over whatever order is temporarily established. Orders arise from all sorts of functions including legal practice, social convention, governing structures or cultural preferences to name a few. During the sixteenth century, the sciences challenged established religious paradigms that essentially opened unifying structures to variance. With the Copernican Revolution, scientists realized that the infinitely expanding universe is not just the realm of God but the material state of existence. With this new cosmological view, '[b]aroque artists reacted with depictions of kinetic energy: proliferating figures and motifs in expansive, dilating spaces; theatrical spaces opening onto infinity; blurred boundaries between real and pictorial spaces; spaces filled to overflowing' (Zamora 2014: 26). Given an ever-expanding universe, still surety seems artificial. Since possibilities expand such that any person could be president, monarch or pope, whom we choose must be surrounded by the frills of ceremony in order to obscure our anxieties of that arbitrary selection. We see this call to ceremony supported in Sarduy's characterization of the baroque spectacle as one that 'postpones conveying meaning, delaying it as long as possible through its theatrical apparatus and its multiple readings, disclosing at last not a fixed and univocal meaning, but glimmerings and ambiguities' (Malcuzynski 2009: 299). While one might be accustomed to thinking pejoratively of the baroque as decorative excess, that excess could be the marker of the larger concern it tries to stave. The décor looks like an overcompensation motivated by fear and anxiety over one's position. In this case, the major strategy combats the *horror vacui* by covering it with gold. The baroque is not empty spectacle and ornament but a response to the void that reminds us of life's infinite and arbitrary nature (Spadaccini and Martín-Estudillo 2005: xxix).

While spectacle and ornament constitute the major strategy, neobaroque critics offer up another visual analogy from cosmology that grounds the minor strategy. Celorio employs Johannes Kepler's discovery of elliptical rather than circular planetary orbits to alter our perception of the baroque against the classical. Instead of seeing the ellipse as a deformed circle, we could consider the circle as a collapsed ellipse (Celorio 2010: 490). To see the baroque as a deformation rather than the prevailing state casts it as disorderly. This seems seeded in the original meaning of the baroque as a non-universalizing syllogism, which is particularly telling of the baroque's relationship to the concept of reason. The baroco syllogism is not chaotic, but it does not universalize truth like the barbara syllogism. The baroco contains one universal affirmative and two partial affirmatives, whereas the barbara has three universal affirmatives (Zamora 2006: 234). Baroco syllogisms only provide 'contingent truths dependent upon the particularity of the propositions' where the affirmatives 'open up alternatives and raise questions about where to stop' (Zamora 2006: 234–35, original emphasis). The baroco syllogism enacts in logic what is visualized in the ellipse, where there is not a universalizing force focused on the correct answer, the single center point. Instead, the baroco syllogism offers up contingent conclusions just as the shape of the ellipse is dependent upon the placement of its second focus.

Kaup adopts the image of elliptical orbits to describe how a minor language stretches the circle into an ellipse because it revolves around two points: the dominant or major language and the minor language of the smaller group. While minor literature must be written in the major language, its authors show how ostracized they are from the major language either by swelling it up with symbolism and signifiers or by chipping away all but its most intense bits (Deleuze and Guattari 1986: 16, 19). Minor authors must write in a language that is not their own heritage or past. They are outsiders to the major language group and face the guilt of turning against their own language. They have to deny their past and their present, so it is not a surprise that minor literature utters new statements, since it is essentially pushed into the future.

Developing around two languages displaces the singular and opens the product to its construction process. The placement of the second focus alters the contour of the ellipse, shifting emphasis to the process of creation rather than only its product. For minor literature, establishing the setting and context is crucial because neither constitute a neutral background. They define positions of power and politicize place. For major literature, the position of the author is never in question, so the choice of setting, for instance, does not equate to a political statement. For minor literature, every choice made is a clue to understand the position of the author. With fewer such authors, their statements cannot be ascribed to them as individual masters but as representatives of a marginalized community. Minor authors solidify their community's existence and reveal the potential for revolution and alternative priorities or sensibilities (Deleuze and Guattari 1986: 17).

Minor literatures oppose the major view that 'language and writing is an attempt to put order to chaotic thoughts' (Wittrock 2010: 107) by charting overlaps in what was perceived as separate, of drawing an ellipse around two distinctly different foci. Deleuze provides one such example by describing Yiddish as a derivative of Middle-High German. Yiddish is so attached to High German that the major language of German is a 'stranger *within* his own language' (Deleuze and Guattari 1986: 26, original emphasis). Minor literature is not outside of major literature 'but the revolutionary conditions for every literature within the heart of what is called great (or established) literature' (Deleuze and Guattari 1986: 18). Such revolutionary potential is in language that returns words to sounds and abandons the sense they mean to represent. Minor literature essentially unlearns the ordered system, so without the prescriptive structure, an individual word or sound could become meaningful in a different way, pushing language back to a state of becoming rather than being.

We can see this disintegration of meaning by repeating a word over and over again until it becomes arbitrary and strange. The sound made by f-o-r-k does not attach to the object with the transparency it did before, and we can lay the object and the sound apart from one another. The poverty of the major language reveals itself when minor writing achieves its goal: '[T]o make language vibrate, to induce disequilibrium, to activate from within a language itself the lines of continuous variation immanent within its grammatical, syntactic and semantic patterns' (Wittrock 2010: 108). When we wrest signs from meaning with minor literature's deterritorialization, reading and meaning-making from these signs seem akin to hallucinating (Lambert 2011: 28).

By this logic, the quickest way of denying our agency is to treat what appears superficial superficially. If we want to be minor rhetoricians, we are obliged to take seriously the superficial, turning the distractions of the major strategy against itself. The minor strategy is so potent a criticism of the major strategy and its master narratives precisely because the minor strategy lives inside of the major as a vaccine is made from the virus itself. Unlike a major literature that starts by filling content into given forms (Fletcher 2011: 60), the minor does not take forms or content already made and fit them together, but considers its process and position and 'learns by doing'. For Jean-Jacques Lecercle, 'the point of minor literature is not to make recognisable sense, but to express intensities, to capture forces, to act' (Fletcher 2011: 61). By creating new forms, a major language stays alive. Jerome Fletcher uses this idea to argue that e-literature is a minor reading of print-based literature by transforming and performing language. However, it is not the novelty of the medium that minors, but the attention to the medium as more than a content container.

While much of the critical literature has looked at the possibility of a baroque minoring within the context of twentieth-century postcolonial literatures of Latin America and the Caribbean, its relevance extends to the implications of digital media on literary and textual studies more broadly. While crossing temporal and geographic boundaries offers up new meanings, so too does crossing media boundaries. While this leads to a potential emptying out or excessively broadened meaning of the term 'baroque' or even 'literature', it also means those terms are no longer static. Certainly answering, 'what is baroque?' becomes harder when Gehry and Verano de Arcimboldo can both be called baroque just as 'what is literature?' seems like an increasingly pointless question if the label includes HOOKED Chat Stories and Thomas Mann's *The Magic Mountain*.

However, baroque reason and its tendency for 'ands' offer up opportunities to blend or juxtapose what seems contrary to revise or augment major narratives. Rather than think through the 'thus' of linear progression or the 'or' of definitive conclusion or clarity, this additive model of a major and minor strategy build up and challenge realism as an artificial interpretation of reality. Such a dual-focused criticism is not a mechanism for judgment or correction but for an increased attention to process that sets back into motion concepts that appeared settled or definitive. Herein lies the conceptual challenge of the ellipse as a cosmic structure. There is not one truth to revolve around, but there is always order and its undoing, its wobbly doppelganger that proves the former's constructive relativism. If we are concerned with process and networks, each choice we make, while seemingly superficial, may be more deeply meaningful. Even in our consumer lives, what appears superficial has real meaning to economies as much as to self-identity. Our choices are performative rather than purely pragmatic, so we cannot rationalize away their impact. Similarly, minor literature reconsiders language as performative rather than semantic, which explains why its authors will swell and strip bare language to its extremes to show their range as artifice-creators and realism-benders. To examine these functions in literary work, we will consider a double minoring project: Bruno Schulz's *The Street of Crocodiles* and Jonathan Safran Foer's *Tree of Codes*, a redaction of Schulz's short story collection. Schulz's work – contemporary with Franz Kafka, the focus of Deleuze and Guattari's *Kafka: Toward a Minor Literature* – demonstrates an oversaturated language mixed with surrealist delirium. Meanwhile, Foer's redaction transforms the language performance to a minimal lyricism even while it already lives in the story it unravels and augments.

The Artificiality of Language

Foer's 2010 book *Tree of Codes* die cuts Schulz's 1934 collection of thirteen semi-biographical short stories, *The Street of Crocodiles*. This physical manipulation of an existing book forefronts the artificiality of *Tree of Codes*. Readers see words from later pages peeking through the cut page. They see how much was removed from Schulz's story and by extension how much culture and history are lost to trauma, time and forgetfulness. Foer's book enacts sculpturally what Schulz's did conceptually. Schulz foregrounded constructedness by rendering stories of his childhood in Drogobych through 'collage-like memories [...] interspersed with metaphors of labyrinthine structures and meditations on the nature of space and time' (Michel 2014: 168). Schulz's dense, poetic style that blurs reality and fiction has garnered him many labels despite his short life as an author, including 'a tragic writer, a comic writer, an absurdist, a satirist, an autobiographer, a mythographer, a poet, a modernist, and a post-modernist' (Benjamin 2011: 47). Schulz's rich style is what drew Foer to create *Tree of Codes* from *The Street of Crocodiles*.

While Foer maintains that *Tree of Codes* is his book, distinct from Schulz's *The Street of Crocodiles*, he also admits an intimate connectivity between his book and Schulz's and between Schulz's and yet other books. Foer writes: 'At times I felt that I was making a gravestone rubbing of *The Street of Crocodiles*, and at times that I was transcribing a dream that *The Street of Crocodiles* might have had' (Foer 2010: 139). Given the material constraints of his choice to die cut an existing book, this observation is not surprising. By literally taking on a source text, Foer reimagines the divide between reading and writing, where all writing is a rereading, reworking or performance of words already in existence. Inhabiting the language of Schulz's book propels Foer to imagine that even Schulz's book is exhumed from another performance wrested from inside another text, leading eventually to an all-encompassing *Book of Life*. Foer imagines that this ultimate book 'is the Temple that our lives strive to enter, but instead only conjure' (Foer 2010: 139).

While Foer may seem to support an idea of a complete or ultimate book, his writing by erasure shows reading as a complex negotiation among the narrative, the author's and reader's context and the history between the text's creation and its consumption. Reading is not the transparent accessing of truth, the 'unmediated portal to a narrative that transcends time and place' (Rager 2012: n.pag.). Meanwhile, for Schulz, stories offer 'alternative ways of viewing one's relationship to the world and, even more radical, of alchemically creating new fields of vision' (Benjamin 2011: 47). To see narrative as a way to uncover meaning and shift one's vision is to cast writing as a practice of minoring that dodges criticisms of superficiality or artificiality, such as Michel Faber's review of *Tree of Codes*: '[Y]et another example of his characteristic blend of whimsy and hubris – the same artifice-dazzled unawareness of being out of one's depth' (Faber 2010: n.pag.).

While Foer may literalize the idea of exhuming a text from a text and rewriting from a fragment, his attitude to the project and at times, the resulting poetic prose, leaves the minoring process incomplete. For instance, in his interview with *The White Review*, Foer responds to questions on the difficulty of writing *Tree of*

Codes: 'It was difficult in the way that, like, an enormously hard crossword, any kind of puzzle, is difficult. It was not difficult like novel-writing difficult, where the difficulties arise from self-consciousness or self-doubt or fear. With this, it was just technical' (Foer 2012: n.pag.). Here there is still a veneration for the expressive individual set apart from the surrounding textual or lived environment even while he is reassembling fragments of Schulz into his own story.[4] *Tree of Codes* does not come from a fount of individual creative genius, but why would it in his other fictional works? He admits that *Tree of Codes* is one of hundreds of potential stories exhumed from *Street of Crocodiles* (Michel 2014: 180), but if all books are essentially a reworking of some great book or a rearrangement of the dictionary, then why do we not imagine all writing as technical in the way that *Tree of Codes* is?

Admitting the artificiality of story is the prerequisite of minor literature. One must know that the story is a construct and that each fragment of that story can spin its own version. While Foer compares two methods of sculpture to differentiate how he writes fiction and how he wrote *Tree of Codes* – the first a sculpture of clay piling on layers and the second a chipping away at marble (Wagner 2010: n.pag.) – these analogies also show the potential minor performances of language that Schulz and Foer adopt. Schulz treats language as material to pile on, swell up and exaggerate, while Foer treats language as material to minimize and chisel away. Lauren Benjamin describes Schulz's writing style as recognizable by its

> ineffability; in both content and form, its fantastic turns of phrase and eloquent propositions require many re-readings. In its multifariousness, it lends itself to almost any reading the reader should allow herself, but with one catch: Never will any one reading be complete.
>
> (Benjamin 2011: 55)

On the other hand, Faber writes of Foer's *Tree of Codes* that 'what seems like an audacious coinage is already there in the original; Foer has merely excised hunks of Schulz's luxuriant verbiage and exhibited a slimmed-down version of the master's vision' (Faber 2010: n.pag.). These are two sides of the minoring coin, both their own performance of applying either extreme exaggeration or extreme minimalism. Either method unravels master narratives that deny or obscure their artificiality and multiplicity.

These differences between the piled and chiseled techniques of minoring are evident in the style of writing that surfaces in *The Street of Crocodiles* and *Tree of Codes*, but let us look to each version of 'Pan' to probe these differences in approaching minoring. In 'Pan' Schulz's narrator, a young boy, pries loose a fence plank that leads to a garden in the middle of the city. While the boy is moving further toward the middle of the city and into a hidden garden, Schulz describes the move as one where 'the prisoner of the courtyard could squeeze through the crack and let himself out into a new, wider world of fresh breezes' (Schulz 1963: 77–78). Foer keeps this concept of a wider inside of a narrower world but adds another contradiction saying, 'i loosened one of its planks, opening a window to a new, wider world. There, spread out, was a profusion of geography, of atmosphere, of full empty air. wild with shamelessness' (Foer 2010: 68–70). Placing 'full' immediately next to 'empty' distills the core contradiction that Schulz finds between the garden and the factory's shadow. The space is heavy, and the world in its materiality is empty, which resonates well when considering geography (the nature and relative arrangement of places and physical features) with atmosphere (the pervading tone or mood of a place, situation or work of art).

Foer's redacted version abstracts the deeply sensual description of the garden that Schulz entertains and even variegates into a range of zones and climates of increasingly dense growth. Foer cuts to the idea that a place has its geography and atmosphere and despite its density, a place can be void of what we may call 'meaning' or 'moral standing'. It cuts to the paradox that Schulz approaches through thick layers of description in a prolific outpouring of language. Schulz's description of the garden contains this paradox but presents it as a saturated mass of descriptive language.

> When you lay in the grass you were under the azure map of clouds and sailing continents, you inhaled the whole geography of the sky. From that communion with the air, the leaves and blades became covered with delicate hair, with a soft layer of down, a rough bristle of hooks made, it seemed, to grasp and hold the waves of oxygen. That delicate and whitish layer related the vegetation to the atmosphere, gave it the silvery grayish tint of the air, of shadowy silences between two glimpses of the sun. And one of the plants, yellow, inflated with air, its pale stems full of milky juice, brought forth from its empty shoots only pure air, pure down in the shape of fluffy dandelion balls scattered by the wind to dissolve noiselessly into the blue silence.
>
> (Schulz 1963: 78)

Even in the lightness of air and sunrays, what we see is the proliferation of hairs there to catch the air we do not see, and the dandelion stems are both full of milk and hollow.

Schulz's 'Pan' also contains characters divergent from Foer's version that augment rather than replace or contradict one another. Schulz puts a child in the garden who pursues butterflies that lead him to the wild abyss near a factory building. There he encounters a mentally unstable vagrant described as a gorilla.

Schulz's child faces what seems the edge of reason in a chaotic place with an animalistic man detached from society's mores and overpowered by primal feelings:

> [D]ark eyes bored into me with the fixedness of supreme despair or of suffering. He both looked at me and did not, he saw me and did not see. His eyes were like bursting shells, strained in a transport of pain or the wild delights of inspiration.
> (Schulz 1963: 80)

Foer turns the drunken vagrant into a worker, saying, 'suddenly, I saw him. Submerged up to his armpits. I saw his broad back, his shoulders hunched as under a great burden. he seemed to be working very hard, struggling. He saw me and did not see' (Foer 2010: 70–71). What else could this man in the garden become in other fragmentations of the text? Beyond his potential for multiple identities, he turns both times into a figure who reveals the plight of minority groups, first as homeless and mentally ill and then as a gardener or potential factory worker, should we import our knowledge of the proximity of the garden to a factory in Schulz's *The Street of Crocodiles*. The discomfort of confronting this figure remains, and the various versions of the man augment the meaning of their coexistence. Is the worker mentally ill as a result of industrialization and consumerism? Is the mentally ill homeless man a slave to another oppressive system, not neurologic but economic?

Minor literature does not let one escape master narratives because there is not an 'outside' to be had. Instead, minoring perverts the major by staking out other perspectives from within the major text. Multiplying perspectives calls into question the veracity of the assumed perspective passed off as stable in the major text or master narrative. For Schulz, Foer manifests such a challenge to the major text by inverting the narrator or character's perspective in 'Tailors' Dummies' and 'Mr. Charles' but still reinforcing a common message of our fragile understanding of life.

Perspectives Fragment Master Narratives

Taking up a perspective with purpose is the saving grace of the minor strategy. While it does not provide an escape from the major or modernity's crisis of representation, it can inoculate one against its numbing effects by seeing the world in oppositional ways. We see such a practice in the father character of 'Tailors' Dummies'. Schulz's father character is life-affirming while Foer's father character is life-denying, but they ultimately say the same thing. In the father figure's treatise on tailor dummies, Schulz writes about a God-like power each human has to undermine authority. We hear the father claim, '[w]e have no ambition to emulate him. We wish to be creators in our own, lower sphere; we want to have the privilege of creation, we want creative delights, we want – in one word – Demiurgy' (Schulz 1963: 61). Coming from the mouth of a senile man, the treatise wins little attention from the women who listen to him during their late-night sewing sessions. To the seamstresses, he is idle entertainment as they work, praising creation while he is the only person not creating a thing.

While it may seem like he is not contributing to or living in the 'real world' by spinning words rather than thread, his public performance of language in his spoken treatise shows an understanding of the liveliness of objects. Alternatively, the seamstresses have no connection to the sentience of the objects around them, despite their role in creating objects. The father laments,

> [w]ho knows [...] how many suffering, crippled, fragmentary forms of life there are, such as the artificially created life of chests and tables quickly nailed together, crucified timbers, silent martyrs to cruel human inventiveness. The terrible transplantation of incompatible and hostile races of wood, their merging into one misbegotten personality.
>
> (Schulz 1963: 69)

In these increasingly dramatic descriptions of liveliness in the dummies and furniture around him, Schulz's father character introduces delirium through the density of his words. He is lost in ideas that connect him to the world around him. This extreme example of empathizing with a table makes it easier to imagine that we might recognize the misfortunes of objectified people and not just objects (Benjamin 2011: 52).

To make a similar claim about agency and empathy, Foer minimizes life rather than espouse Schulz's view that life spills out from everywhere. Instead of fusing life into everything, Foer's father sees the same glass half empty. Rather than focus on the sentience of tables and dummies, he turns to how humans are not as omnipotent and lively as they believe. There, 'In the emptiness of evenings, serious and unequivocal, he would say: "How beautiful is forgetting! what relief it would be for the world to lose some of its contents!"' (Foer 2010: 47–48). While Foer's father character still maintains that there is 'no dead matter' (Foer 2010: 49), he advocates for silencing its force, saying, 'All attempts are transient and easy to dissolve. reducing life is not a sin. It is sometimes necessary' (Foer 2010: 49). Furthermore, liveliness and potency are not desirable in the first place, since this delusion makes humans forget that 'We are not [...] long-term beings. not heroes of romances in many volumes' (Foer 2010: 51). Foer turns down the volume of human sentience so much that, by the end of 'Tailors' Dummies', the father 'suddenly collapsed and folded up. Or perhaps he had been exchanged for another man?' (Foer 2010: 54). Foer's narrator retreats from the mother who wants to realize her dreams because he recognizes dreams as illusory.

Reversing perspective from Schulz's view of life brimming up from everything to Foer's positive view of death also appears in the critical literature of the Foer/Schulz pairing. Though we literally see Foer removing textual material from Schulz's original with the die cut, that eradication is not ultimate. Instead, Jon Catlin argues that Foer's *Tree of Codes* cannot be read outside the context of Schulz's work and life (Catlin 2015: 36). Not only does Foer's version remain entwined with Schulz's, it demonstrates that the fragments of Schulz that pepper each story are encrypted into and recall further stories that are 'not the romantic ruins of history, but the emergence of a new fictional approach to historical memory' (Randall 2013: 86). In this way, a minoring through language is not a direct critique or refutation but an obfuscation of what points of reference might exist. What difference is there in seeing the glass half full with overwhelming descriptions of life everywhere or the glass half empty stripped of life force by the hubris we act out as a species? To see the glass from either perspective is to say the same thing: that there is not one history that recovers the truth. Instead, our perspective, subjective as it is, can always recover and unravel from within another fragment or memory that balloons out of any master narrative.

Seeing perspectives within a master narrative opens up a minor practice of performing order's undoing within that very order. In Schulz's 'Mr. Charles' we see this performance in the description and actions of the Charles character. In 'Mr. Charles', Schulz writes of his uncle and his fitful sleep. As he is waking up, the narrator begins to describe the growing tumor inside of his uncle, and Charles's discomfort in a room he feels is judging and rejecting him. After dressing, he slinks away from the judgmental room.

> [H]e then walked toward the door slowly, resignedly, hanging his head, while someone else, someone forever turning his back, walked at the same pace in the opposite direction into the depths of the mirror, through the row of empty rooms which did not exist.
>
> (Schulz 1963: 84)

Charles is not comfortable in his home, but the mirror offers an alternative interior. Charles can walk out of his home while simultaneously walking into its depths. In the mirror, his prison and his escape are the same, as the minor inside of the major.

We anticipate the story closing with simultaneous opposites because Schulz already establishes Charles's duplicitous reality by describing him from external and internal vantage points. Schulz opens the story with Uncle Charles thrashing in his bed:

> He fought in his sleep against the bed like a bather swimming against the current, he kneaded it and molded it with his body like an enormous bowl of dough, and woke up at dawn panting, covered with sweat, thrown up on the shores of that pile of bedding which he could not master in the nightly struggle. Half-landed from the depth of unconsciousness, he still hung on to the verge of night, gasping for breath, while the bedding grew around him, swelled and fermented – and again engulfed him in a mountain of heavy, whitish dough.
>
> (Schulz 1963: 82)

While this twisting and engulfing happen outside of Charles' body and beyond his consciousness, the same turmoil rages inside of his body where

> there in a thoughtless, vegetative stupor, completely surrendered to circulation, respiration, and the deep pulsation of his natural juices, there formed inside his perspiring body an unknown, unformulated future, like a terrible growth, pushing forth in an unknown direction. He was not afraid of it, because he already felt at one with that unknown and enormous thing which was to come, and he was growing together with it without protest, in a strange unison, numb with resigned awe, recognizing his future self in those colossal exuberances, those fantastic tumors which were maturing before his inward-turned sight.
>
> (Schulz 1963: 83)

Charles is not aware of his undoing where within him are nightmares and tumors whose force threatens to burst through him since his consciousness is less solid than the growth and movement around him. Schulz shows us the latent minority always under the surface of conscious reason.

On the other hand, for Foer, the treatment of the main character results in a more self-assured sense of purpose and identity that could be read as tame or traditional in comparison. Foer keeps his rewriting of 'Mr. Charles' as a more tightly controlled first-person experience of self. He turns the subject from a distinct character, Uncle Charles, to the first-person pronoun, and in that transformation, creates a self-assured subject. Rather than treating the mirror as an actual mirror on the wall, Foer adopts this object as a function of the knowing subject, writing, 'with eyes like miniscule mirrors, i could not contain the groaning, swelling, deep pulsation of the enormous awe, those colossal exuberances. the only living and knowing thing was me' (Foer 2010: 73–74). This assuredness comes out again in Foer's choice to maintain the concept of turning inside out, repurposing it as the instigator to record. He writes, 'out of the depth of yesterday i wanted to turn inside out. I wrote in a notebook, added it all up' (Foer 2010: 73). In contrast, Schulz's story reads, 'Charles yawned out of his body, out of the depth of all its cavities the remains of yesterday. The yawning was convulsive as if its body wanted to turn itself inside out' (Schulz 1963: 82). Here the act of yawning overpowers Charles and acts upon him. Charles' body has more power than his thinking self. An involuntary gesture, a near instinct, threatens to undo Charles while in Foer's version the narrator seems capable of mastering time itself. Regardless, both Schulz's and Foer's versions undo themselves. Schulz splits his character of Uncle Charles into himself and his reflection, but he remains depressingly unaware of the division. Foer seems to maintain that his first-person narrator possesses a sense of all-knowing, but he admits that he cannot contain the force of that knowledge. Schulz internalizes the loss of self, while Foer tries to show this loss as an external force that cannot be incorporated.

In their divergent approaches to undoing order, Schulz burrows into his character with probing and dense language, whereas Foer externalizes this undoing not just in his narrator's perspective, but in the material choice of his book. To die cut Schulz's book refigures something as superficial as reading a flat page into a dimensional choice. While the subject matter of his book may be less controversial, its presentation demonstrates an unraveling from within that captures what a minor literature might achieve. While Foer's character may seem more self-assured, the delicate pages cut with more voids than matter externalize the character's internal conflict. Just as we read of the first-person narrator's confidence as a knowing being, we also look down on a page that is fragile and dislodged from a clear temporal location. On the same page where Foer describes writing in his notebook, we can look through the windows of the die cutting to access words printed on pages 73 through to 84. Some of what peeks through the windows undermines the sense that the first-person narrator has control over his environment as his efforts to document all thought in his notebook first suggests. In fact, the lower right-hand corner of page 73 reads, 'the se was nawing life. This would take me' (Foer 2010: 73–79). We see words that belong to the narrator's future. Depth is not digging into an archeological past but at 'burrowing into the future [at] glimpses of what's to come shaping your interpretation of where you are' (Rager 2012: n.pag.).

Just as we turn toward thinking of Foer as romanticizing individual genius, we recall how delicate and lively the medium of paper can be when turned to a three-dimensional sculpture of pages that create many potential word combinations. Foer's use of die cutting to remove portions of pages creates a three-dimensional book object that moves beyond seeing time as purely linear since it offers two ways of reading the book, which Berit Michel calls the linear and the visual reading.

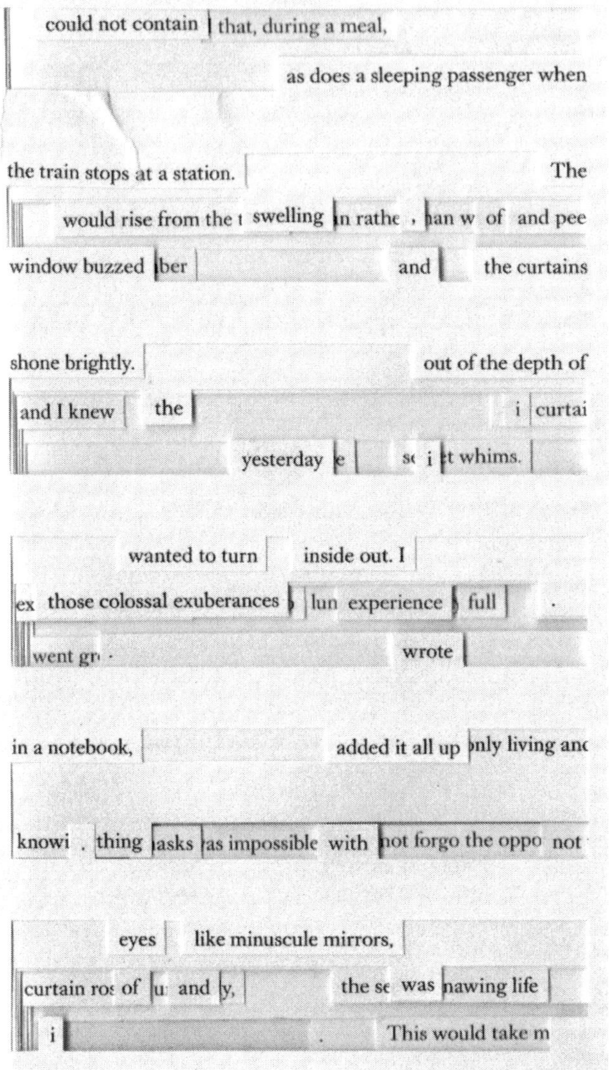

FIGURE 19: Jonathan Safran Foer, *Tree of Codes*, 2010. Die-cut print codex. Use courtesy of Visual Editions.

The first entails reading the content of one planar surface at a time, the reading intended by the author, and the second a reading through multiple pages while moving left to right across the now topographically diverse surface of the opened book. The construction of the book challenges readers in how the linear and visual reading methods affect one another, recalling a long tradition in book arts to take on the codex as a sculpture from Brian Dettmer's carved encyclopedias to Andrea Dezsö's tunnel books. The die cuts make it so readers cannot immediately experience the linear story because future pages interrupt the temporal line. Even so, that interruption reminds readers that the linear reading of *Tree of Codes* is one of many possible strings that could have been *the* linear story, but is so evidently just *a* story (Michel 2014: 179). Schulz's and Foer's interwoven versions hint at infinite further derivations and spin-offs and demonstrate how it becomes harder to think of a story disciplined into one line, much less a point. These revelations in narrative mirror a similar lack of faith in periodicity and the illusion of progress over time. While Foer's material choice makes immediate the sense that time is not unilinear and neither is a story, we also see a critique of progressive historical linearity in the content of the short story, 'Cinnamon Shops'.

Valuing the Surface of Representation

'Cinnamon Shops' does not treat time and space as linear or stable. Instead, both are mercurial in Foer's and Schulz's version of this story, though Foer shows much more enthusiasm for such a fluid sense of time and space. Foer's version of 'Cinnamon Shops' shows a first-person narrator venturing out in an attempt to lose himself, saying, 'This would take me even farther from home. I ran rather than walked, anxious to lose my way. All I wanted was to be unsure. I found myself lost. Everything was full. time passed unevenly' (Foer 2010: 79–81). With this nonmechanical and nonbiological suspended time, the world stands still. Instead of having to wait for time, one can move in and out of it.

While Foer's narrator values being lost as a method to find himself, in this section of the story, Schulz's narrator decides to make a stop at the cinnamon shops but underestimates how long it will take to find them. The space of the city begins to morph in the night, and while the narrator remains calculating, he is frightened of getting lost in the dark, unrecognizable streets. He is not comfortable with the shifting sense of time and place that Foer's narrator sought out.

> I passed three or four streets, but still there was no sign of the turning I wanted. What is more, the appearance of the street was different from what I had expected. [...] I was walking faster now, rather disturbed, beginning to give up the idea of visiting the cinnamon shops. All I wanted now was to get out of there quickly into some part of the city I knew better [....] Looking more closely at one of the buildings, I realized that what I saw was the back of the high school which I had never seen from that side.
>
> (Schulz 1963: 90)

Even as the narrator enters the high school, the deeper into the building he goes, the more extensive the interior becomes until he eventually ventures down an arcade, into a living room that becomes a loggia, which opens onto a square. The further in he goes, the sooner he arrives at the outside.

Before the narrator gets lost in the streets, the story opens with the mother's desire to get the father away from his tightly domestic world and his detachment from reality. Ironically, she decides to take him to the theater. On the stage, curtains are masks and stellar constellations that Schulz considers: 'I knew that the moment was imminent when the tension of mystery would reach its zenith and the swollen skies of the curtain would really burst open to reveal incredible and dazzling events' (Schulz 1963: 87). This interior, artificial sky promises the surprise of a false world, all of which the mother casts as part of real life. Instead of enjoying this little false universe on the stage, the narrator has to run back home to retrieve his father's wallet. After he gets lost looking for the cinnamon shops, he eventually takes a cab ride outside of the city. Space expands as he gets further out. From there he sees an inverse of the spectacle that the theatergoers expected to see behind their starry curtains:

> The transformations of the sky, the metamorphoses of its multiple domes into more and more complicated configurations were endless. Like a silver astrolabe the sky disclosed on that magic night its internal mechanism and showed in infinite evolutions the mathematics of its cogs and wheels.
>
> (Schulz 1963: 97)

From the outside world, the narrator can see the internal functions of the universe, while the theatergoers see artificial worlds contained within a domestic existence. Treating the curtains as the sky and the sky as the curtains blur differences between the real universe and representational space of the stage.

Foer maintains a similar indistinction in his version of 'Cinnamon Shops' but does it by having his narrator step through the theater curtain into representation. In Foer's version he writes,

> i went in silence through the crowd of painted masks, swelling with pathos, with the tremor of moments of revelation. The masks whispered voicelessly, and I knew the curtain would open to reveal experience and honesty. the curtain rose and I stepped into the illuminations. I could feel waves of laid bare, of dreams.
>
> (Foer 2010: 76–78)

Rather than Schulz's unveiling of the cogs of the universe behind the curtain, a peeking behind the *pargod*, Foer imagines unmasking human thought. As he does this unveiling, he feels farther from his home and accepts that he is lost without the contextual markers of time or space so that 'Without transition and full of secret silent moments. i went groping into the deep completely unknown. at each Turn I found myself in an even wider, more sumptuous interior' (Foer 2010: 82–83). The narrator goes on to reminisce about a journey to the outskirts of the city where he seems to shed all his worries and burdens and feel light again. Traveling inward emotionally results in the same feeling Schulz's narrator experiences by escaping the interior of a city. One could travel about in a psyche as one moves through a town, so a person's boundaries are not much different from a city's. 'Cinnamon Shops' deranges our spatial arrangements since we cannot trust that there are discernible differences between what inside or outside of a city is, what representation is and what reality is. Without these hierarchies, time and space appear suspended and flattened.

The title story 'The Street of Crocodiles' acts out this indistinction between reality and representation by making an industrial neighborhood in Schulz's town of Drohobych into a paper construct. Schulz introduces the neighborhood by saying:

> On that map, made in the style of baroque panoramas, the area of the Street of Crocodiles shone with the empty whiteness that usually marks polar regions or unexplored countries of which almost nothing is known. The lines of only a few streets were marked in black and their names given in simple, unadorned lettering, different from the noble script of the other captions. The cartographer must have been loath to include that district in the city and his reservations found expression in the typographical treatment.
>
> (Schulz 1963: 100)

The nefariousness of the area and the cartographer's distaste for it comes through clearly. Regardless, what follows in Schulz's exploration of the area is not a criticism of the region's reality, but a description of it as its own paper construct. Schulz writes of the buildings 'when wandering in those parts, one in fact gained the impression that one was turning the pages of a prospectus, looking at columns of boring commercial advertisements' and '[t]he large gray windows, ruled like the pages of a ledger, did not admit daylight' (Schulz 1963: 102). Such connections between paper media and the region continue until it arrives at a summary comment:

> It is, as usual in that district, a gray day, and the whole scene seems at times like a photograph in an illustrated magazine, so gray, so one-dimensional are the

> houses, the people and the vehicles. Reality is as thin as paper and betrays with all its cracks its imitative character.
>
> (Schulz 1963: 105)

Where we see comparisons and similes before this summary comment, afterward, the area becomes unabashedly artificial: 'The appearance of these trams, though, is pitiful, for they are made of papier-mâché with warped sides dented from the misuse of many years' (Schulz 1963: 106). No longer only like paper, the region's architecture and infrastructure are flimsy paper constructions. Reality exists as a veneer, and since there is nothing behind the veneer, the neighborhood turns to paper.

In Foer's redaction, the map that opens the story is called a 'tree of codes', composed of a few sparse markings of streets and gaps between buildings. We inhabit the map such that 'we find ourselves part of the tree of codes. Reality is as thin as paper. only the small section immediately before us is able to endure, behind us sawdust in an enormous empty theater' (Foer 2010: 92–93). Similarly, this too is not a criticism of superficial representation or detachment from lived experience. Instead, the story closes with Foer praising the map as

> the last secret of the tree of codes is that nothing can ever reach a definite conclusion. Nowhere as much as there do we feel possibilities, shaken by the nearness of realization. the atmosphere becomes possibilities and we shall wander and make a thousand mistakes. We shall wander along yet not be able to understand. The tree of codes was better than a paper imitation.
>
> (Foer 2010: 95–96)

Reality is not a colorful and lively version that hides behind the flat representation of the black-and-white map. The map is not 'a screen placed to hide the true meaning of things, a facade behind which there was an overintense coloring' (Foer 2010: 91). Rather the representation is as close as we come.

Making reality and representation one and the same is not just an aesthetic effect but becomes a tool to question modernity and the concept of progress itself. What progress is possible if our workings are confined to a space that is not 'real'? Schulz's narrator admits the falsity of progress, saying, 'the misfortune of that area is that nothing ever succeeds there, nothing can ever reach a definite conclusion. Gestures hang in the air, movements are prematurely exhausted and cannot overcome a certain point of inertia' (Schulz 1963: 109). The illusion of progress, wrested away from the myth of realism, appears as stopped time. While modernity's promise of progress is something that the Street of Crocodiles cannot afford, its appeal remains 'a concession of our city to modernity and metropolitan corruption. Obviously, we were unable to afford anything better than a paper imitation, a montage of illustrations cut out from last year's moldering newspapers' (Schulz 1963: 110). Time does not progress and reality has no substance. It even infiltrates the readers' experience with Schulz's prose. Rather than press forward, the density of his style requires that readers stop and reread (Gordon 2004: n.pag.). We do not walk in straight lines through his stories but spiral in recursive arcs as we move laterally. While it seems depressing, being outside of the illusions of realism, progress or unity means one is not burdened with supporting a major agenda.

However, undermining the major narrative is not a purely narrative endeavor. Seeing remakes of *The Street of Crocodiles* as rereadings across media, of which *Tree of Codes* is just one, requires that one consider both the narrative and narrative media. Even in the most bookish-appearing books like *Tree of Codes,* what is cached inside is the digital practices and machines that make them possible. In the case of Foer's *Tree of Codes*, this includes cutting-edge printing technology, an aesthetic of sampling or remixing and even replicating binary code as the thematic backbone of a book that relies solely on two functions: inclusion and omission, 1 and 0 (Rager 2012: n.pag.). The digital is in the book and to ignore that is to retreat from the book's reality. As the codex gives way to electronic platforms and is no longer the 'primary conveyor of narrative', it can articulate what its medium adds to narrative, as painting did when freed from realism with the advent of the photographic camera (Rager 2012: 13). Raymond Federman goes so far as to say, 'the whole traditional, conventional, fixed, and boring method of reading a book must be questioned, challenged, demolished' (Lanham 1993: 47). Taking up a book as a geography ripe for recomposition shows how readers could not only make a book their own through the process of reading but also reappropriate and build from the book, as any book is the raw material of another.

Foer's questioning of and experimenting with the inscription medium of the codex and its digital substrate is made ideologically distinct in what Kenneth Goldsmith calls uncreative writing. Rather than focusing on originality or creativity, Goldsmith argues that our digital tools support other priorities and skills such as manipulating or managing the present dearth and continued expansion of language (Goldsmith 2011: 15). Uncreative writing is an exploration in other author functions that digital technologies offer to humans. Writing is no longer married to the page or book and has attained unprecedented flexibility and mobility, in that the digital mediascape is made up of lines of written code. Even as the layperson thinks of the digital space as one of images more than of text, Goldsmith reminds us that all digital files are written in code, so what appears as an image on our screen is a .jpg file written in alphanumeric code (Goldsmith 2011: 17). By converting a .jpg into a .txt file, one can see the code behind the image and by adding content one can alter that image. Because writing is everywhere and the abundance of written content available for use and cached in code is so great, writing needs to reconsider itself in a digital space. Now different material aspects of writing have come forward. Earlier reading the print codex was like reading the code, but now we read the performance of code (Goldsmith 2011: 27). The author function can resemble that of a programmer, archivist or database manager as much as that of a writer, and the computer takes on functions that look like that of a writer, such as generating the paratextual and metatextual layers marking the travel of an email (Goldsmith 2011: 31). As Schulz and Foer show how master narratives undo themselves from within and thus reality and representation bleed into one another, digital technologies in literature reveal how the human and computer intersect and even overlap.

NOTES

1. Christopher Johnson's project is a defense of the baroque rhetorical and aesthetic practice of hyperbole and the baroque writ large from being discounted by literary taste. While he briefly mentions a congruous point with the media hype that floods our daily lives, he limits his comments on hyperbole to those employed during the historical baroque era.
2. Alejo Carpentier claims that to talk about the baroque, one must do so in a baroque way rather than continue with a classical academism. In this vein of thought, Peter Zhang can claim Marshall McLuhan is a minor rhetorician because he refigures academic writing as social poetry (Zhang 2011: 221). This shift in style encourages readers to be more mindful of the text as a representation (Zhang 2011: 222).
3. Certainly, those in positions of power can and have used baroque tropes to consolidate their power. Nicholas Spadaccini and Luis Martín-Estudillo use the baroque to understand mass culture as propagating the power of the Spanish monarchy and the Catholic church through sermons, plays and picaresque fiction, which all solidified a morality reliant on the continued existence of the current power structure. They cite Miguel de Cervantes's accusation that Félix Lope de Vega created populist plays of a commercial and formulaic nature. Predictable character types, constant plot twists, and stunning special effects formed the backbone of vulgar theater and the veneer covering the status quo moral lesson to maintain one's place in society rather than become the 'unhinged' *picaro*, wreaking havoc on the social order to only fail in his typically material goals.
4. A similar contradiction arises when Jonathan Safran Foer observes literature's comparative conservatism and traditionalism next to that of other expressive media:

> Literature is the most conservative art form by a long shot [....] If you look at what's happened in the visual arts in the last century, what's happening in music, what's happening in dance – there's been so much change. Whereas most novels that are

> published now are only the slightest degree different from the *Odyssey*, really. They're different in content but not so much in form.
>
> (Wagner 2010: n.pag.)

While characterizing literature as inherently resistant to change and complicit with majority, Foer still endorses a conservative view of authorship and expressive individualism that can boomerang a minor intent back to a major outcome.

CODE

My last name and mixed ethnic background repeatedly spark the question: 'Where are you from?' When I answer 'California', the curious acquaintance is disappointed and revises the question to 'No, I meant what is your background?' They are satisfied with the equally formulaic answer 'My mother is Icelandic, and my father is Japanese-American.' While the inquisitor feels resolved on my identity, these markers feel less relevant to my life experience. I know little about Icelandic or Japanese culture, history or politics. Instead, my ethnicity seems more a genetic expression, a feeling only deepened by my experience as an egg donor. After completing an intake form, I received a call the next day. A couple was interested in my application because I had nearly the same ethnic background as the hopeful mother. After a full panel of genetic tests, the rest of my DNA was deemed desirable, and I became genetic material. Of course, I always was a sequence of genes, but on the day my eggs were extracted, I was only that. In one sense, they know more about me than my most intimate companions and in another, they never knew me. That day I left one children's book with the nurse to pass along to the couple so I could be more than a cell. I am a cell who read Le Petit Prince *to all of my babies.*

***

Gene artists or bio artists participate in a conceptual cleft between pragmatic functions and aesthetic possibilities. Glow-in-the-dark rabbits and poetic bacteria are quickly labeled useless and decadent (Tomasula 2002: 143). However, in this supposed superficiality is a call to reexamine what belongs in the foreground versus the background of one's thinking. For instance, where do our motives or priorities of pragmatism and efficiency lead? Such questions are often categorical or based on perception, with bio artists spurring on many more.

> What does it mean to alter a natural evolutionary process millions of years old? How will people think of themselves, and their relation to others, once boundaries such as 'plant' and 'animal' have been eroded? How will we think of conventions such as 'humanness' once we are able to customize people?
> (Tomasula 2002: 138)

The speculative answers to these questions constitute a baroque thought project that moves rapidly between *zuhanden* and *vorhanden*. For instance, in customizing humans, we rethink their function and how their function is not exclusive, but programmable. Christian Bök is among this group of bio artists. He considers genetic code and the process of RNA replication as a way to compose poetry. When we see something as basic and essential to our lives as cellular replication imagined otherwise, those *zuhanden* moments let us see the procedural and expressive as one and the same in language – natural, computation or biological.

To get down to the database and strip away the narrative is to cut back to the original code and for Bök that is to go back to genetics as language. Bök's project, *The Xenotext*, takes this stripped-down version of language and approaches it in two ways. First, he writes on a bacterium's genetic code, making his poem not an object-based product but a part of a generative procedure: cellular replication. Second, he writes the companion book, *The Xenotext Book 1* to exercise poetically what Bök tries to accomplish through biochemistry. With the poem, 'Orpheus', Bök creates a poetic bacterium by injecting a string of DNA into a *Deinococcus radiodurans*, an extremophile, that triggers the production of a protein that, when decoded, reveals a poem, titled 'Eurydice' (Davis 2013: n.pag.). The added layer of having the bacterium write back means that Bök is not only using the organism's DNA to publish and store his poetry to survive an apocalypse, but he also wants the bacterium to become a poet as the human poet becomes a biochemist. Bök describes this layer of the project as an attempt at 'transforming the organism into a machine for writing a poem in response [...] I am trying to make my poem a living thing that in turn writes a poem' (Barber 2010: n.pag.). This required that Bök not only cipher the 26 letters of the English alphabet onto nucleotides but also create a double cipher where the translation back from nucleotide to English would make sense (Lista 2014: n.pag.). For the trillions of available ciphers, precious few make for sensical phrases with some poetic unity. For instance, if Christian Bök wanted to use the word 'language' in his line of poetry, the bacterium only had three sensical words it could write back: toxicoid, foxtrot and copy boys (Barber 2010: n.pag.). In the end, Bök's poem 'Orpheus' reads, 'any style of life is prim' to which the bacterium responds with the poem 'Eurydice', which reads 'the faery is rosy of glow'.

Part of Bök's motive behind creating poetry-writing machines out of bacteria is to move beyond humanistic sources of inspiration. He states, 'I am amazed that poets will continue to write about their divorces, even though there is currently a robot taking pictures of orange ethane lakes on Titan' (Davis 2013: n.pag.). Bök claims poets 'tend to write about what they do know: themselves, their own subjectivity', essentially because they do not look past the humanities to other disciplines (Voyce 2007: n.pag.). Doing so could mean that the future of poetry might not be in expressing human subjectivity but in creating poems that work 'by exploiting unthinking machines, by colonizing unfamiliar lexicons, or by simulating unliterary art forms' (Voyce 2007: n.pag.). When we break up the master narrative of human exceptionalism, literature finds a much larger database of what it could express beyond humanness. For instance, in the visual arts, Marc Quinn's *DNA Portraits* move the portrait form away from surface resemblance to genetic essence in the code. This brings up the question of where one's identity lies: in the code or in the expression of that code (Stracey 2009: 497).

Eradicating humanity is not the point, but humanness finds a new context, given scientific and technological advancements. To find new understandings of humanness, Bök still writes a book, but one that looks to other compositional processes, displays and structures than what we imagine as poetic compositions. *The Xenotext Book 1* opens each collection of poems with a pair of QR codes. While the left QR code is functional and brings readers to a text file containing the title of the collection of poems, the right QR code has been subjected to John Conway's 'Game of Life' algorithm and so QR readers can no longer process the image. Another code has corrupted the code. Ultimately, a process will consume an object.

Part of seeing process before product comes from Bök's treatment of natural language as a code. Here language is an executable process before it is semantic content. For instance, in 'Nocturne of Orpheus', Bök produces a poetic anagram of John Keats's 'When I Have Fears That I May Cease to Be'. In this case, Keats's poem is first a pile of letters to be rearranged, not a semantic unity to be interpreted. Dissolving Keats's poem into a jumble of letters does not counter the pull of destruction and arbitrariness. Instead, Bök writes the continuation of Keats's piece, picking up with the lonely lover Keats left standing on the shore. However, now the lover is writing this sonnet to stand against apocalypse. In Bök's continuation, an angel delights in Keats's sonnet with 'EACH SONNET A RHYTHM

FOR HER TO DECIPHER, / MAKING LEGIBLE A KEY IN HER DREAM OF DUSK' (Bök 2015: 22). These lines reference 'Orpheus' and 'Eurydice' where the 'HER' that deciphers the sonnet is the *Deinococcus radiodurans* deciphering Bök's cipher into an amino acid. While by the end of 'The Nocturne of Orpheus' the hero is burning in hell, he at least sees the universe unveiled by facing the abyss. He has looked down into the code, and though he dies, cellular replication in the *Deinococcus radiodurans* continues.

Not only does Bök treat natural language as fodder to recycle, but he also writes poems that radically translate natural language into genetic code. 'The March of the Nucleotides' creates a string of nucleotides from the letters that are left of the gap in each line. These words always end in A, T, C or G to indicate a nucleobase. These nucleobases are labeled to the right of the poem such that

A TREASURY
IT AMASSES
VIA TWISTS

(Bök 2015:100)

becomes ATA – one RNA codon made of three nucleobases. Given the fifteen lines in each poem, one poem creates a string that makes five RNA codons each three nucleobases long. ATA nucleobases result in AUA in RNA, producing the protein isoleucine. That RNA codon and resulting protein equate to the letter 'I' according to Bök's 'The Genetic Code', the cipher for the project. Ultimately, each RNA codon makes a protein that Bök visually represents with the help of a supercomputer, showing its folded structure, atomic backbone, entire molecule and charge envelope. What Bök challenges us to consider in this series is if language is everywhere in invisible layers of code and constantly executed, churning whatever we imagine is solid, then does language lead us anywhere? Darren Wershler says that Bök's *The Xenotext*

> raises that incredibly paranoid possibility that there might be messages embedded in the real world all around us [....] It raises the question of whether or not we're missing things, or whether something has been left for us that we just don't see.
>
> (Barber 2010: n.pag.)

For all our writing, we always find ourselves again at the *horror vacui* – the fear that behind all of our representations is nothing. No truth, meaning or reality.

Rather than those who would instrumentalize the world and see all for its function, Bök aims to show that what means everything also means nothing, and for a poet, language means everything. However, when seen as encoded into all elements of life, language is so ubiquitous it seems negligible. Caught in the cleft between being the result of genetic processes and the engineer of our own life experience, humans find themselves in the quagmire of intentionality and agency. While bio art may display human hubris and delusions of control over nature, their products also question the primacy of human liveliness. In 'Orpheus' and 'Eurydice', the act of writing that seems to affirm human subjectivity also deludes one into thinking that humans must persist. But in the end, we rot, and our plastic diapers go on longer than we do. Rather than see ourselves as less lively, we can see our objects as livelier. What lies beyond our narratives are the stories of other entities swirling about in the universe. We are not alone and hopeless in our pursuit of meaning; there is an entire universe of options and entities beyond our individual perspective. Humans are a process, part of other processes and, further still, irrelevant to so many processes that press on without us.

Collections and Navels: The *Horror Vacui* of the Database

Surviving the Horror Vacui

Seeing the database behind the narrative reveals the material realities behind story. While minor authors work to undo master narratives by essentially denying their unity and exposing the constructed nature of realism, one does not have to turn to a negative criticism to undermine master narratives. One could also positively embrace the presence of the *horror vacui* as a way to defeat realism's hold on our perception. This involves replacing an encompassing realism with a raw exposure to the database underlying all our stories. Facing the *horror vacui* requires a profound acceptance of the idea that no meaning or truth value underlies our representations, which are indistinguishable from our realities.[1] As we tire from running up and down the staircase of the baroque house,[2] we sit on the steps and realize that in making representations we are only moving furniture, but the furniture's placement is crucial.

What the *horror vacui* reveals more than all else is that we participate in a performance for ourselves. In order to shield ourselves from the *horror vacui* of knowing all potentialities in the world and the smallness of our self-enveloping narrative, we double down and try to reaffirm ourselves. The baroque's comfort with the *horror vacui* may be a part of why its critical potential is underestimated.[3] However, if we stared into the *horror vacui* long enough, we could be more critical of our state as performers by accepting the arbitrariness of meaning without being defeated by such knowledge. However, achieving this means that we must wrench ourselves from a singular perspective and refuse closure in order to see the codes that dictate performances of self-representation.

Narrative performance in digital environments is partly driven by the algorithms programmed into software that process input from the hardware and generate an output legible to humans. We are not the only ones reading, writing or performing. Opening ourselves to our digital tools offers us new methods and techniques of arranging, understanding and processing information that adopt computation's interest in systems and patterns rather than narrative design (Berry 2011: 13). Digital technotexts, aware of the computer as inscription medium, could create narratives that function as interfaces to databases, capturing Lev Manovich's concept of narratives as links stored in a database that cast the database as material and the narrative as virtual (Manovich 2001: 231).

Disrupting the through-line of the narrative text gives other voices and stories a place in the less linearly arranged database. While reflecting on building the *Walt Whitman Archive*, Ed Folsom supports Manovich's call to think on a 'poetics, aesthetics, and ethics of this database' (Folsom 2007: 1574). For Folsom, the database is a new genre and one that profoundly affects literature because it destabilizes narrative structures.[4] In constructing a database biography of Whitman as part of his archive project, Folsom states:

> Our biography presents a traditional chronological narrative of Whitman's life and career, but the database hovers behind the biography and, as we develop it, will be made accessible with active links throughout the narrative. These links will dissolve the narrative back into the data out of which it was constructed, and the data that were left out of our particular narrative will be available to the reader as well.
>
> (Folsom 2007: 1576)

While databases and archives of objects will infiltrate, dilute or dissolve our narratives, narrativizing helps stave off symptoms of what Jacques Derrida calls 'archive fever' – a pathology that afflicts researchers who, overwhelmed by information, must write narratives as a survival mechanism (Folsom 2007: 1577).

Perhaps a direct example of this narrative and database cycle appears in Orhan Pamuk's novel *The Museum of Innocence* and the accompanying museum described in his book *The Innocence of Objects*. The novel was first conceived as an annotated catalogue, but, in the midst of collecting physical artifacts for his museum, Pamuk realized that

> writing my novel as an annotated catalogue would not allow me to adequately explore or express the full import of Kemal and Füsun's romance and the entire culture or the period through objects. Yes, I was going to set up the museum, and the novel was going to tell the stories of the objects in the museum and of the making of the museum itself. But I no longer had much need for an annotated

> museum catalogue. I now wanted to write the story of Füsun and Kemal in the form of a classic novel.
>
> (Pamuk 2012: 17)

The objects in the museum needed to be balanced with the narrative antidote, but Pamuk still had to write *The Innocence of Objects* to catalogue not the romantic relationships of the characters so much as the spirit of the museum as an entity independent of the novel. For Pamuk, the objects he collected communicate with one another because of their proximity and the resulting relationships thus formed. Also, being pried from previous contexts, the objects hold a shamanic sense of possessing their own spirit (Pamuk 2012: 52). While the museum and the novel are bonded together by a shared origin, they are not illustrations or explanations of one another (Pamuk 2012: 17). The museum and novel, like a database and narrative, coexist on a flat mediascape.

As we increasingly write and read on the computer rather than in the codex, the more fitting fragmentary and diverse content is to the form.[5] An organizational archetype other than the book helps us see digital literature otherwise. Manovich adopts cinema as his organizing paradigm for understanding new media, but before he did so, he provided a much broader view:

> Contrary to popular images of computer media as collapsing all human culture into a single giant library (which implies the existence of some ordering system), or a single giant book (which implies a narrative progression), it is perhaps more accurate to think of the new media culture as an infinite flat surface where individual texts are placed in no particular order.
>
> (Manovich 2001: 77)

Knowing that we are part of a flat mediascape of representations is a way to feel like part of an extended ecology, where the database could be its own narrative rather than a recounting of some chronological process of collecting (Bal 1994: 100). When the computer acts on us and the digital's programmability and increased capacity for learning enliven its objecthood, we can see as the digital computer processes data and thus imagine ourselves and our world differently.

To examine the database as a kind of guard rail against the void, we could consider its analogue ancestor: collecting. Collecting, like the database, is about accumulating with the potential for a meaningful sequence or arrangement. Collecting is the fallout of baroque minoring. After the minor shatters the major, the major must rebuild by gathering the pieces in hopes that a stable collection might form. As baroque reason is concerned, the sense of stability is not the goal; it is the death of curiosity.

Collecting and the Rise of the Object

One of the great pleasures of reading comes from ignoring the representational divide of fiction and projecting ourselves into the story. We do this to the point of narcissistically searching for ourselves in what we read (Motte 2005: 786). Moreover, these pathologies of narrative immersion can be applied to collecting objects. Collectors try to reaffirm their identity by collecting to express self or crafting their own context. After decades of gathering mirror scenes in literature, Warren Motte fears the motives of his collection. He does not recognize himself in the collection and suspects that his drive is 'a will to totalize', despite knowing that the goal is impossible and the mentality itself is dangerous (Motte 2005: 782). Philip Blom observes collectors guarding and discussing their collections in narcissistic ways, going as far as to retreat therein to imagine the world existing just for them (Blom 2003: 216). In this light, the collector is a bit like Mieke Bal's interpretation of Narcissus. Bal claims that Narcissus died because he could not recognize himself in his reflection or acknowledge that representation, not reality, was at play with the mirrored surface of the water. In the end, the story is not about the dangers of self-love but of the dangers of naïve realism (Bal 1999: 237–38). Collecting is like its own worldbuilding where collections eventually encompass collectors to become their reality.

Alternatively, Walter Benjamin in 'Unpacking my library' characterizes acts of obsession as 'a state of suspense above the abyss' and that '[e]very passion borders on chaos, that of the collector on the chaos of memory' (cited in Blom 2003: 207). Collectors turn outward to the objects that fill the world, and in their desire to possess those objects, they fetishize them. Collections both produce fetishism by cutting off objects from their context and induce fetishism by encouraging further collection spurred on by the feelings of domination that come from ownership (Bal 1994: 105). Susan Stewart develops this vein of fetishism, saying, 'the fetishist's impulse towards accumulation and privacy, hoarding and the secret, serves both to give integrity to the self and at the same time to overload the self with signification' (Stewart 1984: 162–63). The collection saturates us with meaning and shows the monadic subject as both affirmed and expressed by her collection and its arrangement – the second floor of the baroque house – and overcome or undone by the universalizing desire of collecting – the first floor of the baroque house.

This individually motivated collecting cast as identity formation is perhaps partly associated with consumerism, but Pamuk claims that aspiring writers and artists begin their work in much the same way as collectors – not to preserve the past or contribute to a culture but to make themselves a new identity (Pamuk 2012: 46). In this vein, the idiosyncrasies of the individual fold into cultural memory and not vice versa. In his reading of Tan Lin, Thomas Claburn and Georges Perec, Kenneth Goldsmith claims

> [b]y inventorying the mundane – what we eat and what we read – we leave a trail that can say as much about ourselves as a more traditional diaristic approach, leaving room enough for the reader to connect the dots and construct narratives in a plethora of ways.
>
> (Goldsmith 2011: 188–89)

Accumulating the insignificant ultimately constructs identities. Documenting the banal becomes autobiographical.

Alexandra Nemerov's essay 'First, my Motorola' epitomizes the idea of identity formation through possession. She lists in chronological order every brand she touched in a day. The essay is an exercise in metonymy, replacing her branded objects for herself. While a list of consumer products in one's possession might seem more like metadata that has nothing to do with the content of one's identity, metadata is quite telling. The entire essay follows the same format: 'First, my Motorola / Then my Frette / Then my Sonia Rykiel / Then my Bulgari / Then my Asprey / Then my Cartier / Then my Kohler / Then my Brightsmile / Then my Cetaphil' (Nemerov 2011: 457–58). Throughout her essay, we learn that she purchases several luxury brand items, so we assume she has considerable financial means. She eats healthy food and snacks on fruit. She chews gum after her snacks. She always brushes her teeth before and after having coffee. She drinks bottled water but refills the bottles. She exercises. She carries a Blackberry and has an Apple desktop at home with top-of-the-line speakers. She also clearly cares about her appearance with the number of cosmetic brands she touches. Without action or description, only possession, readers can already make a judgment about this person.

Further, these little narcissistically motivated identities, formed through the process of collecting, eventually build up to shape a culture. While knowing others by their possessions may seem like a superficial practice, that does not discredit its effectiveness. Unlike portrait artists such as Vanessa Bell and Francis Bacon, who look to find a nonmaterial resonance in the subject of portraiture, Peter Menzel finds identity alternatively via the mass of things. It is common in portraiture to use objects as markers of social class or occupation, but for Menzel, objects in portraits are more than symbolic markers. Objects act as an inventory of material facts and a direct way of knowing a person. Menzel is concerned that 'with the pervasive influence of modern media, people can be manipulated into thinking they know a rock star or a movie actress, artificially created personalities. Real people remain invisible' (Grossman 1996: n.pag.). His response to this and the west's unawareness of its privilege is to show the possessions of a family laid out in front of their home. Not only does the image represent the family, but more broadly, the country of their origin. This use of objects as definitional traits is not a clear-cut relationship, as James Elkins articulates while explaining away the idea of 'just looking' while we shop. The object will look back. While shoppers hunt for a desired object, they also feel as though they are being hunted, given that each object tries to attract the shopper's attention (Elkins 1996: 18–20). The distinction between the hunter and the hunted is not as crisp as we care to believe. We cannot completely instrumentalize our objects.

While the object can relieve the collector from a sense of social alienation and offers collectors space to construct a discourse they dictate and that signifies themselves (Baudrillard 1994: 24), the perceived intrusion of the object as defining the subject is often a source of embarrassment for the collector. It is not unusual that collectors deny having a pointed intention for a collection. Pamuk could not be honest about his intentions for his *Museum of Innocence*, saying,

> whenever anyone asked what I was going to do with the stuff that I was accumulating, I was unable to answer them. 'I will build a museum, and its catalogue will be a novel' seemed too ambitious a response. Instead, I gave the same answer as the broken-hearted Istanbul collectors I described in the book: I'd say that I was really fond of this teacup, but I would act as if I didn't know what I was going to do with them. This seemed to be a relatively harmless eccentricity. (Pamuk 2012: 21)

To keep collecting as an unmotivated eccentricity rather than a pointed construction of the collector's identity seems major in its mindlessness but its intent to regard the idea of human independence from objects as pathological and dangerous could be its own minor critique. A collector's sense of embarrassment at being enraptured by an object is a way to underplay the power of the object. For Bal a baroque perspective is one where the subject is vulnerable to the object and transgression focuses on the object rather than the subject (Bal 1999: 28), a point Octavio Paz makes in 'Baroque and Romanticism' when he claims that 'while the romantic transgression centers on the subject, the baroque transgression focuses on the object' (Bal 1999: 231). Recognizing the object as its own entity with its own prerogatives and stories could help humans see differently.

Our objects do much more than alter us; they reanimate their purpose. In 'The system of collecting', Jean Baudrillard claims that an object has two states mutually exclusive of one another where it can be seen for either its function or its symbolic meaning as a possession (Baudrillard 1994: 8). Once an object is a possession, it is an 'absolute singularity [...] which means that it is equivalent to a human being'

(Baudrillard 1994: 10). This object state opens reality to 'limitless substitution and play' (Baudrillard 1994: 10). For Bal, this is how objects come to tell stories. Their interchangeability with subjects means they can be 'inserted into the narrative perspective', given their semiotic weight (Bal 1994: 111). Pamuk takes note of the same narrative sentience of objects in his explanation for his *Museum of Innocence*. He briefly discusses the work of Ármin Vámbéry, who studied Tatar rituals to honor the souls of objects like weapons, trains and clocks. Pamuk even quotes Fuat Köprülü's rewriting of a poem found on a clockmaker's calendar:

> I am both a clock and a thing. When you see me as a clock, do not forget that I am also a thing. Whenever you realize that I am a thing, think of the spirit of Time. Mine is the soul of a thing, but also of a clock. It shines brightly during the night, and when in daytime it folds into itself, I too turn inward.
>
> (Pamuk 2012: 140–41)

An object's function erases its story, and when cut from its function, its story arises again. In collecting objects, we do not just desire to possess the thing but 'to know the object's secrets [....] As our soul focuses on objects, we can feel in our broken hearts that the whole world is one, and we come to accept our own suffering' (Pamuk 2012: 195). Collecting is a way for humans to find a synergy between their limited perspective and the overwhelming scale of the universe. For instance, humans can see themselves differently after seeing the world as the digital computer processes data. The digital's programmability and increased capacity for learning enlivens its objecthood.

Synergy with our objects is far from unprecedented. Humans develop profound relationships with their environment and the objects therein. For instance, Aaron Rosand, a renowned concert violinist, says of his violin, '[i]t's almost like a living thing. You treat it carefully; you treat it gently. It talks to you [....] You're caressing your instrument all the time' (Wakin 2012: n.pag.). Laurence Lesser, a concert cellist, continues this line of thought: 'For us string players, our instruments are our environment. It keeps stretching us, it keeps demanding of us, it keeps us aspiring to grow' (Wakin 2012: n.pag.). However, this connection between object and subject, environment and organism, is not strictly typical of (or exhausted by) artistic experience. N. Katherine Hayles describes the heavily mediated environment of the currency exchange broker by highlighting how brokers do not view the currency exchange market as abstract at all. She quotes one trader who calls the market 'a lifeform that has being in its own right ... it has form and meaning [...] as a greater being' (Hayles 2008: 98). Hayles cites others who describe trading on the market as similar to sexual and physical vulnerabilities or violent bodily penetration. When our objects and environments gain agency, we are not being robbed of our humanity. Instead, we are reconnected to our sensual abilities, which we use to reconsider rational faculties. Collections, once they gain mass and momentum, expose the collector to the presence of objects who possess their own stories, flattening the hierarchy between collector and collected.

Exceeding Categories, Navel Reading and the Polyhistor's Wunderkammer

This force of the object intruding into the realm of the subject constitutes only part of the perceived threat of the *horror vacui*. A more systemic threat arises from its sheer mass and the effect of that mass on organizational paradigms. Even small collections can demonstrate this phenomenon on a more localized scale. While collections begin haphazardly before establishing a meaningful sequence, once established, they expand networks rather than limit them. To see an object raises the question of what else accompanied it and that ring of association and relation quickly radiates far beyond the perceived intent of the collection. In describing his collection of packaging materials, Robert Opie shows how beginning with one object expands to the universal with barely a nudge:

> Take the *Oxo* cube. How extraordinary that they got all that flavour into a little cube in the first place, then they've got to fit six *Oxo* cubes into a tin, then that tin is put into a larger box which is sold out of a display carton on the shelf in the shop, which it's got to get to; then they've got to sell it, they have to put up great hoardings everywhere, point-of-sale material, eventually publicize it on television to get you into a shop to actually buy it; then you've got the competition, the twenty other brands that were competing with it, twenty imitators – you need to have representations of all those, and you need to understand how the *Oxo* cube came out in 1910. In fact, there were *Liebig* cubes before *Oxo* cubes. One needs to understand all that history and then how it all fits into the shopping list. It's not just *Oxo* that someone goes out to buy, but there's everything else. So there's the shopping basket; and then some people would telephone their orders through or they would send their servants down to pick it up, and how does that all work, and when did the motor car come in, and all these other differences in the social framework. But you also want to see what the kitchen looked like and so on, you want to understand the whole circle of life.
>
> (Opie 1994: 40, original emphasis)

As a collection grows, it collapses under its own weight. For the collection to stand in for the universe, each object must be metonymic, a part of a whole that keeps expanding. The collection creates its own universe but rarely feels satisfied or complete.

Even trying to close the collection with the catalogue is a labor-intensive process (Stewart 1984: 162). Objects do not always fit cleanly into a defined category or only one category of the collection (Opie 1994: 28). This comes in part from the origin of the object competing with the relationships it now forms with other objects catalogued. Further, as collections expand, the limited value and limiting character of categories become more evident. We become less confident in the predictability and distinction of categories as individual items or entries fall under more and more categories, and newly minted categories force collectors to reconsider all their other categories. The digital computer is readily permissive of such bendable categories particularly in how it can store a digital file in a database to be tagged with multiple categories rather than a physical object that is limited to its single iteration. Of course, this introduces another problem of having too many categories to reasonably navigate. The physical archive approximates this multiplicity in making more indices, yet another time-intensive endeavor.

While catalogues, indices, lists and databases predate our digital technologies, our digital tools and content creation have outpaced our human processing power. Human anxiety about computers lies not just in how computers process information differently than humans, but in the very fact that we need computers at all. Their existence proves we have collected beyond our ability to order. Computer programs and webbots, which now often perform the labor-intensive work of indexing data, remind us that human interpretation is not the only reading. While this is easy to interpret as dehumanizing, we must remember that 'human' is not a fixed concept. Adapting to computers, database models and algorithmic readings is a 'part of a long history of the "human" adapting to new technological possibilities and affordances' (Hayles 2012: 30). We must think like and with our digital technologies so we can face a barrage of information – a veritable data frontier of lists, metadata, logs and tweets – in ethical ways. Humans cannot be left to their own devices and neither can our digital tools.

Hurbert Burda claims the founding of Google in 1998 was when the computer replaced the human curator. As the largest indexer of the Internet, Google receives 63,000 queries a second and accounts for approximately 87 percent of online searches worldwide, resulting in 110 billion dollars in revenue as of December 2017 (Duhigg 2018: n.pag.). Despite these massive numbers, Google is tiny. According to its website, Google has indexed only 100,000,000 gigabytes of data from the surface web, which only accounts for a tiny fraction of what exists on the Internet. With so much information even in just one index representing so little of the existing content, there seems to be no way for humans to understand the totality of their products without adapting to models of reading with our computers that handle mass well. And with that mass of data, today it is not adventurers and explorers who travel to the far reaches of the world gathering artifacts for the *wunderkammer* at home. The *wunderkammer* comes to the user with a quick keyword search. What we find instead are information giants like Google, Facebook and Amazon creating a heterotopic experience where users see their browsing history on Google reflected back to them in the ad content on YouTube.[6] With a database mindset, we create an aesthetic of density that necessitates machine reading. The collector cannot recall, organize or understand the objects collected as a whole. However, coherence and unity are not the guiding principles of textual formation or reading for the database mindset of collectors. They lean on an index, as Google users search an index, not the Internet itself.

To approximate such a machine reading, humans can practice a navel reading that traces peculiarities and their patterns through the collection. Bal's idea of navel-gazing constitutes a process of looking to potent details that transfix our gaze despite their seemingly minor role in the larger representation. Even more, because navels both capture viewer's attention and frighten or revolt, a navel reading that searches out such conflict offers space for idiosyncrasies, curiosities and unincorporated difference. To illustrate the function and force of the navel, Bal examines Michelangelo Merisi da Caravaggio's 1601–02 *The Incredulity of Saint Thomas* and Jeanette Christensen's reappropriation of Caravaggio in her 1995 *Ostentatio Vulnerum*. Christensen identifies the wound in Jesus's side as the navel of the painting and crops Caravaggio's painting to include only the hands, wound and Thomas's face. The wound's surgical precision, along with the presence of the four men staring into it, draws viewers into the wound as the navel of Caravaggio's painting. Below this cropped image Christensen places an identical frame of strawberry Jell-O 'to create the sensation of creeping inside and touching, while simultaneously offering a magnified glimpse under Jesus's skin' (Bal 1999: 34). Christensen's Jell-O frame allows viewers to penetrate the painting. The decay of the Jell-O over time even lives out the rot of the wound. Focusing on this navel alters how Christensen's viewers would view Caravaggio's *The Incredulity of Saint Thomas*, which now has a much stronger erotic presence. While Caravaggio's painting is a religious representation, the erotic reminder helps viewers recall the importance of the bodily in religious tradition.[7] Navel readers can thus move from text to text like a quotation, gathering meanings from all its placements, not unlike allegory as a communicative function between monads.

The associative nature of navel readings exposes the ever-slipping grasp of ordering categories. Such categorical transgression is both invigorating and fear-inducing, where, even in Late Antiquity, St. Thomas Aquinas feared curiosity, as it 'might transgress the approved boundaries set for knowledge and the methods for its attainment, and had sought to circumscribe enquiry in order to block the road that led to mortal danger' (Shelton 1994: 181). Curiosity produces a moral quandary, as it could be considered 'a healthy passion that may produce legitimate pleasure, even admirable knowledge' (Castillo 2005: 6) or 'an essentially feminine passion that threatens the moral and social order' (Castillo 2005: 7). Such curiosity is what motivated collections during the baroque era, then called *wunderkammern*, whose idiosyncratic orderings and flexible categories leave room for the unknown.

The *wunderkammer*, or cabinet of curiosity, was produced out of a sense of wonder. Their displays were not transparent as their contents were often hidden in 'nested drawers, shelves, niches and boxes, behind internal doors, frames and partitions', so that exploring and revealing the artifacts were important to their display (MacLure 2006: 737). *Wunderkammern* often included optical devices to manipulate reality like 'lenses, mirrors, optical games, paintings and clockwork automata' to produce an interactive and playful multi-sensory experience unlike the masterful and detached observer of the modern museum (MacLure 2006: 737). More importantly, for Maggie MacLure, the *wunderkammer* encouraged visitors to connect to a collection through seduction rather than argument. Visitors were to change, expand and cross the categories of a *wunderkammer*'s taxonomies. Thus, the thought imperative is not to analyze what is there, but to add to those objects (MacLure 2006: 738). Further, the *wunderkammer* strove to show visitors similarities across difference and 'otherness that confounds reductionism and abstraction' (MacLure 2006: 738). This openness could be perceived as an ethical practice, which, of course, is historically complicated by the baggage of colonialism and exoticism that comes along with building *wunderkammern*.

Still, the idiosyncratic arrangements of the *wunderkammer* built on the whims and tastes of the owner did not hold for long. By Napoleon Bonaparte's reign and his appointment of Vivant Denon as Director General of Museums, the arrangement of collections focused increasingly on 'chronology, on national schools and on the evolution of styles' (Blom 2003: 118). *Wunderkammern* shifted from spaces of wonder and the unknown to projects of conserving and cataloguing known specimens and phenomena (Blom 2003: 121) such that collections went from gathering the 'rare and monstrous' to displaying illustrations of human knowledge (Blom 2003: 122). Instead of surprising viewers, museums instructed them. The apparent disarray of the *wunderkammer* is read as the chaotic replication of the collector's mind stretched out across too many fields of study (Westerhoff 2001: 643).

The move from *wunderkammer* to museum reveals an ontological conflict between the baroque polyhistor who desires encyclopedism and universalism and the enlightenment specialist who means to essentialize and divide categorically. For the polyhistor, knowledge is broad, covering many fields. As such, the polyhistor approaches inquiry from a range of disciplinary perspectives, often seemingly disconnected. From this position, a specialist's inquiries appear 'hopelessly incomplete' (Westerhoff 2001: 641). However, the polyhistor's methods and goals could result in 'total failure or [...] extremely superficial results' (Westerhoff 2001: 640). Jan Westerhoff nevertheless claims the *wunderkammer* has an order. These *wunderkammern* 'were supposed to mirror the innermost structure of the world' (Westerhoff 2001: 646) and bring 'out clearly the web of significations which connected all phenomena' (Westerhoff 2001: 649). Rather than by categories of similarities, the *wunderkammer* arranges objects to encourage communication across categories to make hidden relations visible (Westerhoff 2001: 645).

While one could see the *wunderkammer* as the stepping stone to scientific inquiry, it can also be the image of another mode of thought that accommodates experiences and feelings commonly suppressed in the public sphere (Arellano 2015: 18), not to mention the Academy. To recapture the collector of the baroque *wunderkammer* is to put the human no longer in the position of the master. Even if that *wunderkammer* is a kind of externalization of the collector's minds, the curious collector does not definitively categorize and arrange objects but must follow them to 'hear what the objects themselves have to say about who they are, how they relate to one another, and what they are trying to do' (Miller 2013: 17). The collector's mind is full of objects that have their own stories and trajectories, which do not abide by the categories humans, and especially experts, apply to them.

Incomplete Inventories and Sensed Presence

Lording over a collection allows us the illusion that we exert some control over our world, but as collections expand, they do more than serve as a narcissistic or fetishistic display of self-expression. Placing objects in a collection may start as a way to symbolize ourselves or our culture; however, by turning to the symbolic, we end up lending more narrative power to the object. Ultimately, we did not explain ourselves better but discovered many more stories beyond our own, that even eclipse our own. We understand ourselves as part of a larger ecology rather than as separate or objective. Of course, we cannot fully release ourselves from our subjectivity or perspective but see that there are views other than our own that spur curiosity and transgress order and category. Narrative works dissolve or explode into the database just below the surface of representation. Two salient examples exist in Georges Perec's *An Attempt at Exhausting a Place in Paris* and Chris Ware's *Building Stories*, both of which spatialize narrative to destabilize the viewpoint of the narrator who cannot achieve a totalizing view and through the force of the *horror vacui* as database, no longer strives for such life-denying control.

Perec's *An Attempt at Exhausting a Place in Paris* admits the limits of human perspective when he documents the happenings at Place Saint-Sulpice from 18–20 October 1974, by taking perch in the cafés, tabacs and on benches in and around the square. Rather than turn his attention to the notable events and buildings, he describes 'that which is generally not taken note of, that which is not noticed, that which has no importance: what happens when nothing happens other than the weather, people, cars, and clouds' (Perec 2010: 3). Each log opens with a date, time, location and for most, a weather summary to frame what follows as the result of a near scientific observation that considers the world as a still set of facts and clear states.

The first log opens with what is visible from his seat as a baseline test to prepare him for the experiment. He lists the known facts beyond the scene, 'The 96 goes to Montparnasse station / The 84 goes to Porte de Champerret' (Perec 2010: 6), and momentarily looks for specific items like colors. Both serve as a way to give purpose and context for the viewing, but more to transition him away from seeing as a human sees. The mass of information quickly overwhelms the tendency to categorize observations and order space in a comprehensible way. Near the end of his first day, Perec candidly admits defeat, writing '(*fatigue*)' (Perec 2010: 24, original emphasis) to mark a loss of time. Several entries throughout the book end with 'Pause' (Perec 2010: 9, 17, 21, 31). By admitting his physical and mental incapacity to log the inconsequential actions of the square, he reminds us that a human perspective is limited and points to the existence of much more information that has slipped by him. How long did Perec break from logging events? What might we have missed in that time? He must have done something during that time. The more he works to log the entirety of events, the more we notice the log and the ultimately impossible task it represents. The resulting inventory exposes the conflict between such a volume of emergent minutiae and the human perspective that must grapple with such details.

Just as Perec admits that his experiment documents the unimportant and forgotten, Ware readily describes the content of *Building Stories*, as 'a decade's worth of work, with dozens of "never-before published" pages (i.e., those deemed too obtuse, filthy or just plain incoherent to offer to a respectable periodical)' (Ware 2012: n.pag.). The larger conceit of the book is to examine the unhappy and disconnected lives of four tenants of a Chicago building: a young woman with a prosthetic leg on the third floor, an unhappy couple on the second floor and an isolated elderly landlady on the first floor. Beyond hearing from the narratorial voices of these four individuals (though potentially all through the voice of the nameless third-floor tenant who functions as the protagonist),[8] we see Branford the Bee and the apartment building gain narratorial control in some segments of the 'book'. Now, the 'book' itself is a box resembling a board game that contains fourteen variously formatted comics.[9] The description on the back of the box provides brief instructions on how the reader ought to 'set down, forget or completely lose any number of its contents within the walls of an average well-appointed home' (Ware 2012: n.pag.). Despite being packaged, shrink-wrapped and sold at the precious price of $50, Ware still hopes that readers will treat the contents of the box as scraps that should infiltrate one's lived space. As the chapter will continue to refer to separate booklets, I have enumerated them below in order from the shortest to longest height with folded pieces left folded. Following a description of the format is the opening few words of unbound pieces:

1. 3-inch by 9¾-inch staple-bound booklet
2. 3½-inch by 7-inch accordion folded strip ('Her laugh is like')
3. 3½-inch by 7-inch accordion folded strip ('I don't care')
4. 5¾-inch by 7¾-inch staple-bound booklet, *Branford the Best Bee in the World*
5. 9-inch by 13-inch 2-page tabloid ('Recently, my high school')
6. 9¼-inch by 12½-inch 4-page tabloid, *The Daily Bee*
7. 9½-inch by 8½-inch *Little Golden Book*
8. 11-inch by 8¼-inch 16-page staple-bound booklet of the 2nd-floor tenant ('shit')
9. 11-inch by 8¼-inch 16-page staple-bound booklet of the 3rd-floor tenant ('vvvfffmmmmmmmmmmm')
10. 11-inch by 16-inch 4-page broadsheet ('It all happened so fast')
11. 11-inch by 16-inch 20-page broadsheet ('God…huf, huf')
12. 12-inch by 9-inch staple-bound booklet titled 'Disconnect'
13. 12¼-inch by 9¼-inch clothbound book
14. 16-inch by 10½-inch folded gameboard.

The integrity of the story relies on the reader's care to its preservation, which builds a sense of neurosis, a feeling echoed in the protagonist's experience of the book. On the final page of the 'DISCONNECT' booklet, the unnamed protagonist dreams of discovering her book in a bookstore, which is in pieces like *Building Stories*. The contents of this found book are remainders of the protagonist's life. '[I]t had everything in it… my diaries, the stories from my writing classes, even stuff I didn't know I'd written… everything I'd forgotten, abandoned or thrown out was there… everything' (Ware 2012: n.pag.). All the things we forgot or did not notice, when gathered together, gain the momentum of a life. If we slow down and pay attention to the mundane, we will see all the emergent possibilities that

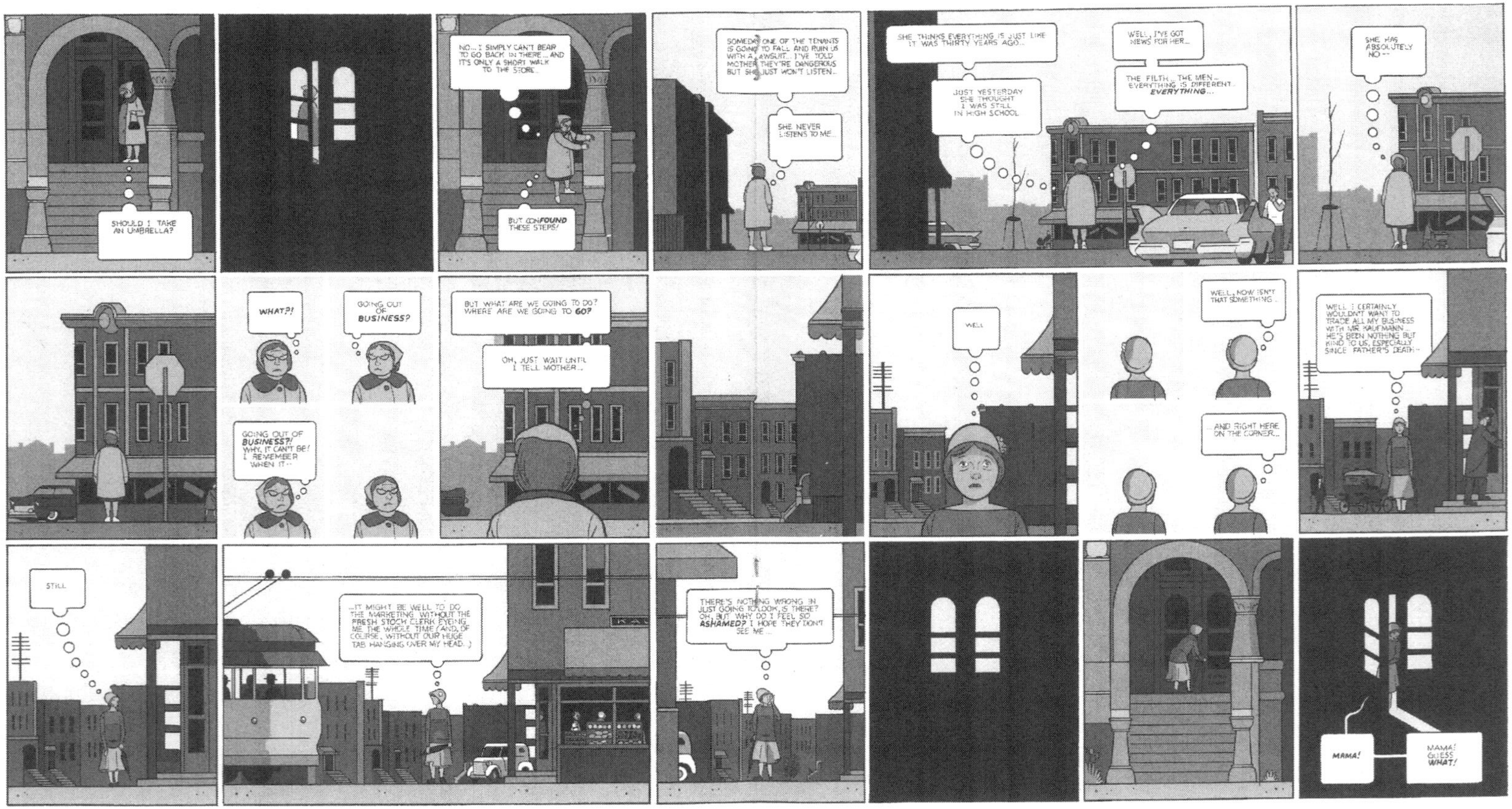

FIGURE 20: Graphic novel excerpt from *Building Stories* by Chris Ware, 'No... no, I never wanted' pages 8–9, copyright © 2012 by Chris Ware. Used by permission of Pantheon Books, an imprint of the Knopf Doubleday Publishing Group, a division of Penguin Random House LLC. All rights reserved.

collide with our narrative perspective, even if that narrative perspective remains unstable and incomplete.

Ware uses perspective and mirroring in the comic panels to make narrative perspective opaque where Perec used visible markers of time passed and a relentless tempo of mundane actions. Ware captures the three women in the building in a repeated frame structure. For the first- and second-floor tenants, we see this repetition in the centerfold page of the two more traditionally sized, coverless comic book pieces devoted to that woman. In both series of panels, we see the near identical moments in these two women's lives. Both leave their apartment frustrated with their cohabiter's mistreatment and disrespect. The landlady escapes from her ailing mother only to return home excited to share news of a new grocery store with her. The second-floor tenant storms out of her apartment to escape her emotionally distant husband, but she returns after realizing her theatrics do not affect his feelings.

Beyond being direct replicas of one another in structure and sharing close affinities, these two stories depict frustration and resignation cinematically, with one lens seemingly at their destination and the other at the origin. When either woman approaches the door of their apartment building, we see them from inside the door and from the street. At times, we look over the shoulder of the character from a distance as though we are trying to assume her perspective. At other times, we face her directly, nearly admitting our stalker-like presence in the scene. These scenes are poignant but distant because they approach memory as what cognitive scientists call *observer memories* seen from the third-person rather than *field memories* that result from the first-person point of view. When we relive memories, we

> remember our past selves not as if we are inhabiting that earlier body, seeing through those younger eyes; instead, we often see ourselves as if from the outside, from a station we never could have occupied in the historical past.
>
> (Sattler 2010: 212)

These *observer memories* are more easily narrativized and 'more conducive to introspection and self-understanding' than *field memories* whose volatility implode into themselves (Sattler 2010: 212). Capturing this composed distancing as a part of the story creates observer memories that play to Ware's belief that a cartoon 'is not an image taken from life. A cartoon is taken from memory. You're trying to distill the memory of an experience, not the experience itself' (Sattler 2010: 206). This blunt admission that what cartoons represent is a representation reveals a baroque worldview aware of the constant performance involved in what we call reality.

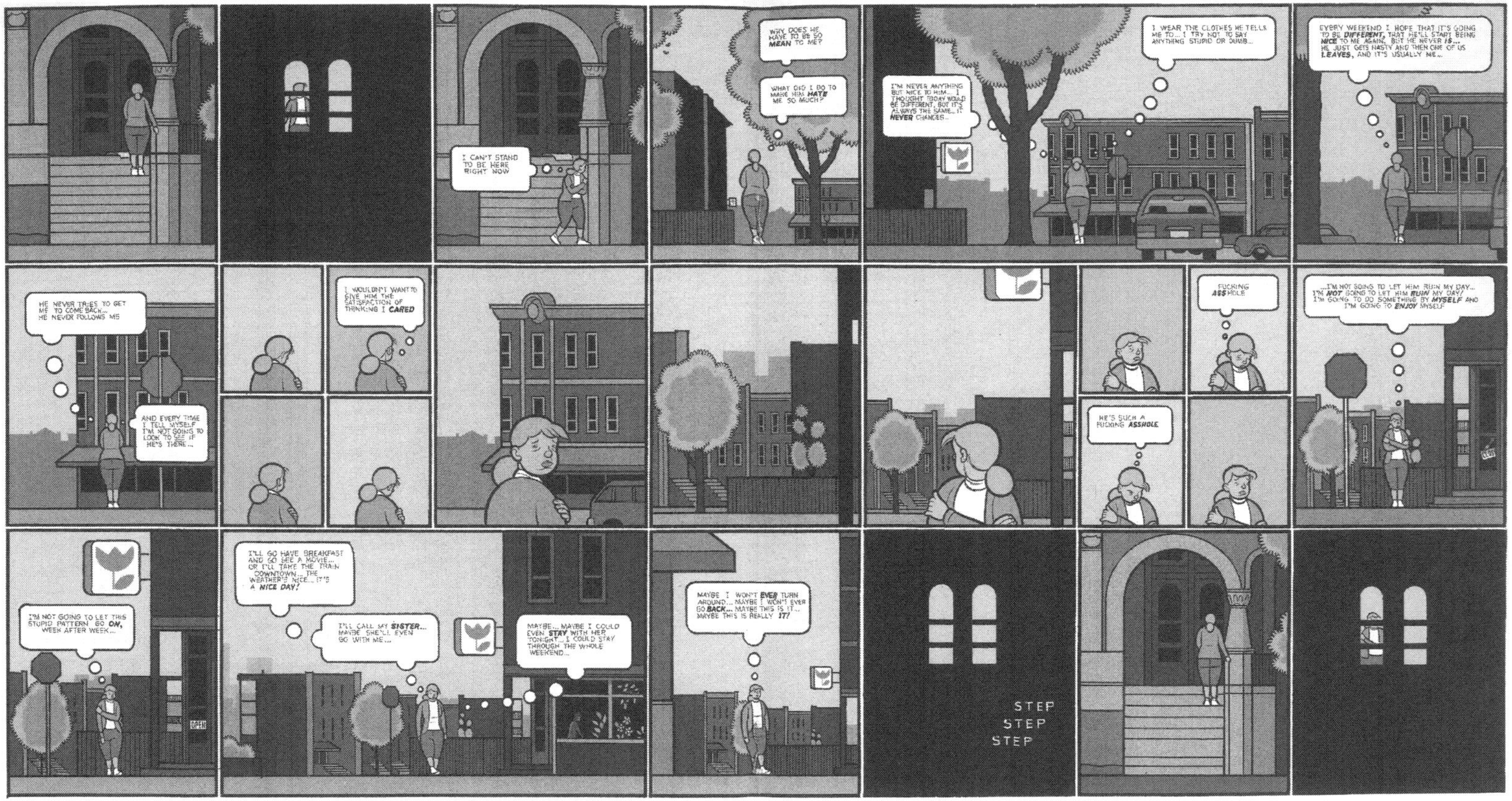

FIGURE 21: Graphic novel excerpt from *Building Stories* by Chris Ware, 'Shit scrape scrape' pages 8–9, copyright © 2012 by Chris Ware. Used by permission of Pantheon Books, an imprint of the Knopf Doubleday Publishing Group, a division of Penguin Random House LLC. All rights reserved.

The same sequence of panels occurs in the third-floor tenant's storyline but in a long, horizontal strip that leverages the medium of the paper by playing on printing the perspective shifts on opposite sides of the paper. Once the woman is away from the building stoop, we see her from behind on one side of the paper and from the front on the reverse as though the reader could walk around the strip of paper as much as he or she could walk around a person. Because each panel was assigned a vantage point either facing the building or back to the building, the paper seems like a slice of time pulled from the three-dimensional action.

These perspective switches between facing and not facing the building occur quickly at the flip of the page when the protagonist enters and leaves the building and when she turns around to face the apartment building that seems to be watching her. The same turn in perspective exists in the panels of the other women, but the protagonist's perspective seems eerier because the opposite side of the page is also oriented to readers who can sense an unknown entity staring at them. When we become so hyper-aware of the effect of perspective we see how even

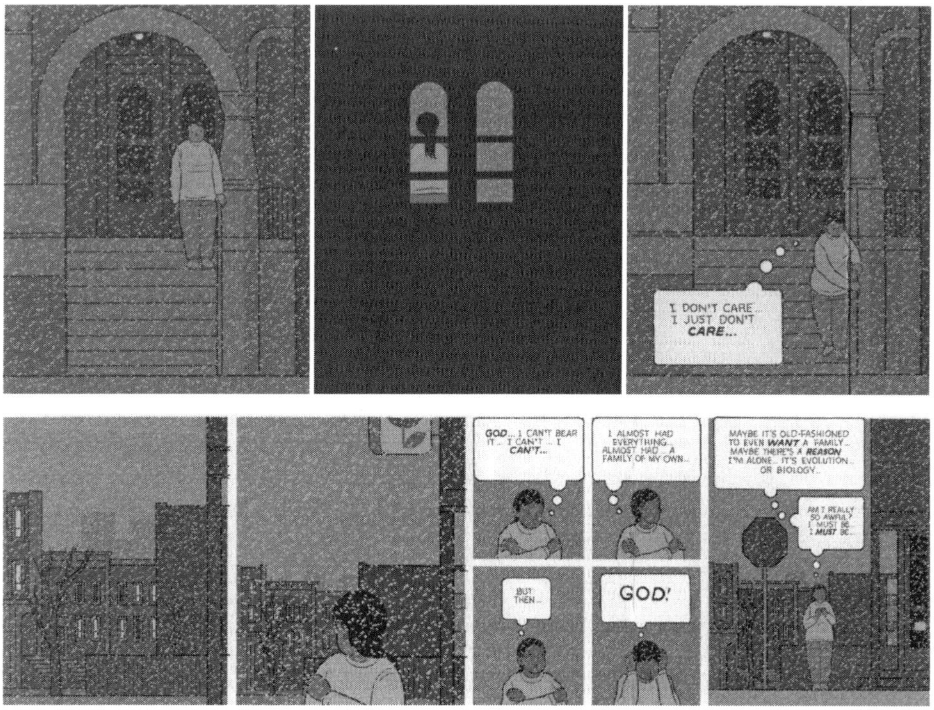

FIGURE 22: Graphic novel excerpt from *Building Stories* by Chris Ware, 'I don't care... I just don't care' panels 1–3 (frontside) and 14–20 (backside), copyright © 2012 by Chris Ware. Used by permission of Pantheon Books, an imprint of the Knopf Doubleday Publishing Group, a division of Penguin Random House LLC. All rights reserved.

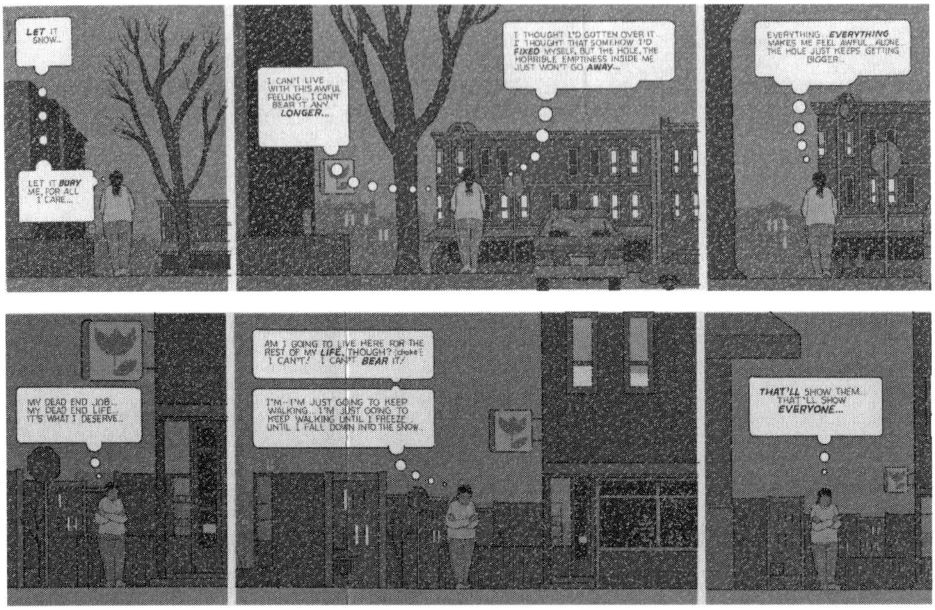

FIGURE 23: Graphic novel excerpt from *Building Stories* by Chris Ware, 'I don't care... I just don't care' panels 4–6 (frontside) and 21–23 (backside), copyright © 2012 by Chris Ware. Used by permission of Pantheon Books, an imprint of the Knopf Doubleday Publishing Group, a division of Penguin Random House LLC. All rights reserved.

in moments of relative solitude we are performing for some unknown observer, inanimate object or are watching ourselves from an outside perspective. While we try to solidify our perspective, we must admit that how we are seen remains out of our control.

Nonhuman Presence and Déjà Vu

Rather than consider a limited or decentralized perspective as a point of human weakness, we could move beyond the boundaries of our human perspective by defining our humanity through our ability to empathize with those unlike us. Recognizing our limits encourages us to look beyond ourselves. Ware gives us ample opportunity to experience this affinity to the nonhuman as perhaps the great insight of the protagonist's depression. Jeet Heer brings this tendency to the forefront in his book review of *Building Stories* calling Ware 'a kind of non-religious animist. For him, animals and physical objects, no less than people, have histories and biographies, and deserve the loving, reviving, liturgical attention that only

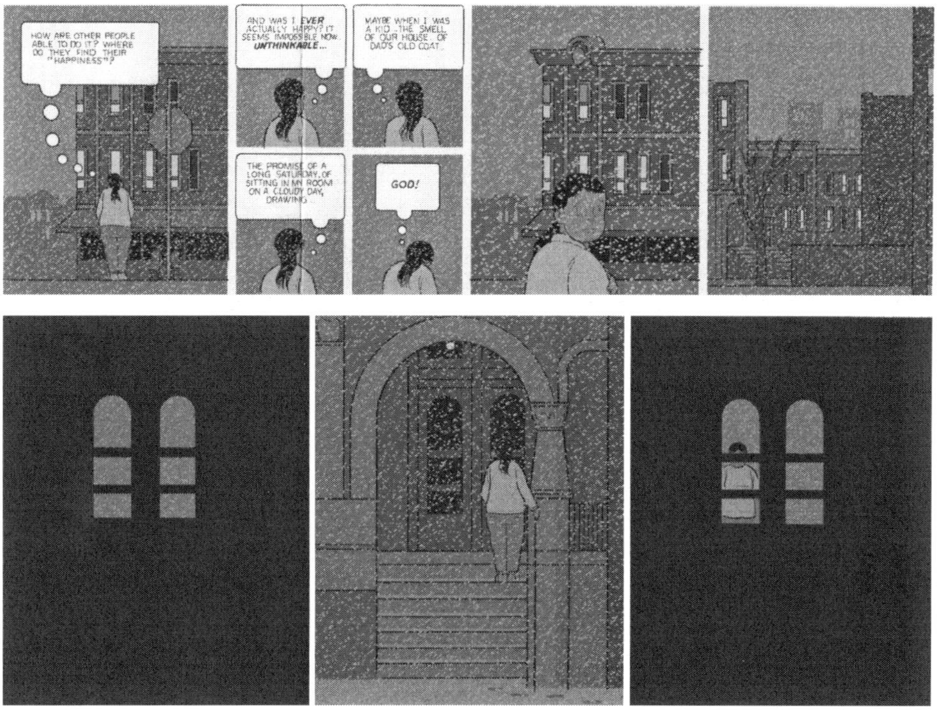

FIGURE 24: Graphic novel excerpt from *Building Stories* by Chris Ware, 'I don't care... I just don't care' panels 7–13 (frontside) and 24–26 (backside), copyright © 2012 by Chris Ware. Used by permission of Pantheon Books, an imprint of the Knopf Doubleday Publishing Group, a division of Penguin Random House LLC. All rights reserved.

art can provide' (Heer 2012: n.pag.). Ware's *Building Stories* extends empathy and sentience to nonhuman entities, a rare feat in narrating urban experiences as most 'dwell in topographical rather than topological space', presenting a seemingly stable environment as a backdrop for human agency (Dittmer 2014: 478). However, in *Building Stories*, the apartment building develops a voice.

To look at a space differently as a networked system of multiple moving parts rather than a background for anthropocentric storytelling broadens the view of space. Because we are more attuned to other perspectives and do not try to unify all experience to our own, we can look into the database of potential narratives without fear of being overcome by the *horror vacui*. Our narratives remain but with a lot more company than we imagined. Ware admits that one of his motives for *Building Stories* was a spatialization process that uprooted temporal organizational models of storytelling, saying,

> I wanted to make a book that had no beginning or end, [...] to try and get at the three-dimensionality of memories and stories – how we're able to tell them starting at this or that point depending on the circumstance, and to take them apart and put them back together.
>
> (Freedman 2015: 337)

To focus on the space rather than the linear progression of time means that we experience all events in that space at once as a catalogue of amassed occurrences whether tragic or mundane (Roeder 2011: 27).

It is not surprising that this inventory is the work of the building, who takes the narrator's position in the *Little Golden Book* piece. The building keeps a meticulous inventory of the many objects that existed or events that occurred in the building, including 74,316 newspapers, 6 suicide notes, 296 birthday parties and 6 moon landings. Ending this accumulation is undesirable because it would mark the building's destruction. In this sense, the inventory serves as the most basic function to avoid complete disappearance. While each of the six suicide notes could have been its own book, here they are just another number. It is both a significant story as a field memory and a statistic as an observer memory. One sees this same effect with repeated exposure to trauma where the ER doctor does not know the name of a patient; she is the third overdose on this shift. The patient's experience is both a tragedy and a statistic, and when seen simultaneously as both, we feel the gape of the *horror vacui* where everything is both brimming with meaning and wholly arbitrary – where toenail clippings are as noteworthy as broken bones.

As the historical record keeper and extensive inventory of potential narratives, the building is frequently referred to in the third-person and personified by an omniscient narrator writing in script font. We discover that 'the building, accidentally catching a glimpse of itself in the glint of the windows across the street, sighed' and 'the building felt it had played a part in defending these young buds from the elements' (Ware 2012: n.pag.). Beyond being endowed with the ability to look, sigh, protect and be self-aware, the building has its own desire to exist without its tenants as a figure rather than the ground. The house's sentience, though, remains decentralized because the house does not have its own booklet, but it interrupts in those of others (Ghosal 2015: 82). On the first and next-to-last page of the *Little Golden Book*, the building speaks through word bubbles, and the exposition in script font moves to the first-person. The building comments on its tenants' lives, saying, '[o]h, the poor thing... I shouldn't make fun of her...' (Ware 2012: n.pag.). In its first-person exposition the building states, 'it may sound heartless, but I can predict with almost 100% certainty that she'll remain unattached for the duration of her time here' (Ware 2012: n.pag.). These moments of hearing directly from the house's voice jolt us into considering that other seemingly inert objects might

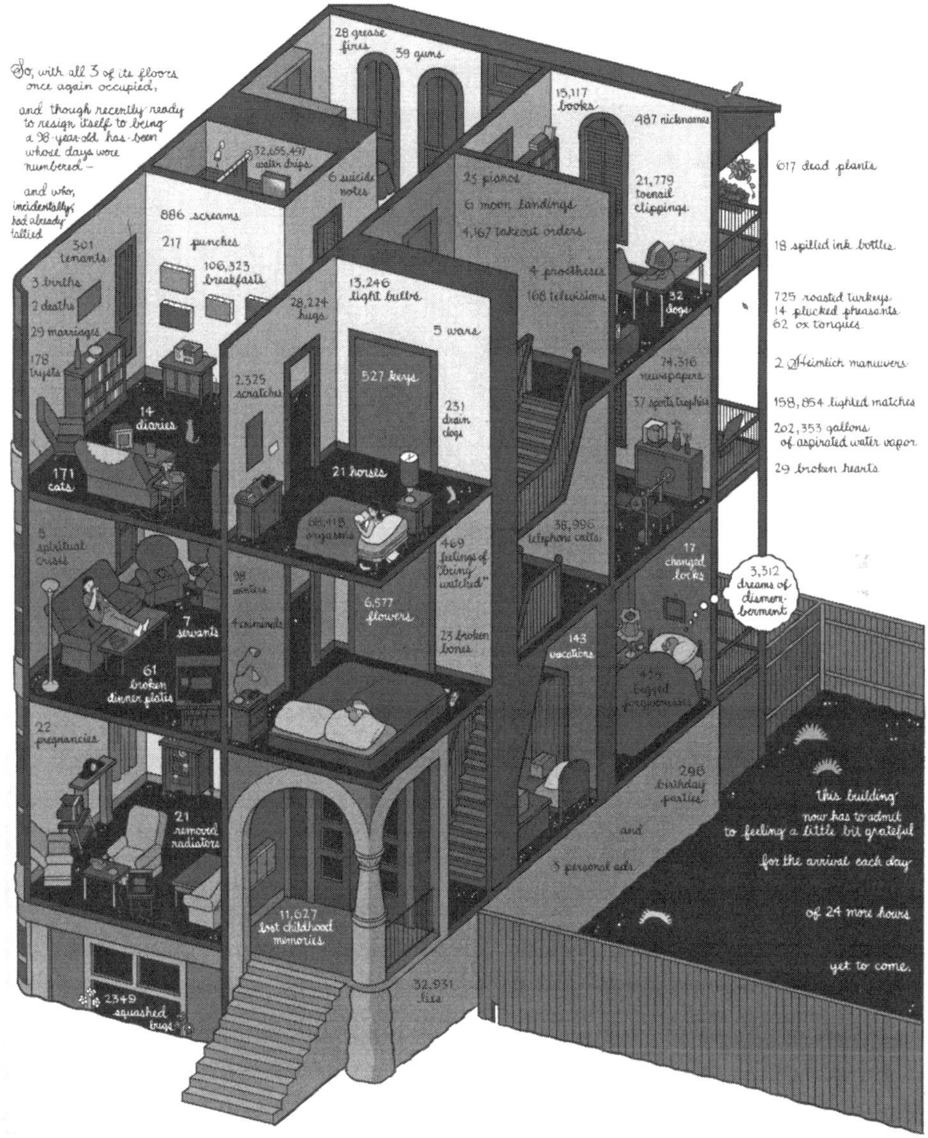

FIGURE 25: Graphic novel excerpt from *Building Stories* by Chris Ware, 'September 23rd, 2000' page 3, copyright © 2012 by Chris Ware. Used by permission of Pantheon Books, an imprint of the Knopf Doubleday Publishing Group, a division of Penguin Random House LLC. All rights reserved.

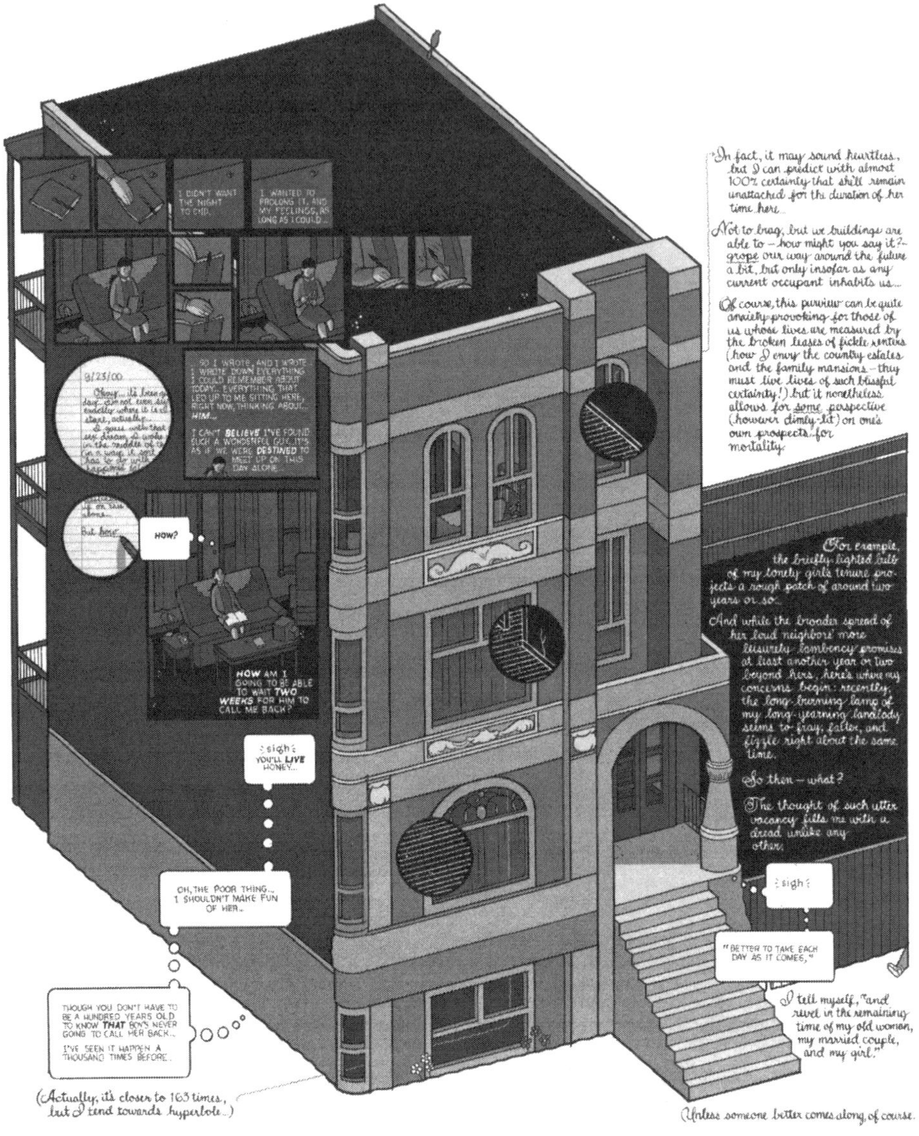

FIGURE 26: Graphic novel excerpt from *Building Stories* by Chris Ware, 'September 23rd, 2000' page 2, copyright © 2012 by Chris Ware. Used by permission of Pantheon Books, an imprint of the Knopf Doubleday Publishing Group, a division of Penguin Random House LLC. All rights reserved.

have biting judgments of our actions and even needs of their own. Not only do we see the characters living in the building, sitting on its stoop, sliding down its stairs, but we also see the building in full without the behaviors of humans coloring the scene. The house as a human dwelling and distinct entity both exist and at times overlap.

The nonhuman sentience registers in the protagonist's experience at her flower shop and at home. She is anxious about trimming stems, convinced that she is causing the flowers pain. She carries this sense of plant sentience home and supposes the building is self-aware, saying, 'sometimes I even imagine the building I live in knows me... though I know that's stupid... [...] and then, of course, I have to wonder: does it even like me?' (Ware 2012: n.pag.). The reader who has read of the building's sentience thirteen pages earlier knows the protagonist is onto the building. Curiously, interrupting her thoughts on the building's sentience is a brief conversation the woman has with her cat, whose needs she acknowledges and then suspends as less pressing than her desire to sit. She is concerned about her environment's sentience and is comfortable talking to her cat as though it were human. Regardless, she still dismisses both the building and the cat.

Beyond nonhuman sentience, Ware introduces several story overlaps, some structural and others seemingly coincidental and inconsequential. The congruities between the human characters' disconnected and depressing lives abound, but they also overlap in the character Branford the Bee, revealing deep connections and dependencies between humans and nonhumans. Despite serving as the comic relief, Branford is perhaps the most direct representation of crushed dreams. His story presents the tragedy of human ignorance of the presence and needs of others chiefly by showing how adept a bee is at considering the workings of his life, species and surroundings. He is not just a bee, given the very human social settings that he faces. As a husband and happy father of two who has escaped the dronish life of repeatedly impregnating the queen, he is cast as a fictional character in the storybook *Branford: The Best Bee in the World* and his existence is documented in the newspaper *The Daily Bee*.[10] There Branford joins the house as the only other being whose thoughts are written in script font, giving the house and bee a hand to write more expressively than humans. Even the bee's diction reaches a more elevated state, surpassing the house that was already more articulate than the humans. The final story in this newspaper is Branford's journal offered as the record of his life and regrets penned while trapped in the basement. Branford writes:

> If I have been placed here to prove – a trial, to confirm my purity – Please, God, show me the way! Is not my anguish evidence of fealty to Thine code? Such thoughts that once crept and frayed the edges of my soul could not even *reach*

> the vast river of tears which now separates my mind from my coil! Please, Lord, give me one more chance!
>
> (Ware 2012: n.pag., original emphasis)

The bee is more than sentient; he is attuned to the workings of his species and the roles that the human and the divine play in his life – seemingly more so than the humans notice their neighborhood bees or observe a deity other than to blaspheme.

We see similar oversights of the human perspective when *déjà vu* moments and collisions in apparent but unclear repetitions foil a global view of Saint-Sulpice. Beyond the obvious frequent repetition of the buses, Perec logs instances whose nature of repetition is unclear. He writes, '[d]emand the real thing, Roquefort Société in its green oval' on page 6 and again on page 7, but is this the same ad on the same bus passing him twice or a repeat of the ad as a separate incidence on a different bus? He has overlooked making such a distinction. The same occurs with people: 'Return (uncertain) of previously seen individuals: a young boy in a navy blue peacoat holding a plastic bag in his hand passes by the café again' (Perec 2010: 12). At other times, he is surer of repetition's presence, saying '[a] little girl goes by wearing a long red hat with a pom-pom (I already saw her yesterday, but yesterday there were two

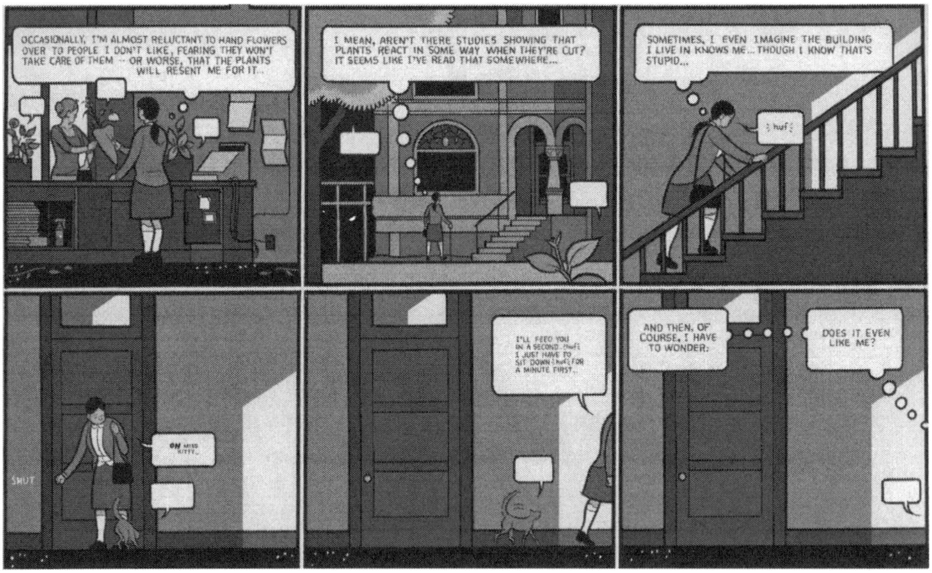

FIGURE 27: Graphic novel excerpt from *Building Stories* by Chris Ware, 'Repulsive to me' page 21, copyright © 2012 by Chris Ware. Used by permission of Pantheon Books, an imprint of the Knopf Doubleday Publishing Group, a division of Penguin Random House LLC. All rights reserved.

of them)' (Perec 2010: 31). These repetitions reveal the potential faults in Perec's observations and raise questions regarding which are direct overlaps and which are separate incidences of a similar nature. We are even led to wonder if it is important that the repeated figure is the same person. These little details on the nature of and relationship to repetitions do less to affirm our understanding of the square's happenings than they do to muddle it. Perec even states outright the limits and doubts of his observations. He writes,

> a crane stands out in the sky (it was there yesterday, but I don't recall making note of it). I couldn't say whether the people I'm seeing are the same ones as yesterday, whether the cars are the same ones as yesterday.
>
> (Perec 2010: 29)

Beyond blurring the distinction between incidences, the repetition tends to simplification. Perec must overlook the potential complexities of passersby's lives to keep pace, so pedestrians and patrons in the square turn into the equivalent of Branford the Bee – just a forgettable thing. Passersby are never more than the objects they wear or carry, as though the objects have more presence. Perec logs: 'Two men with pipes and black satchels / A man with a black satchel and no pipe / A woman in a wool jacket, smiling' (Perec 2010: 12–13). These shorthand identifiers make processing large amounts of data a possibility, but in doing so, they only mark a pure presence where a whole life's story is possible. At times, objects carried or worn stand in completely for humans: 'Capes, turbans, boots, sailor-like caps, short or long scarves, policemen with kepi, furs, suitcases, umbrellas' (Perec 2010: 20). Such scansion is not flippant but instead provides complexity, one more in line with polyhistors enmeshed in the process of amassing perspectives than experts who use perspective to lord over a narrative explanation. The human as unifying narrator slips as nonhuman sentience and its density and pace lay bare the limits of human perspectives. Every entity in that square takes on an absolute presence when we open our eyes to our environment.

Despite knowing that his perspective will never grasp all the mundane events at Saint Sulpice, Perec still must battle his subjectivity, admitting its presence in the inventory process even while actively trying to overcome his limited perspective. By his third entry of the first day, Perec entertains his most prolonged bout of narrative interpretation as a relief to the clipped sentences and fragments that precede and follow.

> Later on, I went to the Tabac Saint-Sulpice. I went up to the second floor, a sad room, rather cold, occupied only by a quintet of bridge players, four of whom were in the middle of playing three clubs. I went back down and installed myself

> at the table I had occupied this morning. I ate a pair of sausages and drank a glass of Bourgueil.
>
> (Perec 2010: 18)

He reminds us of his body, sharing what he eats or drinks and describing his relationship to the space he is in and the people around him. This narrative antidote colors his inventory as hopelessly incomplete and subjective. Following this first-person moment, he gives us another general inventory of his observations but hides it behind his perspective, saying, 'I again saw'. Rather than just listing the item observed, he writes in his subjective presence. To assert himself further he writes his observations in the past tense to tame the immediacy of his environment.

When Perec is more reserved with his presence, he still includes subjective, narratorial thoughts as parentheticals throughout the log, providing the reader a brief reprieve from the deluge of observations. Perec admits the impossibility of creating this inventory with one conscious human mind: '(*Obvious limits to such an undertaking: even when my only goal is just to observe, I don't see what takes place a few meters from me: I don't notice, for example, that cars are parking*)' (Perec 2010: 15, original emphasis). The obvious and mundane are a true challenge to grasp in totality. Despite this early admonition, Perec persists in explicating his thought process. By the end of that first day, he cannot avoid a long parenthetical that rationalizes why he inventories the items he does.

> ([W]hy count the buses? [P]robably because they're recognizable and regular: they cut up time, they punctuate the background noise; ultimately, they're foreseeable The rest seems random, improbable, anarchic; the buses pass by because they have to pass by, but nothing requires a car to back up, or a man to have a bag marked with a big 'M' of Monoprix, or a car to be blue or apple-green, or a customer to order a coffee instead of a beer...)
>
> (Perec 2010: 22–23)

Each of these examples reminds us that despite the relief of his subjectivity, we continually face the reality that his recounting is always overwhelmed by the overflow of information and infiltrated by supposition, estimation or doubt.

Over time his will to narrativize or rationalize his thought process falls away. On the first day, he defined a series of categories that surface from the environment: letters, symbols, numbers, slogans, ground material, but those quickly turn into generalities that he marks with 'inventory remains to be made' (Perec 2010: 6).

By the third day, he no longer narrativizes the opening scene. His last day's logs have little reflection or commentary and close on an objective note:

> The 63
> It is five to two
> The pigeons are on the plaza. They all fly off at the same time.
> Four children. A dog. A little ray of sun. The 96. It is two o'clock.
>
> (Perec 2010: 47)

Regardless of how much attention he pays or the comprehensiveness of his categories, the rhythm of the space and all its goings-on will overpower ordering mechanisms. In a way, Perec admits defeat, but all is not lost. Though comprehension and unity are apparently impossible, the narrative or self-reflective moments amidst the overwhelming mass create an ideal moment for a non-universalizing, baroque reason.

> What difference is there between a driver who parks on the first go and another ('90') who only manages to do so after several minutes of laborious efforts? This provokes attention, irony, the participation of an audience: to see not just the rips, but the fabric (but how to see the fabric if it is only the rips that make it visible: no one ever sees buses pass by unless they're waiting for one, or unless they're waiting for someone to come off of one, or unless the Paris City Transport Authority pays them a salary to count them...)
>
> (Perec 2010: 33–34)

In those brief narrative moments, we are forced to admit our limited perception and are made aware of the larger fabric of space that we inhabit. We see the *horror vacui* is not empty, but teeming with perspectives beyond our own.

Access Denied and the Pleasure of Irresolution

When immersed in one's vantage point but attuned to one's environment, there is room for the potential discoveries and unexpected connections privileged by the *wunderkammer*. Returning to the *wunderkammer* means capturing the polyhistor who encourages broad thinking. Rather than see one passerby's whole life, we see many points that hint at how much remains unexplored and inaccessible. Perec's *An Attempt at Exhausting a Place in Paris* quickly achieves this sense of potential discovery via the questions he poses in his log. His first question on the second page reads: '– Lettuce (curly endive?) partially emerging from a shopping bag' (Perec 2010: 6) marks the place of specificity in the log and raises reader awareness at how many other elements included in the log lack the specificity he tries to achieve with lettuce. He previously listed trees and stone, but what kinds of trees? What kinds of stone? Now each entry raises questions.

Beyond questions that clarify the specifics of an object, others expose elements at play in the square but not limited to that square. Perec asks, '[a] postal delivery tricycle, a postal van (is it time for the mailboxes to be emptied?)' (Perec 2010: 20), reminding us that this mailbox is connected to a system of mailboxes, delivery routes and sorting machines. Related commentary draws on knowledge or data not observable in the square itself, like '[a] man goes by, eating a cake (the reputation of the neighborhood confectioners is not to be doubted)' (Perec 2010: 37). He even begins to suppose the motives and interests of the people he sees passing by, asking questions like '(does a man who goes round Paris on a Friday want to do so again on a Saturday?)' (Perec 2010: 30) and '[p]eople are entering the church (to visit it? Is it time for mass?)' (Perec 2010: 31). By the end of the second day, he even asks a borderline hypothetical question aimed at the reader of the log: 'Also: why are two nuns more interesting than two other passersby?' (Perec 2010: 34). As he projects forward in time imagining his reader, he begins to see his log as part of the space and so a legitimate object to log. Not only do these questions expand the reach of this particular space, but they do so by showing that there is always more seen than recorded and still always more to see.

Furthermore, seeing is done through the filter of one's experience, leaving blind spots and questions at each turn. Perec wants to navigate what belongs in the log and what is beyond the purpose of the log by frequently easing questions and personal reflections into parentheticals as though they are categorically different from the items or events that should be listed objectively. One parenthetical joke is about his profession: '([P]erhaps I have only today discovered my true calling: ticket collector for the Paris City Transport Authority)' (Perec 2010: 26). Other questions bring us to Perec's consciousness and the motives and biases behind his logging. He asks of himself, 'why count the buses?' (Perec 2010: 22), pointing to how his thought process is now entangled with his environment. He even considers the effects of what he has consumed and how that might change how he sees the square, asking, 'I'm drinking a Vittel water, whereas yesterday I was drinking a coffee (how does that transform the square?)' (Perec 2010: 30). In a way, he tries to keep himself out of the log even when he knows that he cannot separate himself from that log. How he sees the square is intimately a part of what he logs about that square and trying to separate them quickly fails. While his last day of logging is much briefer and the questions and parentheticals nearly disappear, the damage is already done. The reader now sees how little is captured and misses hearing about the holes in the observation.

Ware's protagonist also participates in this self-reflection and inquiry that ultimately reveals the limitations of one's perspective. Printed on what is meant to be an inside view of the protagonist's facial dermis is a red oval with opened eye holes looking at a pixelated image of the ex-boyfriend's face. On the other side of the bifold paper is an image of her face with eyes closed. After reconnecting with her high school boyfriend, the protagonist admits:

> The weirdest thing, though, was that no matter how hard I tried, he looked exactly the same to me as he always had...in other words, I couldn't look at any picture of him and not see a seventeen-year-old... it was like there was some kind of scrim in my mind that dropped down in front of my eyes and prevented me from seeing things as they really were.
>
> (Ware 2012: n.pag., original emphasis)

The protagonist's revelation is more than an admission of the limits and trickery of her perception. The paper is her layer of skin, and its feigned transparency deviates from the more typical use of page space in comics to sequence images over time (Dittmer 2014: 494). Rather than fit a story into lines, the story bleeds through the pages.[11] The protagonist's vision is faulty. The reader is confronted with the opacity of a page, which feigns transparency but shows us how much we cannot access or know.

Readers face this lack of access in Ware's treatment of screenic spaces represented in the cartoon drawings. After the protagonist moves from her third-floor apartment, marries and has a daughter, we see her text message interface or an image of an email on her laptop. Even when we do not see the contents of the screen, we frequently see the protagonist and her husband engrossed in their laptops or tablets. There is another layer of textual and visual material on screens accessible to the characters and only hinted at to the reader. Not only are the characters privy to textual layers readers cannot access, but they are also aware that they could be a part of any number of framed environments. The protagonist wonders just how often she appears in the background of some stranger's snapshot, framed and displayed in their homes. This time the reader has access to these images that the protagonist only imagines. Ware even projects layers of connections into the future in the second-floor tenant's booklet with a subway platform scene that comes to pass 150 years later. A student reads a hologram about the second-floor tenants missing each other on that very platform when the husband arrives just as the train leaves the station with his wife on board. It is as though every story is grafted onto its origin point, calling one to wonder about the lost opportunities and histories of one's immediate surroundings. *Building Stories*, like the rest of the world, becomes a body of pulsating networks to explore. The pleasure of reading comes from accumulating or collecting observations that can be linked or grouped in nonlinear even serendipitous ways.[12]

Readers as navel gazers, like bowerbirds, are transfixed by what sparkles and collect those radiant objects. Reading this way creates its own little cognitive collection of scenes that resonate across texts and through rereadings. Divested from searching for meaning or unity, these navel-gazing readers read for pleasure without a pointed purpose. While these little pleasures seem innocent, accumulating too many intriguing links builds up a narrative that is eventually uncomfortable with the mass of grocery goods that opened this book. Having accumulated and collected to the point of saturation, we fall back to our narrative impulse, of choosing and arranging how we perform ourselves as monads containing all possibilities filtered by one subjective perspective, as *matryoshka* dolls of representation in representation aware of our own artifice, as part of illusory worlds indistinguishable from what we call reality, as our own undoing ready to dismantle the narratives we live by, as polyhistors primed to see from many perspectives. Our performances always teeter back and forth on the dual foci of the baroque ellipse of *vorhanden* and *zuhanden*, function and form, material and content, medium and literary text. It was the digital that disrupted literatures settled into the print

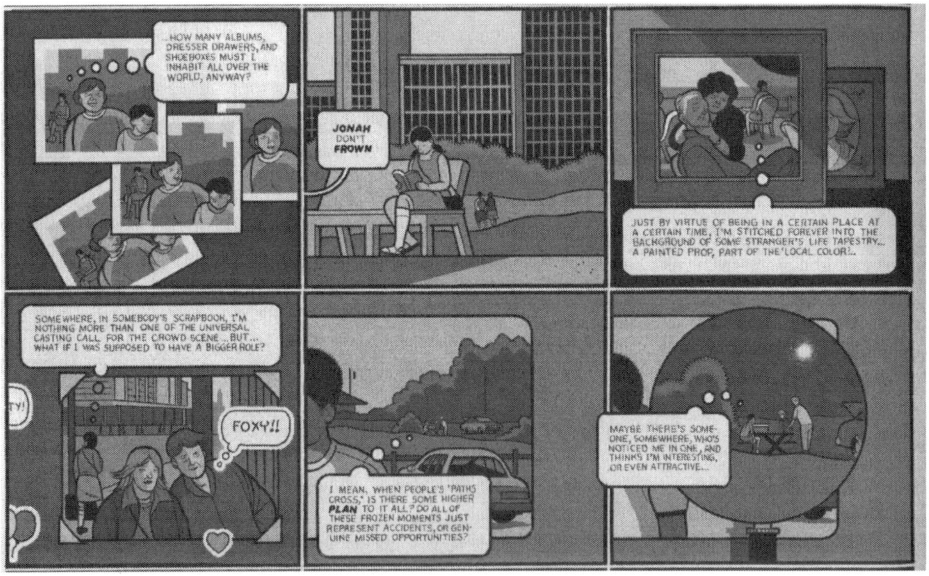

FIGURE 28: Graphic novel excerpt from *Building Stories* by Chris Ware, 'Repulsive to me' page 29, copyright © 2012 by Chris Ware. Used by permission of Pantheon Books, an imprint of the Knopf Doubleday Publishing Group, a division of Penguin Random House LLC. All rights reserved.

medium, and it is through baroque practices and their aptitude for embracing such wobblings that we might understand the technotext's methods and placement in a digital mediascape.

NOTES

1. For David Castillo, the *horror vacui* is a 'fundamental feeling of attraction/revulsion concerning the idea of absence' that defines the modern condition as one 'triggered by a pervasive sense of loss of meaning' and a 'paradoxical longing for the Absolute' (Castillo 2005: 87–88). The *horror vacui* not only frightens readers but challenges them to think about 'the arbitrariness of inherited forms of knowledge, social values and structures.' (Castillo 2005: 100).
2. Thus far in the cyclical journey of this book, we have gone up and down the stairs of the baroque house, building representational practices as we ascend and undermining those practices as we descend. While the monad feigns individualism by caching foundational similarities present on the first floor and the *trompe l'oeil* obscures the reality of representational practice, the *mise en abyme* recognizes the presence of representation, and the minor strategy politicizes representation's presence.
3. The concept for this book began six years ago with a conference paper on the entangled relationship between humans and computers as analogous to Roger Caillois's pseudoscientific essays on anthropomorphism and camouflage. Of course, some of the audience's responses focused on how these ideas are suicidal or life-denying and that seeing agency in the machine takes agency from the human. The same disconnect occurred when I assigned René Crevel's *My Body and I* to an undergraduate class. The suicidal author and his suicidal autobiographical narrator place little value in his life but quite a bit into one passing conversation at a train station café and in a newspaper photograph of a murderess. While most of the class was content to dismiss him, saying they could not read anything so depressing, students who survived difficult bouts of depression understood that even in his suicide, he was not life-denying but rather overrun with life everywhere. A less critical route would call for readers to drop Caillois and Crevel and double down into self-affirming narratives.
4. Of course, Ed Folsom idealizes a kind of pure database without a user interface or file directory where each entry can exist without some interpretation. He also seems to assume our paper heritage is near wholly aligned with narrative despite the categorical system an archival object exists within, not to mention its material state born of its historical context.
5. Differences between media make it impossible to judge a digital literary text by print literature's standards or think of the digital as an enhanced page. Of course, such analogies can and have been frequently drawn such as the codex page to a digital file's page, a webpage to a scroll, or a hyperlink to a footnote. However, such comparisons ask us to look at a medium through the expectations of another, which may prejudice or limit the use of the new medium.

6. Michel Foucault has considered museums, libraries, ships and mirrors as heterotopic spaces. Of mirrors, he writes:

> In the mirror, I see myself there where I am not, in an unreal, virtual space that opens up behind the surface; I am over there, there where I am not, a sort of shadow that gives my own visibility to myself, that enables me to see myself there where I am absent: such is the utopia of the mirror. But it is also a heterotopia in so far as the mirror does exist in reality, where it exerts a sort of counteraction on the position that I occupy.
>
> (Foucault 1986: 24)

7. Despite the pejorative treatment of navel-gazing as narcissistic introspection that discounts one's surroundings, navel myths hold an important place in several religious traditions. Jerusalem and Delphi are both shrines that claim to be earth's navel, and thus its connection to the heavens and the underworld (Terrien 1970: 317, 320). Samuel Terrien examines navel myths and how its heterogenous motifs including snake cults, solar worship, and male prostitution underly 'the ambivalent character of the Zion theology' (Terrien 1970: 332). After the 587 BC destruction of Jerusalem, Ezekiel refers to Jerusalem as the navel of the earth such that it was 'the belief in the myth of Zion as the cosmic umbilic – the eternal bond between heaven and earth – which conferred a shape to the eschatological hope of nascent Judaism' (Terrien 1970: 333–34). The navel is also considered as a symbol for the origin of creation and the 'center of the world' (Becker 2000: 210) as well as the feminine sexual (Online Etymology Dictionary 2019: n.pag.) and the 'universal maternal connection' (Dansky 2015: 26). In more modern terms, Sigmund Freud used the navel to signify uninterpretable dreams that 'contained an inextricable knot' (Dansky 2015: 26).
8. The larger conceit of the story began as braided stories of the four tenants living on the three floors of the building. Ware realized that privileging an imbalance toward the third-floor tenant was more authentic to how humans experience the world via one consciousness (Kelly 2013: n.pag.).
9. Ware wanted to give 'the reader the same feeling of excitement that I get from artwork like Joseph Cornell's boxes and boxes of ephemeral things or objects or papers. There's something about that that I find really thrilling' (cited in Freedman 2015: 340).
10. *The Daily Bee* is even visually cited in the booklet *Branford: The Best Bee in the World*, itself a chapter book meant to entertain children, an interpretation confirmed in the DISCONNECT booklet where on two occasions the protagonist's daughter mentions the character Branford the Bee. The protagonist reads Chapter 4 of *Branford: The Best Bee in the World* to her daughter and the daughter draws a garden for Branford. The book *Branford: The Best Bee in the World* solidifies his status as a fictional character who has a real effect on the daughter's world. However, on the game board and in *The Daily Bee*,

Ware grafts the bee into the human characters' reality – pollinating their flowers, trapped in their basement, drinking their soda – while remaining beyond the purview of humans.

11. The same visual conceit appears in the DISCONNECT booklet centerfold where we see in the gutter the backside of a cheap Halloween princess mask on a page where the protagonist's mother reveals how her husband had an affair in the 1970s. On the reverse side appears the blonde, made-up princess mask's face amidst scenes of the protagonist hiding her marital frustrations. She hides her anger from her husband and her mother, though her mother suspects that she is upset and can see through her mask.
12. I recall feeling satisfied in finding one short description of a cold car trip in the landlady's story and the unnamed protagonist's. Even searching back through the booklets to verify that the story was replicated across storylines made for its own little scavenger hunt.

Coda

I had not planned on writing a conclusion, because it would suggest that a final destination exists. Recursion functions as an implicit assumption behind many of my points: that baroque methods and aesthetic practices rise as crises accumulate and diminish as they usher in new paradigms; that the technotext opens a continuous, dialogic dynamic between material form and linguistic content, between textuality and hermeneutics. I could look back at this book and relay my concern that despite its goals, I hewed too closely to hermeneutic models of literary analysis out of habit and lack of experience in other methods. I could apologize to my readers for thinking that writing this book in a baroque fashion was a worthwhile endeavor. Instead, I will generalize some personal revelations garnered from writing this book.

While writing and revising, I thought more and more of how the cyclical structure without resolution or escape can seem to disempower, and even the thought that I cannot escape my perspective appears to invite apathy and inaction. While editing the book, I was attending a workshop on stylometry in R. On the first day, the instructors displayed the equations for John Burrow's Delta used in author attribution cases. I took one look at it and thought that if I were to embark on this path, I would need to understand multivariable statistics. Though I am always one focus in a baroque ellipse, the other focus could be very far and the arch of my ellipse very shallow but larger for it. So we will all have to reach. Literary studies borrow statistical methods to understand language and authorship as the sciences borrow analogy from moral philosophy. Here are the philologists, polyhistors, illusionists, satirists and monadic harmonies whose curiosity and speculation can chart paths for a future literature imagined in technotextual terms.

Of course, this means communicating with others whose expertise is so focused and rooted in an area of which we may know very little. But this is scaling knowledge and seeing the first floor of the baroque house for the representational processes and disciplinary methodologies it contains. That means we may have to use more metaphors, allegories and analogies in order to reach one another. It means we might feel small in the mirrorish or nearly vanish in illusion. It could mean that our systems of representation implode from the force of a minor criticism or that we may become manic but at least curious about navel details. But a technotextually composed piece of literature knows that these moves are part of the process (*An Attempt at Exhausting a Place in Paris*). The technotext accounts for how it appears in the world and writes the reader into the piece (*Choice of Robots*). It gives the inscription medium a role in meaning-making (*Tree of Codes*). It understands its mode and translates into others (*The Wandering Veil*). It oscillates between figure and ground (*88 Constellations for Wittgenstein*) or between subject and object (*Building Stories*). The ends do not justify the means not because that invites the immoral but because ends do not come. The technotext is how literature will persist rather than petrify as we transition to new media, new models of reading, new understandings of authorship and subjectivity.

So where do we go from this infinite loop? Go through the book again to crowd the margins with your own analogies, comparisons, connections, commentaries or asides. Chart out many potential second foci and draw elongated ellipses that account for not just the meaningful interpretations made through close reading and hermeneutic methods, but also for the material and social contexts that might be better understood from the perspectives of other disciplines, maybe mathematics, maybe sociology, maybe psychiatry and neuroscience.[1] We will incorporate while growing outward if we see the network and process behind each text, each monad, each perspective. There are no loop counters that stop the relay between reality and representation, that solidify the categories we use to describe and understand our objects of study or that reach settling conclusions. Instead, we alter the shape of the loop with each pass, with each new focus we pair with and with every new harmony struck.

NOTE

1. Days before submitting final revisions of this book, I listened to NPR's *Hidden Brain*, ironically as a break from editing. The episode was 'One Head, Two Brains: How the Brain's Hemispheres Shape the World We See' and it discussed Iain McGilchrist's book *The Master and His Emissary*. He spoke of how the differences between the right and left hemisphere of the brain are not based on *what* they do but *how* they do what they do. In short, the left brain processes the world through narrow details and is driven by short-term goals while the right understands the broader picture of dynamic flows and implicit meaning. Had we only the left brain, McGilchrist says our reality would be one of 'predictability, organizability, anonymity, categorization, loss of the unique and an ability to break things down into parts but not really see what the whole is like' (*Hidden Brain* 2019). We would need total control and black-and-white choices because we would be paranoid without the right brain's broader picture view of the world. Ultimately, while we need the left hemisphere, it is the

emissary who lacks the more expansive view of the master: the right hemisphere. That glorious right brain grasps melody and harmony, reads emotional expressions, empathizes with others, determines intent, accounts for broad cultural patterns, understands metaphor and analogy, and can laugh at a joke.

McGilchrist claims our society venerates the detailed, analytical, and rational left hemisphere method of thinking much to our detriment. This conclusion spurred on his choice to include cultural topics in a book on neuroscience. So much of what he said reminded me of what I have said here with 'enlightened reason' and 'baroque reason' in the place of 'left' and 'right'. When he said he had been a scholar of literature before becoming a psychiatrist, my ears perked up in anticipation. Why did he leave? Well, because he felt analytical criticism killed poetry by turning poems into 'explicit, general and entirely abstract entities', when understanding a poem is to grasp its presence as an 'implicit, unique, embodied creature' (*Hidden Brain* 2019). He wrote *Against Criticism* and left literary study. I have mentally placed both of his books at the top of my reading pile and eagerly await the pleasure of seeing how we have drawn similar ellipses with different foci.

References

Aarseth, Espen (1997), *Cybertext: Perspectives in Ergodic Literature*, Baltimore: Johns Hopkins University Press.

Abbott, Kate (2014), 'Mass MoCA will hold and evening of poetry to honor Agha Shahid Ali', *Berkshire Eagle*, 25 April, http://www.berkshireeagle.com/stories/mass-moca-will-hold-an-evening-of-poetry-to-honor-agha-shahid-ali,375986. Accessed 6 June 2017.

Ades, Dawn (2000), 'Dalí's optical illusions', in D. Ades (ed.), *Dalí's Optical Illusions*, Hartford: Wadsworth Atheneum Museum of Art, pp. 10–29.

Ali, Agha Shahid (1996), 'A Muslim snobbery in America: May I?', *Green Mountain Review*, 9:2–10:1, pp. 86–96.

Arellano, Jéronimo (2015), *Magical Realism and the History of the Emotions in Latin America*, Lewisburg: Bucknell University Press.

Bailey, Gauvin Alexander (2012), *Baroque & Rococo*, London: Phaidon.

Bal, Mieke (1990), 'De-disciplining the eye', *Critical Inquiry*, 16:3, pp. 506–31.

——— (1991), *Remembering Rembrandt: Beyond the Word-Image Opposition*, Cambridge: Cambridge University Press.

——— (1994), 'Telling objects: A narrative perspective on collecting', in J. Fraser and R. Cardinal (eds), *The Cultures of Collecting*, Cambridge: Harvard University Press, pp. 97–115.

——— (1999), *Quoting Caravaggio: Contemporary Art, Preposterous History*, Chicago: University of Chicago Press.

Ballard, Thea (2013), 'Painting with tulle: A high-tech veil of illusion', *Modern Painters*, 25:11, p. 40.

Barber, John (2010), 'Bök vs. bug', *The Globe Review*, 28 April, https://www.theglobeandmail.com/arts/books-and-media/bok-vs-bug/article4189363/. Accessed 27 June 2017.

Baudrillard, Jean (1994), 'The system of collecting', in J. Fraser and R. Cardinal (eds), *The Cultures of Collecting*, Cambridge: Harvard University Press, pp. 7–24.

Bazin, Germain (1968), 'Trompe l'oeil', *The Baroque: Principles, Styles, Modes, Themes*, London: Thames and Hudson, pp. 238–84.

Becker, Udo (2000), 'Navel', *The Continuum Encyclopedia of Symbols*, New York: Continuum, p. 210.

Benjamin, Lauren (2011), 'The lost cause of poetry: Resistance and re-creation in Bruno Schulz's "Traktat O Manekinach"', *New Zealand Slavonic Journal*, 45:1, pp. 45–55.

Benjamin, Walter ([1963] 1998), *The Origin of German Tragic Drama*, London: Verso.

Bennett, Jane (2010), *Vibrant Matter: A Political Ecology of Things*, Durham: Duke University Press.

Berry, David M. (2011), 'The computational turn: Thinking about the digital humanities', *Culture Machine*, 12, pp. 1–22.

Birke, Dorothee and Christ, Birte (2013), 'Paratext and digitized narrative: Mapping the field', *NARRATIVE*, 21:1, pp. 65–87.

Blom, Philipp (2003), *To Have and to Hold: An Intimate History of Collectors and Collecting*, Woodstock: The Overlook Press.

Blouin Artinfo (2014), 'Izhar Patkin narrates "The Wandering Veil" at MASS MoCA', YouTube, https://www.youtube.com/watch?v=5pNXvS_W8m8. Accessed 25 June 2017.

Bogost, Ian (2012), *Alien Phenomenology or What It's Like to Be a Thing*, Minneapolis: University of Minnesota Press.

Bök, Christian (2015), *The Xenotext Book 1*, Toronto: Coach House Books.

Bolter, Jay David and Grusin, Richard (1999), *Remediation: Understanding New Media*, Cambridge: MIT Press.

Borsuk, Amaranth and Bouse, Brad (2012), *Between Page and Screen*, New York: Siglio.

Boucher, Bruce (1998), 'The bel composto', in B. Boucher, *Italian Baroque Sculpture*, London: Thames and Hudson, pp. 134–51.

Bromwich, Jonah (2014), 'Make art, not ads', *New York Times*, 26 September, https://www.nytimes.com/2014/09/28/nyregion/an-app-that-replaces-ads-with-art.html?_r=0. Accessed 12 July 2017.

Bruno, Giuliana (2014), 'The surface tension of media: Texture, canvas, screen', in *Surface: Matters of Aesthetics, Materiality, and Media*, Chicago: University of Chicago Press, pp. 73–105.

Buci-Glucksmann, Christine (1994), *Baroque Reason: The Aesthetics of Modernity*, London: Sage Publications.

Burke, Peter (2009), 'The crisis in the arts of the seventeenth century: A crisis of representation', *The Journal of Interdisciplinary History*, 40:2, pp. 239–61.

Calabrese, Omar (1992), *Neo-Baroque: A Sign of the Times*, Princeton: Princeton University Press.

Calé, Luisa (2011), 'Gray's Ode and Walpole's China tub: The order of the book and the paper lives of an object', *Eighteenth-Century Studies*, 45:1, pp. 105–25.

Caillois, Roger (1964), *The Mask of Medusa* (trans. G. Ordish), New York: Clarkson N. Potter.

Carlson, Elizabeth (2011), 'Reflections to projections: The mirror as a proto-cinematic technology', *Early Popular Visual Culture*, 9:1, pp. 15–35.

Castillo, David R. (2005), 'Horror (vacui): The baroque condition', in N. Spadaccini and L. Martín-Estudillo (eds), *Hispanic Baroques: Reading Cultures in Context*, Nashville: Vanderbilt University Press, pp. 87–104.

Catlin, Jon (2015), 'The art of erasure: On *Tree of Codes*', *The Midway Review*, 10:3, pp. 25–36.

Cayley, John (2004), *Translation*, Electronic Literature Collection Volume 1, http://collection.eliterature.org/1/works/cayley__translation.html. Accessed 12 March 2016.

Celorio, Gonzalo (2010), 'From the baroque to the neobaroque', in L. P. Zamora and M. Kaup (eds), *Baroque New Worlds: Representation, Transculturation, Counterconquest*, Durham: Duke University Press, pp. 487–507.

Claes, Koenraad (2010), 'Supplements and paratext: The rhetoric of space', *Victorian Periodicals Review*, 43:2, pp. 196–210.

Clark, David (2008), *88 Constellations for Wittgenstein*, 88constellations.net. Accessed 14 March 2017.

——— (2015), 'Pictures in the stars: *88 Constellations for Wittgenstein* and the online "biography"', *Biography*, 38:2, pp. 290–96.

Chartier, Roger (2004), 'Languages, books, and reading from the printed word to the digital text', *Critical Inquiry*, 31:4, pp. 133–52.

Chartier, Roger and Elton, Maurice (2005), 'Crossing borders in early modern Europe: Sociology of texts and literature', *Book History*, 8, pp. 37–50.

Conti, Flavio (1978), *How to Recognize Baroque Art* (trans. P. Waley), St. Louis: Macdonald Educational.

Coté, Mark (2010), 'Technics and the human sensorium: Rethinking media theory through the body', *Theory & Event*, 13:4, muse.jhu.edu/article/407142. Accessed 2 March 2012.

Crevel, René ([1974] 2005), *My Body and I* (trans. R. Bononno), Brooklyn: Archipelago Books.

Danius, Sara (2003), *The Sense of Modernism: Technology, Perception, and Aesthetics*, Ithaca: Cornell University Press.

Dansky, Steven F. (2015), 'Contemplating the navel', *The Gay & Lesbian Review*, 22.5, pp. 26–29.

Darley, Andrew (2000), *Visual Digital Culture: Surface Play and Spectacle in New Media Genres*, London: Routledge.

Darnton, Robert (1982), 'What is the history of books?', *Daedalus*, 111:3, pp. 65–83.

Davis, Anthony A. (2013), 'Creating the poetry bug', *Maclean's*, 11 January, http://www.macleans.ca/culture/books/creating-the-poetry-bug/. Accessed 14 May 2017.

Day, Gail (1999), 'Allegory: Between deconstruction and dialectics', *Oxford Art Journal*, 22:1, pp. 105–18.

Deleuze, Gilles (1992), *The Fold: Leibniz and Baroque*, Minneapolis: University of Minnesota Press.

Deleuze, Gilles and Guattari, Félix (1986), *Kafka: Toward a Minor Literature* (trans. D. Polan), Minneapolis: University of Minnesota Press.

Derrida, Jacques (1978), *The Truth in Painting* (trans. G. Bennington and I. McLeod), Chicago: University of Chicago Press.

——— (1979), 'The parergon', *October*, 9, pp. 3–41.

Diego, Estrella de (2003), 'Representing representation: Reading *Las Meninas*, again', in S. L. Stratton-Pruitt (ed.), *Velázquez's Las Meninas*, Cambridge: Cambridge University Press, pp. 150–69.

Dittmer, Jason (2014), 'Narrating urban assemblages – Chris Ware and *Building Stories*', *Social & Cultural Geography*, 15:5, pp. 477–503.

Domingues, Diana (2004), 'Day-dreaming states in interfaced environments: Telematic rituals in "Ouroboros"', *Leonardo*, 37:4, pp. 308–14.

Dormehl, Luke (2014), 'Free app swaps New York subway ads for street art', *Cult of Mac*, 30 September, http://www.cultofmac.com/298127/ad-turns-new-york-subway-street-art-wonderful/. Accessed 12 July 2017.

Duchamp, Marcel (1973), *The Writings of Marcel Duchamp*, M. Sanouillet and E. Peterson (eds), New York: Da Capo Press.

Duhigg, Charles (2018), 'The case against Google', *New York Times*, 20 February, https://www.nytimes.com/2018/02/20/magazine/the-case-against-google.html. Accessed 13 May 2018.

Edelstein, David (2012), 'Tolstoy: Keira Knightley and Joe Wright show their work in the overstylized Anna Karenina', *New York*, 11 November, http://nymag.com/movies/reviews/edelstein-anna-karenina-2012-11/. Accessed 8 July 2017.

Egginton, William (2005), 'Of baroque holes and baroque folds', in N. Spadaccini and L. Martín-Estudillo (eds), *Hispanic Baroques: Reading Cultures in Context*, Nashville: Vanderbilt University Press, pp. 55–71.

——— (2007), 'The corporal image and the new world baroque', *South Atlantic Quarterly*, 106:1, pp. 107–27.

——— (2010), *The Theater of Truth: The Ideology of (Neo)Baroque Aesthetics*, Stanford: Stanford University Press.

Elkins, James (1996), *The Object Stares Back: On the Nature of Seeing*, New York: Simon & Schuster.

Elliott, Paul (2010), 'The eye, the brain, the screen: What neuroscience can teach film theory', *Excursions*, 1:1, pp. 1–16.

ELMCIP (2009), 'Exquisite_code', https://elmcip.net/node/941. Accessed 4 June 2017.

Faber, Michel (2010), '*Tree of Codes* by Jonathan Safran Foer – review', *The Guardian*, 17 December, https://www.theguardian.com/books/2010/dec/18/tree-codes-safran-foer-review. Accessed 15 July 2017.

Fletcher, Jerome (2011), '*ha perdut la veu*: Some reflections on the composition of e-literature as a minor literature', *Journal of Writing in Creative Practice*, 4:1, pp. 53–63.

Foer, Jonathan Safran (2010), *Tree of Codes*, London: Visual Editions.

——— (2012), interviewed by Jacques Testard, *The White Review*, May, http://www.thewhitereview.org/interviews/interview-with-jonathan-safran-foer/. Accessed 7 June 2017.

Folsom, Ed (2007), 'Database as genre: The epic transformation of archives', *Modern Language Association*, 122:5, pp. 1571–79.

Foucault, Michel and Miskowiec, Jay (1986), 'Of other spaces', *Diacritics*, 16:1, pp. 22– 27.

Freedman, Ariela (2015), 'Chris Ware's epiphanic comics', *Partial Answers: Journal of Literature and the History of Ideas*, 13:2, pp. 337–58.

Funkhouser, Chris T. (2012), *New Directions in Digital Poetry*, London: Bloomsbury Academic.

Gabriele, John P. (2005), 'Narrative prisms and prisons: Mirror effects and *Mise-en-Abyme* in *Don Quijote*', *Symposium*, 59:1, pp. 31–42.

Gal, Ofer and Chen-Morris, Raz (2010), 'Baroque optics and the disappearance of the observer: From Kepler's optics to Descartes' doubt', *Journal of the History of Ideas*, 71:2, pp. 191–217.

Galloway, Alexander (2012), *The Interface Effect*, Cambridge: Polity Press.

Galperina, Marina (2014), 'Augmented reality app turns subway ads into art', *Animal New York*, 12 September, http://animalnewyork.com/2014/no-ad-subway/. Accessed 12 July 2017.

Ghosal, Torsa (2015), 'Books with bodies: Narrative progression in Chris Ware's *Building Stories*', *Storyworlds*, 7:1, pp. 75–99.

Glazier, Loss Pequeño (2008), *Digital Poetics: The Making of E-Poetries*, Tuscaloosa: University of Alabama Press.

Gold, Kevin (2015), *Choice of Robots*, Albany: Choice of Games LLC.

Goldsmith, Kenneth (2011), *Uncreative Writing*, New York: Columbia University Press.

Gombrich, Ernst H. (1956), *Art and Illusion: A Study in the Psychology of Pictorial Representation*, Princeton: Princeton University Press.

Google (n.d.), 'How search organizes information', https://www.google.com/search/howsearchworks/crawling-indexing/. Accessed 13 May 2018.

Gordon, Jaimy (2004), 'The strange afterlife of Bruno Schulz', *Michigan Quarterly Review*, 43:1, http://www.michiganquarterlyreview.com/2016/07/from-the-archive-the-strange-afterlife-of-bruno-schulz-by-jaimy-gordon/. Accessed 16 July 2017.

Gosetti-Ferencei, Jennifer Anna (2005), '*Trompe l'oeil* and the mimetic tradition in aesthetics', *Analecta Husserliana*, 87, pp. 79–93.

Grau, Oliver (2003), *Virtual Art: From Illusion to Immersion*, Cambridge: MIT Press.

Griffiths, Devin (2016), *The Age of Analogy: Science and Literature between the Darwins*, Baltimore: Johns Hopkins University Press.

Griffiths, Dave, Elggren, Leif, Howell, Brendan, Kemp, Jonathan, Oldfield Ford, Laura, Oreggia, Eleanora and Small, Sabrina (2010), *exquisite_code*, London: Mute Publishing.

Grossman, Ron (1996), 'Material things', *Chicago Tribune*, 25 June, http://articles.chicagotribune.com/1996-06-25/features/9606250013_1_photographers-tel-aviv-peter-menzel. Accessed 13 May 2017.

Guðmundsdóttir, Björk (2011), interviewed by Lisa Robinson, *Vanity Fair*, 614, p. 138.
Guðmundsdóttir, Björk and Snibbe, Scott (2011), *Biophilia* app, One Little Indian, Ltd. and Well Hart, Ltd.
Hayles, N. Katherine (2002), *Writing Machines*, Cambridge: MIT Press.
——— (2007), 'Intermediation: The pursuit of a vision', *New Literary History*, 38:1, pp. 99–125.
——— (2008), *Electronic Literature: New Horizons for the Literary*, Notre Dame: University of Notre Dame Press.
——— (2012), *How We Think: Digital Media and Contemporary Technogenesis*, Chicago: University of Chicago Press.
Harbison, Robert (2000), *Reflections on Baroque*, Chicago: University of Chicago Press.
Hayles, N. Katherine and Pressman, Jessica (eds) (2013), *Comparative Textual Media: Transforming the Humanities in the Postprint Era*, Minneapolis: University of Minnesota Press.
Heer, Jeet (2012), 'What is a book like a building? When it's in the hands of Chris Ware, whose *Building Stories* is a brilliant marriage of art and architecture', *The Globe and Mail*, 5 October, https://www.theglobeandmail.com/arts/books-and-media/book-reviews/when-is-a-book-like-a-building-when-chris-ware-is-the-author/article4591752/. Accessed 12 June 2017.
Heidegger, Martin (1962), *Being and Time*, New York: Harper Collins.
Hénin, Emmanuelle (2010), 'Parrhasios and the stage curtain: Theatre, metapainting and the idea of representation in the seventeenth century', *Art History*, 33:2, pp. 248–61.
Hidden Brain (2019), 'One head, two brains: How the brain's hemispheres shape the world we see', NPR, 4 February, https://www.npr.org/2019/02/01/690656459/one-head-two-brains-how-the-brains-hemispheres-shape-the-world-we-see. Accessed 6 February 2019.
Jackson, Shelley (1995), *Patchwork Girl*, Watertown: Eastgate Systems.
Johnson, Christopher (2010), *Hyperboles: The Rhetoric of Excess in Baroque Literature and Thought*, Cambridge: Harvard University Press.
Joyce, Michael (1987), *afternoon: a story*, Watertown: Eastgate Systems.
Kant, Immanuel (1952), 'Analytic of the beautiful', *Critique of Judgement*, Oxford: Oxford University Press, pp. 35–74.
Kaplan, Louis (2013), 'Mapping Ararat: Augmented reality, virtual tourism, and grand island's Jewish ghosts', *CR: The New Centennial Review*, 13:2, pp. 239–64.
Kaup, Monika (2005), 'Becoming-baroque: Folding European forms into the new world baroque with Alejo Carpentier', *CR: The New Centennial Review*, 5:2, pp. 107–49.
——— (2006), 'Neobaroque: Latin America's alternative modernity', *Comparative Literature*, 58:2, pp. 128–52.
——— (2007), '"The future is entirely fabulous": The baroque genealogy of Latin America's modernity', *Modern Language Quarterly*, 68:2, pp. 221–41.

Kelly, Stuart (2013), 'Chris Ware: "There is a magic when you read an image that moves in your mind"', *The Guardian*, 11 October, https://www.theguardian.com/books/2013/oct/11/chris-ware-graphic-novelist-interview. Accessed 9 June 2017.

Klein, Norman M. (2004), *The Vatican to Vegas: A History of Special Effects*, New York: The New Press.

La Biennale di Venezia Channel (2009), '66th Venice film festival – Jaco Van Dormael', YouTube, https://www.youtube.com/watch?v=dyYwjdrtZuc. Accessed 30 May 2017.

Laerke, Mogens (2010), 'Four things Deleuze learned from Leibniz', in S. van Tuinen and N. McDonnell (eds), *Deleuze and* The Fold: *A Critical Reader*, New York: Palgrave Macmillan, pp. 25–45.

Lambert, Gregg (2008), *On the (New) Baroque*, Aurora: The Davies Group Publishers.

——— (2011), 'The bachelor machine: Kafka & the question of a minor literature', in P. Kouba and T. Pivoda (eds), *Franz Kafka: Minority Report*, Praha: Litteraria Pragensia Books, pp. 7–31.

Lanham, Richard (1993), *The Electronic Word: Democracy, Technology, and the Arts*, Chicago: University of Chicago Press.

Latour, Bruno, Jensen, Pablo, Venturini, Tommaso, Grauwin, Sébastian and Boullier, Dominique (2012), '"The hole is always smaller than its parts" – A digital test of Bariel Tardes' monads', *The British Journal of Sociology*, 63:4, pp. 590–615.

Lebensztejn, Jean-Claude (1988), 'Framing classical style', *Art Journal*, 47:1, pp. 37–41.

Leibniz, Gottfried (1898), *The Monadology* (trans. R. Latta), http://home.datacomm.ch/kerguelen/monadology/. Accessed 6 October 2015.

Lichty, Patrick (2014), 'The aesthetic of liminality: Augmentation as artform', *Leonardo*, 47:4, pp. 325–36.

Lista, Michael (2014), 'Michael Lista, on poetry: Christian Bök and the poetry of the future', *National Post*, 3 January, http://nationalpost.com/entertainment/books/on-poetry-christian-bok-and-the-poetry-of-the-future/wcm/d5ba9983-5bee-4fda-9c20-2cfdcb231654. Accessed 27 June 2017.

Loh, Maria H. (2004), 'New and improved: Repetition as originality in Italian baroque practice and theory', *College Art Association*, 86:3, pp. 477–504.

Lyotard, Jean-François (1990), *DuchampTRANSformers* (trans. I. McLeod), Venice: The Lapis Press.

MacLure, Maggie (2006), 'The bone in the throat: Baroque method', *International Journal of Qualitative Studies in Education*, 19:6, pp. 729–45.

Malcuzynski, Marie-Pierrette (2009), 'The (neo)baroque effect: A critical inquiry into the transformation and application of a conceptual field to comparative American studies', *Comparative Literature*, 61:3, pp. 295–315.

Manovich, Lev (2001), *The Language of New Media*, Cambridge: MIT Press.

——— (2006), 'Generation flash', in W. Hui Kyong Chun and T. Keenan (eds), *New Media,Old Media: A History and Theory Reader*, London: Routledge, pp. 209–18.

Marino, Mark (2013), 'Reading *exquisite_code*: Critical code studies of literature', in N. K. Hayles and J. Pressman (eds), *Comparative Textual Media: Transforming the Humanities in the Postprint Era*, Minneapolis: University of Minnesota Press, pp. 283–309.

Martin, Vincent T. (1994), 'Experimental poetics: A (neo-)baroque paradigm', in J. García, B. Kaplan and C. Lechner (eds), *Literature and Society: Centers and Margins*, New York: Columbia University Press, pp. 97–109.

MASS MoCA (2013), *Izhar Patkin: The Wandering Veil*, exhibition pamphlet, MASS MoCA, North Adams, MA, 7 December 2013–1 September 2014.

McGann, Jerome (1998), 'Textual scholarship, textual theory, and the uses of electronic tools: A brief report on current undertakings', *Victoria Studies*, 41:4, pp. 609–19.

——— (2001), *Radiant Textuality: Literature after the World Wide Web*, New York: Palgrave Macmillan.

——— (2009), 'Our textual history', *The Times Literary Supplement*, 20 November, pp. 13–15.

McManus, James M. (2008), 'Mirrors, TRANS/formation and slippage in the five-way portrait of Marcel Duchamp', *The Space Between*, 4:1, pp. 125–48.

Mellmann, Katja (2013), 'On the emergence of aesthetic illusion: An evolutionary perspective', in W. Wolf, W. Bernhart and A. Mahler (eds), *Immersion and Distance: Aesthetic Illusion in Literature and Other Media*, Amsterdam: Rodopi, pp. 67–88.

Merrill, Christi Ann (2011), 'The lyricism of violence: Translating faith in revolution', *Boundary 2*, 38:3, pp. 119–45.

Michel, Berit (2014), '"PlastiCity": Foer's *Tree of Codes* as (visual) multilayered urban topography – Performing space and time in a twenty-first-century adaptation of Bruno Schulz's textual labyrinths', *Critique: Studies in Contemporary Fiction*, 55:2, pp. 166–86.

Miller, Adam S. (2013), *Speculative Grace: Bruno Latour and Object-Oriented Theology*, New York: Fordham University Press.

Morris, Adelaide and Thomas, Swiss (eds) (2009), *New Media Poetics: Contexts, Technotexts, and Theories*, Cambridge: MIT Press.

Morton, Timothy (2015), 'This huge sunlit abyss from the future right there next to you...', in J. Merry (ed.), *Björk Mid-career Retrospective with New Commissioned Piece for MOMA*, New York: MoMA.

Motte, Warren (2005), 'Reflections on mirrors', *MLN*, 120:4, pp. 774–89.

Murray, Timothy (2008), *Digital Baroque: New Media Art and Cinematic Folds*, Minneapolis: University of Minnesota Press.

Naim, Choudhri M. (2012), 'Urdu poetry', in R. Green, S. Cushman and C. Cavanagh (eds), *The Princeton Encyclopedia of Poetry and Poetics*, 4th ed., Princeton: Princeton University Press.

'Navel' (2019), Online Etymology Dictionary, http://www.etymonline.com/word/navel#etymonline_v_2334. Accessed 12 January 2019.

Ndalianis, Angela (2004), *Neo-Baroque Aesthetics and Contemporary Entertainment*, Cambridge: MIT Press.

——— (2008), 'From neo-baroque to neo-baroques?', *Revista Canadiense de Estudios Hispánicos*, 33.1, pp. 265–80.

Nemerov, Alexandra (2011), 'First my Motorola', in C. Dworkin and K. Goldsmith (eds), *Against Expression: An Anthology of Conceptual Writing*, Evanston: Northwestern University Press, pp. 457–62.

Not-Fig (2010), 'Exquisite_Code', http://notfig.garethfoote.co.uk/exquisite_code/. Accessed 4 June 2017.

Opie, Robert (1994), '"Unless you do these crazy things…": An interview with Robert Opie', in J. Elsner and R. Cardinal (eds), *The Cultures of Collecting*, Islington: Reaktion Books.

O'Leary, Joanna and O'Leary, Shawn Brigid (2010), 'Where "things go the other way": The stereochemistry of Lewis Carroll's looking-glass world', *Victorian Network*, 2:1, pp. 70–87.

Pamuk, Orhan (2012), *The Innocence of Objects* (trans. E. Oklap), New York: Abrams.

Panofsky, Erwin (1991), *Perspective as Symbolic Form*, New York: Zone Books.

Pareles, Jon (2011), 'The science of song, the song of science', *New York Times*, 1 July, https://mobile.nytimes.com/2011/07/02/arts/music/bjorks-biophilia-at-the-manchester-international-festival.html?mcubz=0. Accessed 12 June 2017.

Patkin, Izhar and Agha, Shahid Ali (2007), *The Veil Suite*, San Francisco: Artspace Books.

Perec, Georges (2010), *An Attempt at Exhausting a Place in Paris* (trans. M. Lowenthal), Adelaide: Wakefield Press.

Pope, James (2010), '"Where do we go from here?" Readers' responses to interactive fiction', *Convergence*, 15:1, pp. 75–94.

Pressman, Jessica (2014), *Digital Modernism: Making It New in New Media*, Oxford: Oxford University Press.

Purgar, Kresimir (2007), *The Neo-Baroque Subject*, Zagreb: MeanderMedia.

Pytlik, Mark (2003), *Björk: Wow and Flutter*, Toronto: ECW Press.

Queneau, Raymond (1961), *Cent Mille Milliards de Poèmes*, Paris: Gallimard.

Rafferty, Terrence (2012), 'Degrees of infidelity to Tolstoy's heroine', *New York Times*, 2 November, https://mobile.nytimes.com/2012/11/04/movies/keira-knightley-in-joe-wrights-anna-karenina.html?mcubz=0. Accessed 9 July 2017.

Rager, Matt (2012), '[_]Tree[_] of C[___]od[__]es', *Post45*, 24 May, http://post45.research.yale.edu/2012/05/_tree_-of-c___od__es/. Accessed 19 June 2014.

Randall, James (2013), 'Sculpting in lost time: The fragmentation of Bruno Schulz's *The Street of Crocodiles* in Jonathan Safran Foer's *Tree of Codes*', *Comparative Critical Studies*, 10, pp. 75–90.

Rickert, Thomas (2013), *Ambient Rhetoric: The Attunements of Rhetorical Being*, Pittsburgh: The University of Pittsburgh Press.

Roeder, Katherine (2011), 'Seeing inside-out in the funny pages', *American Art*, 25:1, pp. 24–27.

Ross, Alex (2015), 'Beyond delta: The many streams of Björk', in J. Merry (ed.), *Björk Mid-career Retrospective with New Commissioned Piece for MOMA*, New York: MoMA.

Ross, Deborah (2012), 'This world really is a stage', *The Spectator*, 8 September, https://www.spectator.co.uk/2012/09/this-world-really-is-a-stage/. Accessed on 9 July 2017.

Saemmer, Alexandra (2011), 'Writing the ephemeral [...] and re-enchanting the remnants: The lability of the digital device in literary practice', *Journal of Writing in Creative Practice*, 4:1, pp. 79–91.

Salgado, César Augusto (1999), 'Hybriditiy in new world baroque theory', *The Journal of American Folklore*, 112:445, pp. 316–31.

Sarduy, Severo (2010), 'The baroque and the neobaroque', in L. P. Zamora and M. Kaup (eds), *Baroque New Worlds: Representation, Transculturation, Counterconquest*, Durham: Duke University Press, pp. 270–91.

Sattler, Peter R. (2010), 'Past imperfect: "Building Stories" and the art of memory', in D. M. Ball and M. B. Kuhlman (eds), *The Comics of Chris Ware: Drawing Is a Way of Thinking*, Jackson: University Press of Mississippi, pp. 206–22.

Saul Steinberg Foundation (2019), 'Murals', *The Saul Steinberg Foundation*, http://saulsteinbergfoundation.org/essay/murals/. Accessed 1 June 2019.

Schulz, Bruno (1963), *The Street of Crocodiles*, New York: Penguin.

Sefami, Jacobo (2011), 'Avant-garde and neo-baroque', *Confluencia*, 26:2, pp. 2–12.

Shelton, Anthony Alan (1994), 'Cabinets of transgression: Renaissance collections and the incorporation of the new world', in J. Fraser and R. Cardinal (eds), *The Cultures of Collecting*, Cambridge: Harvard University Press, pp. 177–203.

Siegel, Tatiana (2012), 'The making of Anna Karenina', *Hollywood Reporter*, 16 November, http://www.hollywoodreporter.com/news/making-anna-karenina-391219. Accessed 9 July 2017.

Siegert, Bernhard (2015), 'Figures of self reference: A media genealogy of the trompe-l'oeil in seventeenth-century Dutch still life', in *Cultural Techniques: Grids, Filters, Doors, and Other Articulations of the Real* (trans. G. Winthrop-Young), New York: Fordham University Press, pp. 164–91.

Simanowski, Roberto (2011), *Digital Art and Meaning: Reading Kinetic Poetry, Text Machines, Mapping Art, and Interactive Installations*, Minneapolis: University of Minneapolis Press.

Spadaccini, Nicholas and Martín-Estudillo, Luis (2005), 'Introduction: The baroque and the culture of crises', in N. Spadaccini and L. Martín-Estudillo (eds), *Hispanic Baroque: Reading Cultures in Context*, Nashville: Vanderbilt University Press, pp. ix–xxxvi.

Stanitzek, Georg (2005), 'Text and paratexts in media', *Critical Inquiry*, 32:1, pp. 27–42.

Steinberg, Leo (2002), 'Reflections on the state of criticism', in B. W. Joseph (ed.), *Robert Rauschenberg*, Cambridge: MIT Press, pp. 7–37.

Stewart, Allison (2015), 'Björk's "Vulnicura" is a rewarding listen if you can handle the heartbreak', *Washington Post*, 16 January, https://www.washingtonpost.com/entertainment/music/bjorks-vulnicura-is-a-rewarding-listen-if-you-can-handle-the-heartbreak/2015/01/26/281f557c-a56f-11e4-a7c2-03d37af98440_story.html?utm_term=.244e5f9179c3. Accessed 30 August 2017.

Stewart, Susan (1984), *On Longing: Narratives of the Miniature, the Gigantic, the Souvenir, the Collection*, Baltimore: Johns Hopkins University Press.

——— (1990), 'Reverse trompe l'oeil: The eruption of the real', *Public Culture*, 3:1, pp. 67–76.

Stracey, Frances (2009), 'Bio-art: The ethics behind the aesthetics', *Science & Society*, 10, pp. 496–500.

Terrien, Samuel (1970), 'The omphalos myth and Hebrew religion', *Vetus Testamentum*, 20:3, pp. 315–38.

The Wandering Veil (2013), MASS MoCA, North Adams, MA, 7 December 2013–1 September 2014.

Timpano, Kiara R. and Shaw, Ashley M. (2013), 'Conferring humanness: The role of anthropomorphism in hoarding', *Personality and Individual Differences*, 54, pp. 383–88.

Tomasula, Steve (2002), 'Genetic art and the aesthetics of biology', *Leonardo*, 35:2, pp. 137–44.

toutlecineTLC (2010), 'Interview de Jaco Van Dormael – Mr. Nobody', YouTube, https://www.youtube.com/watch?v=egtcJQyMZbk. Accessed 30 May 2017.

Travers, Peter (2012), 'The man in the arena', *Rolling Stone*, 1170, pp. 86–87.

Trubek, Anne (2001), 'American literary realism and the problem of trompe l'oeil painting', *Mosaic*, 34:3, pp. 35–54.

Turner, Bryan S. (1994), 'Introduction', in C. Buci-Glucksmann, *Baroque Reason: The Aesthetics of Modernity*, London: Sage Publications, pp. 1–36.

University of Iceland (2012), 'Biophilia awarded best science communication project', http://english.hi.is/frettir/biophilia_awarded_best_science_communication_project. Accessed 9 October 2012.

Van Dormael, Jaco (2009), *Mr. Nobody*, USA: Magnolia Home Entertainment.

van Reijen, Willem (1992), 'Labyrinth and ruin: The return of the baroque in postmodernity', *Theory Culture Society*, 9:1, pp. 1–26.

Van Wer, William F. (2007), '*Close*: Voyeurism and the idea of the baroque', in M. Tschofen and J. Burwell (eds), *Image and Territory: Essays on Atom Egoyen*, Waterloo: Wilfrid Laurier University Press, pp. 295–305.

Voyce, Stephen (2007), 'The xenotext experiment: An interview with Christian Bök', *Postmodern Culture*, 17:2, http://pmc.iath.virginia.edu/issue.107/17.2voyce.html. Accessed 14 May 2012.

Wagner, Heather (2010), 'Jonathan Safran Foer talks *Tree of Codes* and conceptual art', *Vanity Fair*, 10 November, http://www.vanityfair.com/culture/2010/11/jonathan-safran-foer-talks-tree-of-codes-and-paper-art. Accessed 12 July 2017.

Wakin, Daniel (2012), 'Dispossessed', *New York Times*, 13 January, https://www.nytimes.com/2012/01/15/magazine/bernard-greenhouse-cello.html. Accessed 14 May 2012.

Ward, David (2013), 'The space of poetry: Inhabiting form in the ghazal', *University of Toronto Quarterly*, 82:1, pp. 62–71.

Ware, Chris (2012), *Building Stories*, New York: Pantheon.

Wei, Lilly (2014), 'Izhar Patkin', *ARTnews*, 113:6, pp. 102–03.

Westerhoff, Jan C. (2001), 'A world of signs: Baroque pansemioticism, the *polyhistor* and the early modern *wunderkammer*', *Journal of the History of Ideas*, 62:4, pp. 633–50.

Wilks, Christine (2008), *Fitting the Pattern*, Electronic Literature Collection Volume Two, http://collection.eliterature.org/2/works/wilks_fittingthepattern.html. Accessed 12 March 2016.

Wittrock, Mary Cobb (2010), 'Frankétienne's spirals: Chaos theory, minor literature and generic limits', *International Journal of Francophone Studies*, 13:1, pp. 103–29.

Wollen, Peter (2006), 'Baroque and the neo-baroque in the age of the spectacle', *Point of Contact*, 8:1/2, pp. 8–21.

Woodland, Malcolm (2005), 'Memory's homeland: Agha Shahid Ali and the hybrid ghazal', *ESC*, 31:2–3, pp. 249–72.

Wright, Joe (2012), *Anna Karenina*, USA: Focus Features.

Zaidi, Nishat (2008), 'Center/margin dialectics and the poetic form: The ghazals of Agha Shahid Ali', *The Annual of Urdu Studies*, 23, pp. 55–66.

Zamora, Lois Parkinson (2006), *The Inordinate Eye: New World Baroque and Latin American Fiction*, Chicago: University of Chicago Press.

——— (2013), 'Eccentric periodization: Comparative perspectives on the enlightenment and the baroque', *PMLA*, 128:3, pp. 690–97.

——— (2014), 'Exuberance by design: New world baroque and the politics of postcoloniality', *Canadian Journal of Continental Philosophy*, 18:1, pp. 22–41.

Zamora, Lois Parkinson and Kaup, Monika (eds) (2010), *Baroque New Worlds: Representation, Transculturation, Counterconquest*, Durham: Duke University Press.

Zhang, Peter (2011), 'Gilles Deleuze and minor rhetoric', *ETC*, 68:2, pp. 214–29.

Index